U.S. SHARPSHOOTERS

Berdan's Civil War Elite

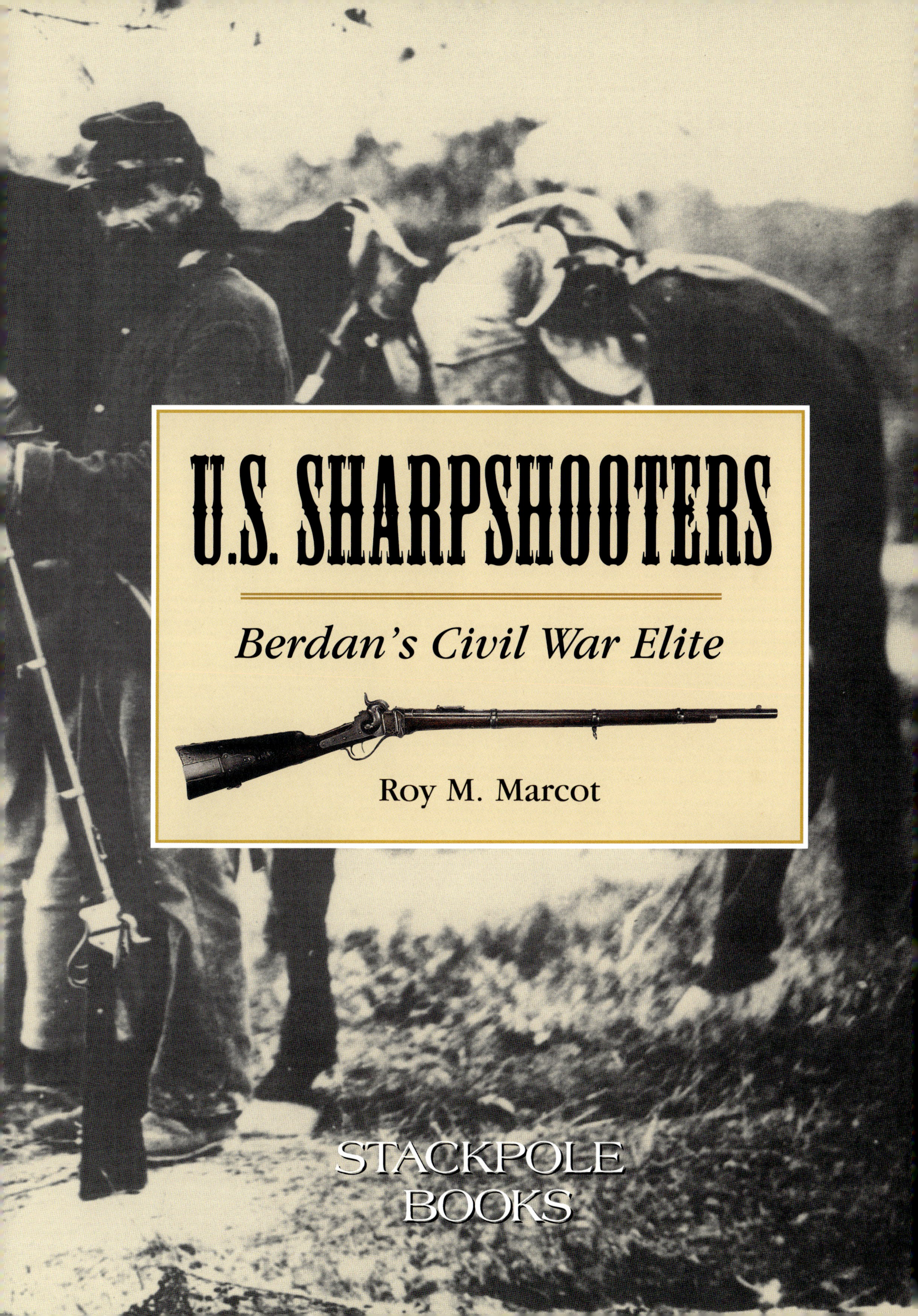
U.S. SHARPSHOOTERS
Berdan's Civil War Elite
Roy M. Marcot
STACKPOLE
BOOKS

Designed by Philip Clucas MCSD

Printed in China

Published by
STACKPOLE BOOKS
5067 Ritter Road
Mechanicsburg, PA 17055
www.stackpolebooks.com

ISBN 0-8117-0271-5.

10 9 8 7 6 5 4 3 2 1

Contents

This photograph of Berdan was taken by Matthew Brady sometime after the Colonel's recovery from the wound he received in 1862. His military records state that his weight dropped from a robust 210 pounds to 180. The pressures of warfare are seen in his face, especially when compared to pictures of him from 1861.

Introduction

Colonel Hiram Berdan's two regiments of United States SharpShooters are recognized as being among the most colorful and effective units of the Civil War. They took part in some of the bloodiest battles and are reputed to have "inflicted more casualties upon the enemy than any other unit in the Civil War."

Dressed in distinctive gray and green uniforms, the SharpShooters were carefully selected from across the United States, with each man needing to demonstrate high standards of accurate shooting before being accepted for the corps. They became expert skirmishers, operating in loose formations ahead of the rest of the army, relying on their individual initiative, field skills, courage and marksmanship to inflict damage on the enemy out of all proportion to their own strength.

This book tells the story of that short-lived unit, separating the historical facts from the legend that has surrounded the SharpShooters. But the story of the SharpShooters is inextricably tied up with that of the man who created and led them – Hiram Berdan.

Berdan was born in Phelps, Ontario County, New York, on September 6th, 1824. He was the third of seven children, born to a relatively prosperous landowning family. When Hiram was only six years old the family moved to the newly settled area of Plymouth, Michigan where the young boy grew up working on the family farm. He was fortunate enough to be given formal schooling and eventually studied mathematics and mechanical engineering at Hobart College in Geneva, New York.

Hiram's engineering inventiveness was demonstrated from an early age, when he invented an improved threshing machine which he patented in 1847. This was only the first of many inventions.

In 1853, now living in New York, Berdan invented and patented a simple machine for extracting gold from ore for the mining industry. Berdan was an astute businessman as well as inventor, and sold manufacturing rights to a group of New York investors for the staggering sum of $550,000, then separate rights in California and even international rights for another $200,000. The device was simple, effective and cheap, and many were still in service around the world right up until World War II.

Berdan continued to invent, and developed such things as: a folding lifeboat, a device for laying undersea telegraphic cables, bakery apparatus and even a pen and pencil holder. His farming background meant that he was brought up around guns, so along with his engineering skills he was an expert marksman – an ability that inspired the formation of the SharpShooters.

By the eve of the war, Hiram Berdan was living in New York with his wife and two children. A prosperous and successful inventor and businessman, he had extensive personal contacts in the higher echelons of politics and industry. But as with so many Americans, the coming Civil War was to change his career and his life. And as will be seen, as a military commander he was to become a controversial figure.

Berdan Organizes the SharpShooters

On April 12, 1861, Fort Sumter, a brick stronghold built near the mouth of South Carolina's Charleston Harbor, was fired upon by forces of the new Confederacy of Southern States. Federal relief expeditions had not arrived, and the undermanned and poorly provisioned fort could not withstand the bombardment. One day later, Fort Sumter surrendered to the jubilant attackers. The final blow had been struck against efforts to keep the Union intact, and war began.

Abraham Lincoln, inaugurated only a month earlier on March 4th, was compelled to use his powers as President of the United States to call up 75,000 volunteers to augment the small standing army. This action resulted in a fever of enthusiastic recruiting throughout the North. Nationalism, a call to arms, and the promise of adventure quickly filled the ranks. These idealistic untrained men and boys were soon to feel the unforgiving sting of battlefield agony, illness, disease and daily campsite boredom. Leaders of the North and the South were totally unprepared for what would follow.

State militia units responded to President Lincoln's call. State trained and equipped, they were eager to come to their country's aid, brimming with the confidence common to those who have yet to taste battle. Trained primarily in parade-ground drill, the uncohesive assembly of troops tried to retain local hometown individuality, with their flamboyant names and even more gaudy dress. Each state unit elected its own officers notwithstanding their lack of experience in anything military. Local politicians, hardware shop proprietors land owners, and the like were pressed into leadership roles, often with only a copy of *HARDEE'S TACTICS* to differentiate them from the raw troops they commanded

***Above:** The ruins of Fort Sumter after its surrender .The Confederate batteries fired some 4,000 rounds and claimed 600 direct hits on the fort but despite this no-one was actually hurt.*

Hiram Berdan likewise felt the call of patriotism, and responded to President Lincoln's modified call on May 3rd for 42,034 three-year volunteers. Berdan believed that he could channel his own ability as a leading marksman to organize a contingent of the best rifle shots from each state. Indeed, if the governors of each loyal state would send their best marksmen, he thought he could mold them into a special, elite fighting unit, the likes of which the Army of the United States had never before seen.

***Above:** A careworn Abraham Lincoln who, on the outbreak of war, was compelled to use his powers to call up volunteers to augment the standing army. At this point he could not have envisaged the horrors that were to follow.*

Encouraged by several business leaders from New York, Berdan wrote to the governors of each of the Northern States, asking them to convey authority to him to recruit companies of skilled marksmen. The following article from the *NEW YORK POST* newspaper, dated June 4, 1861, is one of the very earliest references to Berdan and his quest to form a regiment of SharpShooters.

SKIRMISHERS
Mr. H. Berdan of this city calls for volunteers to form a corps of skirmishers for the Army, which shall consist of the best marksmen in the country.... The target rifle is said to do execution at the distance of more than a thousand yards, and such men as Berdan proposes to enlist in the corps of skirmishers will be able to kill a man at the distance of a quarter of a mile.

The Spirit of the Times recently published a list of the best rifle shots in the country for fifteen past years. Mr. Berdan's name stands at the head as the best shot, and it is remarkable that in the entire list there is but one name from the slave states, and he is by no means among the crack shots!

The Corps of SharpShooters will be used not in the midst of battle, but on the outskirts, where, beyond the smoke and fury of the engagement, they will act independently, choose their objects, and make every shot tell. Posted in small squads at from one-eighth to three-eighths of a mile from the field, firing a shot a minute, and hitting their mark with almost a dead certainty, they will be a great annoyance to the enemy. They will combine their attention to the officers, and by picking these off, will bring confusion into the enemy's line.

These rifle skirmishers propose to devote themselves entirely to picking off the rebel officers. They will have the best opportunities for this kind of work. They will be out of range themselves. They will probably be mounted, and can thus change their locality quickly, and take advantage of every movement of their forces. They will be a most valuable addition to our forces, and, we trust, their proposed organization will receive such encouragement and pecuniary support from the public, as will place them in the field, ready for service, in time for the first great battle.

Favorable responses from the Adjutants General of several states made Berdan realize that he needed official Federal approval before actual recruiting could begin. Therefore, he drew upon the political influence of the same New York businessmen who first encouraged him, each writing a letter of introduction to the Secretary of War. No response followed, and Berdan realized that if he was to succeed, he had to journey to Washington to meet with President Lincoln, Secretary of War Cameron, or anyone in authority who might listen to his proposal.

Whether Berdan had known Lincoln prior to their meeting on June 13 is not known, but the following letter, written by Berdan to Lieutenant General Winfield Scott, mentions this important encounter:

Washington
June 13, 1861

Lieutenant General Winfield Scott
Commander-in-Chief United States Army
Dear Sir:
The applications I am every day receiving from persons anxious to join a regiment to be formed entirely of first class rifle shots, are so numerous that it is obvious but a slight effort is needed to secure, at once, a most important addition to our military machinery.

I propose to form a regiment of 750 men, to serve for three years, or during the War, to be divided into ten companies of 75 men each. Each company to have a Captain, First and Second Lieutenants, four Sergeants, and four Corporals. I propose, also, to divide each company into three detachments of 25 men each, and to forward the same as soon as mustered-in under Lieutenants, etc., wherever directed by the proper authorities.

These men will be required to supply themselves with everything in the way of arms and uniforms, with the expectation that the Government will supply them with camp and garrison equippage.

No man is to be mustered in who cannot, when firing at rest at a distance of 200 yards, put ten consecutive shots in a target, the average distance not to exceed five inches from the center of the bulls-eye, to the center of the bull.

I had a short interview with the President this morning, on the subject. He expressed great interest in the project, and thought it would be a very valuable arm to the military machinery. And that he had no doubt that they would be received as fast as they were ready to be mustered into the service. But he must refer me to the Secretary of War, so that anything he did in connection with the matter would be endorsed by him, or words to that effect. He seemed very much interested with the targets I had, one of which I promised to return to him, at his request.

I then called on the Secretary of War, and found him too busy to read my letters of introduction. He said that he had no doubt but that the SharpShooters would be a valuable acquisition. But, as it was something entirely new to him, at least he thought it proper to have your views on the subject, as to how they could be placed. He desired me to call on you for that purpose.

Trusting this explanation will make an apology for troubling you unnecessarily, I remain,

H. Berdan

Berdan was rewarded with a favorable reply to his request for Federal authority to muster his SharpShooters, as he called them. Winfield Scott's Military Secretary confirmed this on June 14:

Headquarters of the Army
Washington
June 14, 1861

H. Berdan, Esq.
Sir:
The General-in-Chief, under the reference to him of the subject of SharpShooters by the Honorable Secretary of War, as set forth in your letter of the 13th of June, desires me to say that he was very favorably impressed with you personally, and that a Regiment of such SharpShooters, as are proposed by you, and instructed according to your system, would be of great value and could be advantageously employed by him in the public service.

Schuyler Hamilton
Lieutenant Colonel
Military Secretary

A *NEW YORK TRIBUNE* newspaper account of Berdan's success came out the very same day, and shed the first light on the initial uniform proposal for the SharpShooters, and on the unusual request that his marksmen be mounted:

> THE BERDAN RIFLE CORPS
> Mr. Berdan's proposition for a mounted Rifle Corps has been accepted.... This new arm to the service is exceedingly popular here. The Secretary of War would have been willing to suspend the three year rule, to oblige those who cannot leave their families more than a few months, but such must take the chances to be elected officers in the regiment, so they can resign at pleasure.
>
> The uniform will be heavy, dark blue flannel sack coat, metal buttons, and black fringe round the bottom, with black velvet collar, soft crown hat, with small black feather. The rifle is to be the well known target rifle, with cast steel barrel, swedged balls, false muzzle, and either globe or telescopic sights.

Even four months later Berdan still fostered the idea of mounted SharpShooters to augment his initial proposal for infantry SharpShooters. This is, perhaps, the last mention made of mounts for Berdan's men. The mobility that the horses would have afforded would have significantly altered the eventual disposition of Berdan's men as skirmishers. Note the fascinating, yet naive weaponry that Berdan envisioned for these mounted men:

> Camp of Instruction Washington, D.C.
> October 1861
>
> Captain Wells:
> Your letter of the 4th instant, offering to raise a regiment of mounted SharpShooters for my Corps has been received, together with strong letters from General Johnny Dix and Assistant Secretary of State and others, as your ability to raise and command such a regiment. I propose organizing a regiment of mounted SharpShooters in every respect up to the standard adopted for this Corps, to be armed with sabres, and the improved Volcanic rifle (carbine size), capable of being fired 15 times without lowering it from the shoulder.
>
> This regiment is to be employed in time of action in two battalions, each firing and retreating, to load alternately. The first is to be outfitted specially with reference to weapons, saddles, and trappings, according to Army Regulations. The uniforms will be green, with yellow trimmings. My authority for the same will be forwarded with the next correspondence to the Secretary of War.
>
> H. Berdan

Official approval of Berdan's proposal to form a regiment of the best marksmen came from the Secretary of War on June 15, as an endorsement to Lieutenant Colonel Hamilton's letter:

> The regiment within named is accepted in accordance with the within proposal, provided the whole of the regiment shall be mustered into service within 90 days of this date. The first detachment to be mustered within 20 days, and so one detachment after the other, as the War Department may order. And provided also, that the regiment shall come into service armed and equipped with no expense to the [Federal] Government.
>
> Simon Cameron
> Secretary of War

In a highly strategic move, Hiram Berdan enlisted the services of prominent businessmen in each of the "Loyal States" to recruit for him. William Y. W. Ripley from Vermont was just such a leader. Eighteen years after the war ended, he was to author a book on his company of Berdan SharpShooters. An excerpt from the book described these early days:

> The detail of the recruiting and organization of this regiment was entrusted to Hiram Berdan, then a resident of New York City, an enthusiastic lover of rifle shooting, and an expert marksman.
>
> It was required that a recruit possess good moral character, sound physical development, and in other respects come within the usual requirements of army regulations. But, as the men were designed for an especial service, it was required of them that before enlistment, they justify their claim to be called SharpShooters, by a public exhibition of their skill as would fairly entitle them to the name, and would warrant a reasonable expectation of usefulness in the field.
>
> To insure this, it was ordered that no recruit be enlisted who could not, in a public trial, make a string of ten shots at a distance of two hundred yards, the aggregate measurement of which should not exceed fifty inches. In other words, it was required that the recruit be able to place ten bullets, in succession, within a ten-inch ring at a distance of two hundred yards.
>
> Any style of rifle was allowed, however use of telescopic sights was not permitted. The applicant was allowed to shoot from any position, as long as he shot from the shoulder.
>
> Circular letters setting forth these conditions and Colonel Berdan's authority, were issued to the governors of the Loyal States.

Announcements sent by Hiram Berdan to each state's Adjutant General called for the formation of independent companies of volunteer SharpShooters. He hoped that at least one company could be raised from each of the "Loyal Northern States." It was Berdan's intention to maintain individual state pride by keeping each company autonomous and by not mixing marksmen from other states into any unit already mustered. To assure that only the best marksmen were chosen, Berdan set extremely high, but attainable standards, from which he would not waiver:

> ...no man will be received into the Corps, who does not come fully up to my requirements: every man must be good for a 50 inch string. Such a Corps would, I consider it safe to say, be relied upon, firing at rest, to hit a man of ordinary size: every time at 1/8 mile twice out of three times at 1/4 mile; and three out of five times at 1/2 mile. Many of them would do as well, if not better than this, off-hand.
>
> The arrangements made at Washington provide for their entry into the service as fast as ready, in detachments

of twenty-five. The applications for admission are so numerous, that I feel confident that every regiment of this State can be furnished with its complement of SharpShooter. All that remains to be seen done is to provide for equipping the men with arms and uniform, and this, I must respectfully suggest, properly devolves upon State Governments.

The arms will require $60 for each man. What the uniform will cost, I have not been advised. It is, however, an expensive though a very serviceable one, consisting of a loose sack coat of heavy blue flannel, trimmed with black fringe round the bottom, black velvet collar, and regulation buttons, loose trousers, a single-breasted vest of the same cloth, and a soft felt hat with a small black feather.

I respectfully suggest that this State send with each regiment, a detachment of 25 SharpShooters, and provide each man with his uniform, and give him $60 to furnish himself with arms. Each man should get his gun from such maker as he shall select, and to adopt each style of rifle as he can use with best effect. He should be required, however, to justify his selection by the actual performance in his own hands.

Several Governors accepted Berdan's challenge, and issued specific orders to commence marksmanship trials in different cities within their states. The following General Order from the Michigan Adjutant General's office is typical of the strict conditions and requirements of these trials:

Military Department – Michigan
Adjutant General's Office
June 25, 1861

GENERAL ORDER NO. 37

A proposition having been made by H. Berdan, Esq., to the War Department to raise a Corps of Rifle SharpShooters, to be taken from the best rifle shots in the Loyal States of the Union; and which proposition was accepted by the Secretary of War, June 15, 1861.

It being very desirable that Michigan should furnish and equip such a company for the above Regiment, the Commander-In-Chief hereby calls for volunteers for one company to comply with the requirement, here-in-after mentioned, to consist of one captain, one first lieutenant, one second lieutenant, four sergeants, four corporals, and eighty-nine privates. They are to be mustered into the service of the State, subject to being mustered into the service of the United States, for the period of three years, or during the war, unless sooner discharged in accordance with the provisions of the Military Force Law, approved May 10th, 1861. They are to receive such pay and emoluments as are allowed to officers and soldiers of the United States, which will be furnished by the State when the Company is rendezvoused.

The arms will be rifles, and each man will have his own rifle from such maker as he shall select, and adopt such style of rifle as he can use with the best effect, being required, however, to justify his selection by the actual performance of the gun in his own hands. He will also furnish the necessary equipments, consisting of a leather waist belt, cartridge box and cap pouch, which will be the same grade as those in the army of the United States. The members of the Company will have the right to select their own officers, to be approved by the Commander-in-Chief, and the Captain will appoint the non-commissioned officers.

No man will be accepted who cannot, when firing at a rest, at a distance of two hundred yards, put ten consecutive shots in a target, the average distances not to exceed five inches from the center of the bulls-eye to the center of the ball. All candidates will have to pass an examination by a committee to be selected for that purpose, in a subsequent order.

News of Berdan's plan to recruit the best marksmen from each state spread like wildfire, Newspapers throughout the Union carried the information and there was no want of helpers and applicants:

W. S. Roland of New York was appointed to see the Governors of the Western States, to urge them each to furnish one company of SharpShooters for Berdan's Regiment. He says that he has been successful in every application, as yet.

By July 2, Hiram Berdan had become somewhat unsure of the task he had undertaken. In a letter to the Governor of New York, he stated that if a full company of New York SharpShooters could not be recruited, then he will offer the marksmen already enlisted to other volunteer infantry regiments previously formed in the state. The rigors and disappointments that must have befallen Berdan during these early days of organizing the SharpShooters must have been intimidating. But, the farsighted leader would not be denied. Seventeen days later, and despite Berdan's fears, his associates were successful in raising ten full companies of SharpShooters, one from each of ten different states.

Even this early, Berdan realized that muzzle-loading, heavy-barreled, target rifles that some of his marksmen possessed were a poor choice for the field. In addition to the extreme weight, 14 to over 30 pounds per rifle, each took a different bullet, both in caliber and configuration. To resupply SharpShooters in the field would have been an ordnanceman's nightmare.

Berdan knew that his marksmen could only be as effective as the weapons they wielded. Therefore, he petitioned the Federal Chief of Ordnance, Brigadier General James Wolfe Ripley, for appropriate arms for his men. However, his initial choice, as surprising as it seems, was to arm his SharpShooters with the standard issue, Springfield muzzleloading musket.

Office of H. Berdan,
Civil Engineer

5th Avenue Hotel
New York
July 19th, 1861

General Ripley
Ordnance Department
Washington
Sir:

I have ten companies of SharpShooters selected from ten different states, that will be ready for the field in about two weeks. Every man's skill with the rifle has been tested, and not one has been admitted that did not come fully up to the requirements.

All have superior rifles, but there is such a variation in caliber and sights, that I have concluded to take your suggestion and leave them all at home and take a uniform weapon. I have tried the Springfield rifle-musket, and much prefer it to anything I have seen. I would like seven hundred and fifty of them for my Regiment. Can you arrange to give me this number? You can place them where they will do special service. I will regard it as a special favor. An early reply will oblige.

H. Berdan

p.s. I may have made a mistake in applying to you direct, but I have done so with the feeling that if I could not secure your able assistance in the matter, I should have but little hope of success.

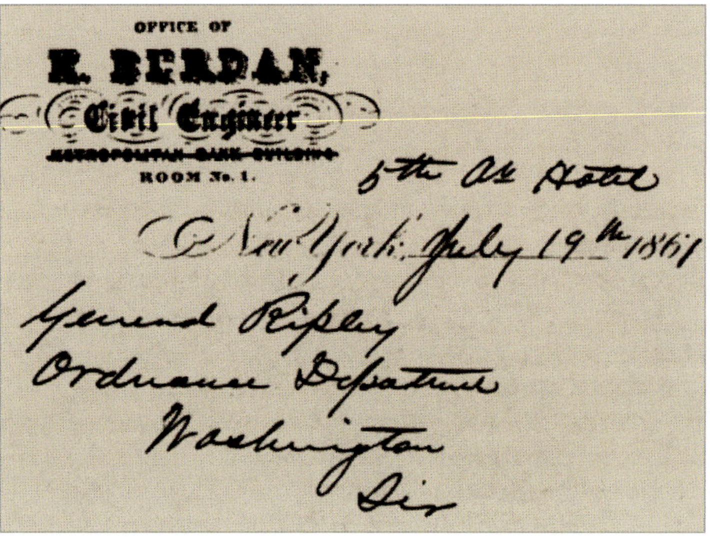

OFFICE OF
H. BERDAN,
Civil Engineer
METROPOLITAN BANK BUILDING
ROOM No. 1.

5th Av Hotel
New York: July 19th 1861
General Ripley
Ordnance Department
Washington
Sir

Ripley responded:

TELEGRAM

Ordnance Office
Washington
July 26, 1861

Colonel H. Berdan
Fifth Avenue Hotel
New York

Can furnish your regiment with 750 rifle muskets, at this place.

James W. Ripley
Brigadier General

However, while the Springfield rifle muskets promised by General Ripley afforded standardization, they could hardly be considered SharpShooter quality, especially at ranges in excess of 300 yards.

Meanwhile, recruiting continued at a rapid pace, and Berdan answered numerous letters from both officials and interested marksmen. It was during the month of July that Berdan changed his mind about uniforming his men in *dark blue flannel sack coats*. He decided, instead, on colors which would allow them to blend into the woodland environment in which they would fight. This decision was a momentous one in American military history, because prior to this, there was little or no effort to conceal troops on the battlefield.

Infantrymen at this time were drilled in mass firepower tactics, with shooters standing or kneeling shoulder to shoulder. Volley upon volley from their black powder, muzzle-loading muskets would meet similar fire from their foe. Berdan's intent was to utilize skilled marksmen as skirmishers, firing from concealed positions to engage the enemy. Not since Ethan Allen's Green Mountain Boys, or Andrew Jackson's Kentucky Riflemen, would American battlefield tactics break so completely with established European battle drill.

The following letter to the Governor of Pennsylvania revealed much about Berdan's revised thoughts of uniforms and firearms for his men:

...On reflection, I have concluded to include a uniform of green cloth, with gray overcoat instead of blue, as first contemplated. The latter color being too conspicuous. The greenness will correspond in the leafy season with the color of the foliage, while the gray overcoat will suit surrounding objects in the fall and winter.

The undercoat is to be made double-breasted, with short flannel up, black collar and black buttons, essentially of the same color, and no vest.

Each man will require two pairs of pantaloons, of Russia twilled linen, very strong, and a shade of gray. One pair of goatskin leggings, up to the knee, with hair outside. Two pairs of heavy, well made, low heel shoes, with leather gaiters. One long waisted green cloth jacket, round about with sleeves and black metal buttons.

The overcoat to be dark gray, with black metal buttons, long enough to cover the knees. Cape to be attached and lined with rubber cloth. Felt hat, same shade as the overcoat. Green cloth cap, according to the shape prescribed by army regulation. Knapsack, etc., to conform, as nearly as possible, to the army pattern. Proper under-clothing.

Arms: no gun should weigh less than 10 pounds, nor more than 15 pounds. The caliber and model, in this case, to be less than 35 long balls to the pound. If any difficulty is found in obtaining guns of this description, the men can be supplied by the United States with Springfield rifles until a first class rifle of uniform caliber, adapted to this special arm of the service, can be made.

In my judgment, the best sights for this service are the plain open sight, consisting of a notch sight, and a silver pin at the muzzle, and a windage globe at the breech. The open sight would be convenient in obscure places. For long service and with good light, the globe may be used in connection with the silver pin forward sight. An extra main spring with nipple for each gun would be desirable.

The drill and signals for SharpShooters differ from all others in the service, and as attachments from different companies may, by accident or design, operate together in action. It is important that all the companies should be collected at the rendezvous, in order that they may become familiar with these, before any are sent forward into actual service. As no time and effort be lost in getting the men to the field, I would suggest that your company be forwarded

Above: *Lieutenant Colonel William Ripley, this Vermont born officer of Berdan's 1st Regiment of U.S. SharpShooters was greivously wounded at the Battle of Gaines Mill in June 1862.*

as soon as possible to the place of general rendezvous at Weehawken, New Jersey, on the North River, opposite the city. And that you empower an adjutant to uniform them here while being drilled. The company from this state will be uniformed before goods can arrive, and our committee for fitting-out this company will gladly render assistance.

Berdan, always cognizant of the necessity of approval from those in high office, kept President Lincoln apprised of the SharpShooters' progress:

The men are all selected, and have come a long way inside of the requirements. I shall have ten companies ready in about two weeks. I have made the standard high, which has had the effect to bring out nearly all of the first class rifle shots.

Should you call for three thousand SharpShooters, all to come up to the requirements of those now being mustered in, I will undertake to give them to you in thirty days. They would be worth thirty-thousand common troops with the common weapon, considering the mode of warfare conducted by the rebels.

H. Berdan

Berdan's plan to raise a regiment of SharpShooters was turning out to be far more difficult a task than he had first envisioned. The sheer logistics of recruiting in each of the 'Loyal States' was more than Berdan's helpers could manage and, therefore, Hiram was forced to secure additional time to ready his men. He requested and received favorable response from the War Department. A fifteen-day extension was given. With this positive response, Berdan redoubled his efforts to recruit marksmen. However, he was not always successful in securing all that he asked from each governor. In early August, for example, Berdan's agent lamented New York Governor Morgan's refusal to pay the newly recruited SharpShooters an additional bounty for their marksmanship skill.

The following letter from the Adjutant General of Wisconsin is representative of the strict entrance requirements for one wishing to be chosen one of Berdan's SharpShooters:

ATTENTION SharpShooters

August 17, 1861

All those men that have been tested and accepted by Captain W.P. Alexander will report themselves to Camp Randall, Wisconsin, on the 25th instant, if possible. Or by the 1st day of September, at the farthest. Those that have not been tested and wish to join the company can do so by reporting themselves to Captain Alexander, who will give them a chance to test their skill.

All persons coming here for trial who cannot fulfill the requirements of Colonel Berdan, will have to pay their own expenses, as the Government will not waste money on a man who cannot do that easy thing. It would be well for every man to furnish his own gun, if possible. Captain Alexander will assist those who wish to procure the proper kind of gun.

...As soon as the company has been filled to the requisite number, an election will be ordered for company officers.

On August 17th, a Wisconsin paper carried news of Berdan's SharpShooters to the populace, calling the yet to be assembled unit: *"The Crack Corps of the Army."*

SharpShooters ATTENTION!

Mr. W .S. Rowland, the accredited agent of Colonel Berdan, whose regiment of SharpShooters is accepted by the War Department, visited the Capital today. He exhibited his credentials and requested of Governor Randall that Wisconsin should furnish one company for the regiment.

The Governor has responded to the call, and issues a proclamation calling for them today. Each state sending six regiments to the war will be entitled to a company of SharpShooters numbering one hundred. A regiment of U.S. SharpShooters has been accepted for special service, upon the earnest solicitation of Lieutenant General Scott.

It is recommended that the states contributing SharpShooters raise subscriptions so that the men shall receive an addition 'to their pay as U.S. soldiers. The company from this state will be forwarded at the earliest moment, in detachments to Washington.

Noted rifle shots in different sections of the state will be selected to act as judges in determining the qualifications of candidates. Adjutant General Utley and Mr. Alexander are spoken of as fit men to be judges, as they cannot easily be excelled in the use of the rifle. Among the places that trials will be held will be Milwaukee, Madison, and New Lisbon.

This will be the Crack Corps of the Army, and it is rendered necessary, by reason of the guerrilla system of warfare adopted by the opposing force. The special mission of the SharpShooters is to pick off the officers of the rebel army. Mr. Rowland was detailed to organize and forward the western division of this corps, and holds his headquarters, at present, in Detroit.

The thanks of the people of the Loyal States are due to Mr. Berdan for this addition of so important an arm to the military service, in this, the hour of peril. And to Mr. Rowland, for his untiring zeal and energy in obtaining the immediate action of the governors of the western states, towards furnishing men and means for this organization, which he predicts will at once become a most powerful one in speedily crushing out this rebellion.

Berdan wrote to Major General McClellan, informing him of the progress made in raising his Regiment of SharpShooters. Berdan realized that the unit lacked a key element, without which they could not hope to become a viable fighting force – a veteran training officer. Such a man was needed to turn his raw, undisciplined recruits into Federal soldiers who would react to orders under fire in an unflinching manner. The unspoken request, it would figure, was that this veteran officer would also teach its leader, Berdan, but would not outrank him. The vacancy was filled, fortunately enough, by Lieutenant Colonel Frederick Mears.

Late in August, Berdan bypassed the chain of command and wrote directly to Major General McClellan, informing him of the status of his SharpShooters. His request for a next-in-command, a Lieutenant Colonel, bespoke of his own ignorance of military tactics and training:

According to instructions from the War Department, the various companies of the First Regiment of SharpShooters have been ordered to rendezvous at Weehawken, to be sworn into United States service. One company has already been mustered in. Of the other companies, one from each state, some are on the way. The rest have been promised by the respective governors [to arrive] in ten days, or a fortnight. I shall thus be able to place at the immediate disposal of the government, a regiment of picked rifle shots, for the test has been rigidly enforced.

Providing this body of men with officers has been a matter of serious concern. [They are] capable, trustworthy and spirited. Officers to whom the care, as well as the command of such men can be committed, with proper regard for their efficiency and safety. I believe that in company officers, I have been very successful in obtaining men who will do themselves, and their country, honor.

I need, however, a competent and efficient Lieutenant Colonel. Many applications have been made to me by gentlemen of my acquaintance, whom I know to be men of decision, intelligence and character, and who, since the opening of the present war, have devoted themselves to the study of the soldier's duty in the field. But I feel that the regiment should have, for the Lieutenant Colonel, a military man.

I, therefore, take the liberty of writing to you to ask that if consistent with your views and your duty, you will recommend to the War Department such a man among the army officers, or the resigned graduates of West Point, as you would like to see in actual command of the regiment.

I am aware that the course which I take in making this request of you is somewhat irregular, but I trust that my motive and your devotion to the cause may ensure my excuse.

H. Berdan

General McClellan forwarded Berdan's request to Secretary of War Cameron, requesting that a competent training officer be assigned to the SharpShooter Regiment.

Recruitment of the finest marksmen from each state continued through the late summer months of 1861. Berdan's appointed coordinators informed him, in detail, of their recruitment efforts and progress with specialized training.

As Berdan made ready to join his newly formed SharpShooters, his wife Mary sold their residence on Long Island. With the uncertainties of war approaching, she and her daughter returned to New Lebanon, New Hampshire, to live with her parents.

An initial point of rendezvous for Berdan's newly formed SharpShooters was established at Weehawken, New Jersey, across the Hudson River from New York City. The companies were ordered to assemble there, and the publicity they received from local newspapers, especially from the prestigious *HARPERS WEEKLY*, helped further their recruiting efforts:

HARPER'S WEEKLY – A JOURNAL OF CIVILIZATION

August 24, 1861

We illustrate, herewith, the exploits of Colonel Berdan and his famous sharpshooting regiment, which will shortly be heard of at the war. On [August] 7th, the Colonel gave an exhibition of his skill at Weehawken, New Jersey, in the presence of a large crowd of spectators:

The "man-target," christened Jeff Davis, was set up at a distance of more than two hundred yards. Colonel Berdan inaugurated the firing. In an easy, business-like way, he loaded his rifle, an ordinary target piece with a telescopic sight, and approached the "rest." The visitors crowded around him in every direction, excepting, of course, that occupied by the muzzle of the rifle. A sense of personal danger preserved a small opening there. The wind blew quite heavily.

Above: *On August 7, 1861, Hiram Berdan gives an impressive display of marksmanship by hitting a life-size target of Jeff Davis at over two hundred yards.*

TO THE

SHARP SHOOTERS

OF WINDHAM COUNTY!

Your Country Calls!! Will you Respond?

CAPT. WESTON has been authorized to raise a Company of Green Mountain Boys for Col. Berdan's Regiment of Sharp Shooters which has been accepted by the War Department to serve for three years, or during the war. Capt. Weston desires to have Windham County represented in his Company.

The Sharp Shooters of Windham County and vicinity who are willing to serve their country in this time of need and peril, are requested to meet at the ISLAND HOUSE in Bellows Falls, on TUESDAY, the 27th inst., at 1 o'clock, P. M., for the purpose of testing their skill in TARGET SHOOTING. There are great inducements to join this celebrated Regiment, destined to be the most important and popular in the Service.

No person will be enlisted who cannot when firing at the distance of 200 yards, at a rest, put ten consecutive shots in a target, the average distance not to exceed five inches from the centre of the bull's eye to the centre of the ball.

GREEN MOUNTAIN BOYS!

"Rally for the support of the Stars and Stripes!"

YOU ARE INVITED TO BRING YOUR RIFLES.

F. F. STREETER, Supt. of Trial.

BELLOWS FALLS, VT., August 19, 1861.

Phenix Job Office, Bellows Falls.

Above: *An original Berdan SharpShooter recruiting poster, dated August 19,1861 seeking a Company of "Green Mountain Boys"!*

It will be conceded that these circumstances were not particularly conducive to careful and unerring aim. But Colonel Berdan is a man of wonderful nerve. The crowd did not at all disturb him. He proceeded in the work with the utmost steadiness. Balancing his rifle for a moment, he fired at the head of the figure. When the smoke cleared away, the hole made by the bullet was observed by the aid of the telescope – the cheek, near the nose.

Again the Colonel loaded and quickly fired at the head, hitting it just over the front piece of the cap, which was painted upon it.

The third shot was fired. "Put his eye out," remarked the Colonel. The ball had struck near enough to that organ to destroy its use, had it been a real one.

The fourth shot hit the face. "I'll try nature's rest," said the Colonel, and he proceeded to a knoll nearby, and throwing himself at its side, accommodated his person to its shape and took aim, but the percussion cap only exploded. "Davis is safe this time," he remarked. "We'll try him again." Another cap was provided, and the image was struck just below the front piece of the cap. The aim was quite as accurate as that he had previously obtained.

The sixth shot hit about two inches lower than the fifth. The seventh hit the top of the head. Loading again, the Colonel made ready to fire. "Where will you have this shot?" he inquired of one standing by. "In the end of the nose," was the answer. "Between the eyes," suggested another. At this moment the rifle discharged. "You spoke too late," quietly remarked the Colonel, "as he has another nostril." A gentleman was called to witness the effect of the shot, and afterward our reporter. The nose has an additional aperture.

"Where shall I put the next shot?" the Colonel inquired of the gentleman at whose request he had spoiled the nose of the image. "Try his right eye," was the answer. No sooner said than it was done. The ball entered the lower part of the eye. The effect of this shot was carefully noted by several persons through the glass.

"Will you tell me where to hit him again?" once more asked the Colonel of the person who had called the last two shots. The individual declined. He was satisfied that the Colonel could hit anything, and it was not worth while to fire at the image, whose face was riddled. "We will hit him once more, and now in the center of the forehead." This shot, the tenth, was the finest of the whole. It took effect midway between the front piece of the cap, and the root of the nose, and directly over that organ. The distances were almost mathematically accurate.

Some idea of the rigidity of the test may be gathered from the fact that no man is admitted who does not shoot, at 600 feet distance, ten consecutive shots at an average of five inches from the bulls-eye. That is, the aggregate distance of the whole ten shots must not exceed fifty inches. Not a man is accepted, under any circumstances, who varies a hair-breadth from the mark. Remarkable though it may seem, many of the men exceed this proficiency. Colonel Berdan, himself, has on a windy day, with a strange rifle, put ten balls within an average distance of one inch and one-tenth each from the bulls-eye, at 600 feet. At 1,000 feet, the Colonel made a string of 22 inches. Sergeant Major Brown, under more favorable circumstances, made a string of 33 inches, or a little more than three inches for each ball, at a distance of 100 yards, with a strange rifle.

In testing the applicants at Albany, about two-thirds were found unfitted, and indeed the general average of incompetent applicants is more than that. The American riflemen prove generally superior, especially the hunters of New England, and the west.

The uniform of the sharp-shooters will be green in the summer, and gray at other seasons, to assimilate, as nearly as possible with the colors of nature. They ridicule the idea of Zouave and Havelock uniforms, as according too splendid a target for marksmen. They will be armed with the most improved Springfield rifle, with a plain silver pin sight at the muzzle, and notch sight, or the globe sight at the breech for long range, or on a dark day, or night shooting. It was, at first, intended to arm them with the Northern target-rifle, but it was found that there were not enough in the country.

Colonel Berdan has invented a ball [bullet] which is superior to the old Springfield rifle ball. It will carry with great accuracy at a distance of 3,000 feet. It is a grooved and conical ball, and is almost certain for a horse [sic] at the distance of three-fifths of a mile. Each man may take his own rifle, if he wishes.

The design of the Colonel is to have the regiment detached in squads on the field of battle to do duty in picking off officers and gunners on the European plan, by which they take the risk of being cut off by cavalry, or executed, as they certainly would be, if taken. It is the first regiment of rifles worthy of the name (i.e. that subjected each member to the rifle-shooting test).

Captain Aschmann reported that the camp at Weehawken was quite pleasant:

> Our tents had the shape of an "A" and were, therefore, called "A-tents." Each was designed to house four men. Great stress was laid on cleanliness in camp, and everyone tried to make his place look really homey and pleasant. The snow-white tents were decorated with leafy boughs and pine branches. Each of the parallel streets had been given a name reminiscent of the fatherland: one was called Tell Street, another Swiss Homeland, a third Winkelried Lane.

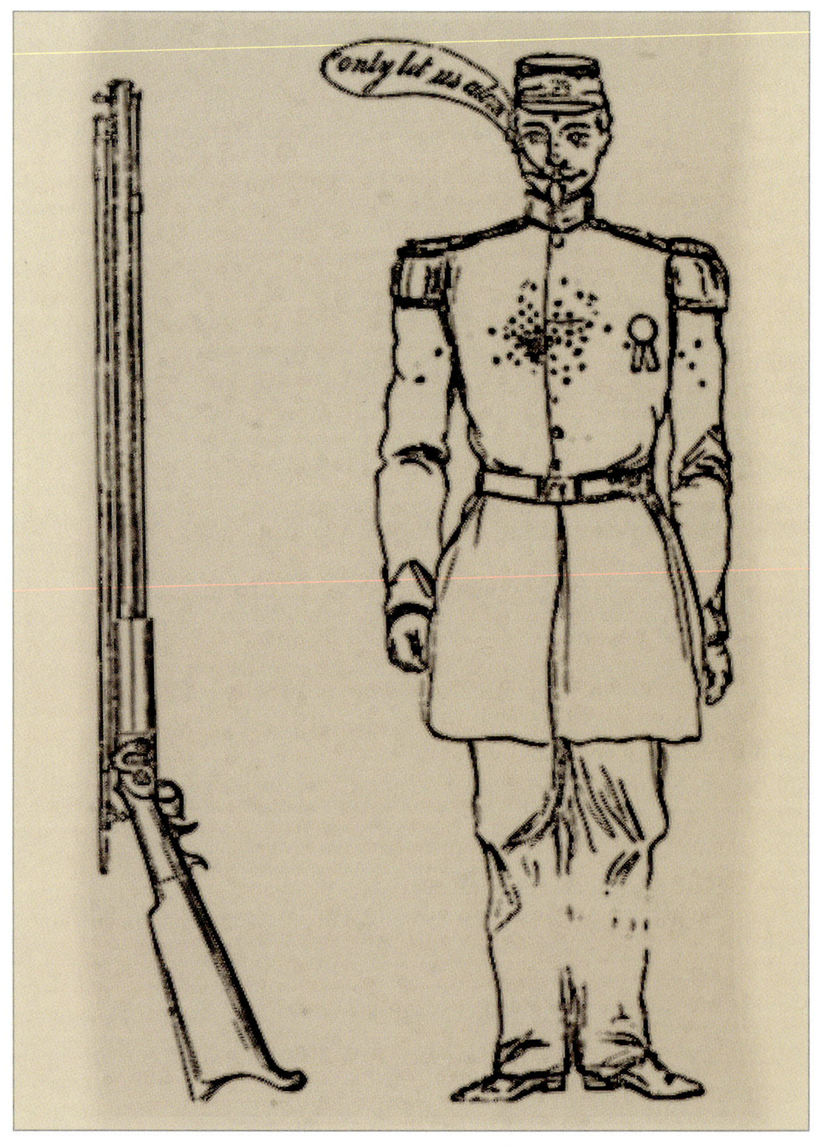

Above: *An amateur artist's recording of the rifle used by Berdan and the life size target said to represent the President of the Confederacy, Jefferson Davis, which he used for his demonstration at Weehawken.*

Not all of the individual companies of Berdan's SharpShooters were sent to Weehawken, as evidenced by this amusing and informative letter from a Wisconsin marksman to his hometown newspaper:

Camp Randall,
Wisconsin
September 6th, 1861

As you are aware, I left the village last Saturday by railroad for this place, and on my arrival in the evening I reported myself on hand to Captain Alexander, for the war. We, however, did not come into camp until Monday, following, although at the time, but few in number, owing to the unavoidable delay of most of the accepted dates, on account of work which detained them.

We are now, however, rapidly filling up, and in about ten days, the Wisconsin Company of the First Regiment, United States SharpShooters, expect to start for the rendezvous at New York City. The Captain, having today received a letter from Colonel Berdan to that effect.

I find things here considerably improved since the time when the Citizen's Guard first came into quarters at this place last spring. The barracks and mess room are now waterproof, while tents are freely supplied whenever needed. As for the victuals, it is enough for me to say that they are in a "sound and healthy condition," and of great variety, such as beef, potatoes, bread and butter, coffee and water, beans, soups and stews, with a good sprinkling of pepper, salt and vinegar, and occasionally fruit, such as melons, etc.

One evil exists, however, which did not, when the encampment was first established, and which should be remedied, which is the sale of Lager beer at the refreshment booths on the ground. This results, sometimes, in the Volunteers imbibing a little too freely (some of them), which is apt to make them ugly and "don't care a damnish."

The soldiers here, at present, are kept busily at work, and we are consequently being rapidly drilled, to use an expressive phrase, "up to the handle."

Captain Alexander's men, at present, employ themselves principally at target shooting and making double-quick march towards the mess room when grub call is sounded on the waiter's drum. Those of the Captain's men who have thus far come to time, show by their behavior, their stout and rugged appearance and their superior marksmanship, that they are certainly good men.

In concluding this letter, I will remark that although there are several companies springing up under the name of SharpShooters, they are nothing, more or less, than Musketeers, while Captain Alexander's company is the real, original SharpShooters from the Badger State, while the so-called "Sharps" are, in I reality, bogus. As for the Captain, he can't be beat, not only at shooting, but in good manner or anything else, or any other man.

Berdan's Camp of Instruction

On September 2nd, the War Department ordered Berdan's newly formed, yet not fully assembled regiment to proceed from its temporary rendezvous at Weehawken, New Jersey, and to set up a new *Camp of Instruction*, just north of Washington D.C.

On September 6, the *NEW YORK WORLD* newspaper reported the departure of the first two companies of Berdan's SharpShooters from Weehawken to *"the seat of war."* Their uniform, the paper went on to say, was:

Peculiarly appropriate for their position as marksmen, consisting of green frock coats, gray pantaloons, and green caps. The dress is made to accord with the colors of nature, as much as possible, and is intended to be worn in summer. In winter, the uniform will consist entirely of a gray pattern.

As late as September 14th, even though many of Berdan's companies had already departed for their permanent Camp of Instruction in Washington, D.C., some others were just arriving in Weehawken from their respective states:

U.S. SharpShooters
The New Hampshire company for Berdan's SharpShooters, 100 strong, reached the camp at Weehawken on Thursday. The Vermont company is expected today. These New Hampshire marksmen are all men of excellent moral character, more than ordinary intelligence, and of good social position. Quite one-third are farmers, the remainder being composed of mechanics and artisans who earn their $2 a day, the year round.

Captain A.B. Jones is a wonderful rifle shot, having made a ten-shot string of seven inches from a rest in a recent public trial of the men. This almost equals the marvelous exploit of Colonel Berdan, himself, at the Weehawken exhibition, and is actually better than the champion string made in 1848, in Kentucky. Let the Colonel look to his laurels.

Captain Jones, in recruiting the New Hampshire company, advertised for candidates to come to headquarters, bringing with them satisfactory certificates of good character and habits as their second qualification for admission. The result was that over 250 applications were made, nearly all of them by men who could "pass the string test."

The Camp of Instruction for Berdan's First Regiment of U.S. SharpShooters was located immediately northwest of the Prospect Hill Cemetery. Today, this site would be east of North Capitol Street and north of Rhode Island Avenue. Period maps of Washington City (as it was sometimes called) show the encampment site on a high flat piece of ground. U.S. SharpShooter historian Charles Stevens mentions the cemetery to the southeast, and states that the camp bordered the Corcoran Estate. Private Wyman S. White, a new recruit for Company F (New Hampshire), 2nd U.S.S.S. stated:

We arrived at the grounds where we were to camp about noon on December 1st, 1861. It was on high ground, and was on the southwest side of a rise of ground between 4th and 7th Streets, west about a mile and a half from the Capitol. The 1st Regiment of SharpShooters were camped on the highest part of the rise, and six companies of the 2nd Regiment were already in camp. Some of the companies were in Sibley tents, some in "A" tents, and some in nice circular wall tents that were furnished by their State, Maine. The right and rear corners of the two camps of regiments came together. We had Sibley tents, which were circular, and at the ground were about fourteen feet in diameter. Twenty men were assigned to each tent. The weather was cool, and it looked rather hard to me to lay down on the cold damp ground with nothing under me but straw and only two blankets over us, each man having drawn a woolen blanket at the Quartermaster, and two of us bunking together, that giving two blankets.

Competitive rifle shooting became a daily affair, with dignitaries frequently visiting on weekends. Of one occasion President Lincoln, General McClellan, and Assistant Secretary of War Scott paid a visit to the camp, and were invited by Colonel Berdan to the rifle range where shooting was in progress. To show off the SharpShooters' marksmanship skills, a target with two figures painted on the canvas was placed at a distance of 600 yards. One hundred men with their heavy target rifles, entered the pit, where each fired one shot. When the target was brought in, it was found that every shot had struck within the outline of the two figures. This was a remarkable exhibition of sharpshooting, a feat that would be difficult to duplicate, even with today's most up-to-date target rifles.

Historian Stevens would later relate:

President Lincoln fired three shots from a globe-rifle, belonging to H.J. Peck, of Company F, while General McClellan and some others tried their skill with more or less success. Abraham Lincoln handled the rifle like a veteran marksman, in a highly successful manner, to the great delight of the many soldiers and civilians surrounding. Once, resting his gun on what he called a sapling, he said: "Boys, this reminds me of old time shooting." Then they waved their hats and cheered him. His visit aroused their slumbering patriotism.

After which, Colonel Berdan being called on, proceeded to execute some difficult shots, by knocking out the right eye of a Zouave painted full length on half of an A-tent. This was done with a James telescope rifle. He fired three shots, all easily found within the parts [of the Zouave] selected, the head, right breast, or left thigh.

Then occurred one of those extraordinary accidents from which great and beneficial results often follow. Thomas Scott, the Assistant Secretary of War, thought to gain a point by attacking me [Colonel Berdan] personally, and asked me what I knew about guns and war, that I should set up my opinion against all these officials, and ended by challenging me to fire (thinking, doubtless, I would decline), or if I accepted, to get the laugh on me by my making a bad shot. I at once accepted, and ordered the men to bring out a target. The only one left was the figure of a single man, full size, with the words Jeff Davis painted above his head. I remarked that I did not think it was exactly the thing to fire at Jeff Davis in the presence of the President of the United States. Mr. Lincoln laughed heartily, and replied: "Oh Colonel, if you make a good shot it will serve him right."

Below: *A woodcut entitled: "Trial of skill of Berdan's Riflemen before General McClellan and Staff at Washington." that appeared in Frank Leslie's:* American Soldier in the Civil War. *A large crowd of civilians gathered to watch the marksmen load their muzzleloading rifles and fire from rifle pits at stationary targets.*

Above: *A commemorative poster recording the various stages of the shooting demonstrations at Weehawken. This kind of spectacle was very much a propaganda exercise aimed at both the U.S. Public and the Confederacy.*

The target was set up and I called for the Sergeant Major's rifle, which I knew to be correctly sighted for this distance.

Thomas Scott then remarked: "Now you must fire standing, for officers should not dirty their uniforms by getting into rifle pits." I replied: "You are right, Colonel Scott, as I always fire from the shoulder." I stepped forward and began to bring the gun to my face, when he said: "What point are you going to fire at?" "The head," I replied. "Fire at the right eye," he shouted.

I was then taking aim and made no reply, and it is hardly necessary for me to say that at that distance I did not aim at the eye, but did fire at the head. The target was brought in, and as good luck would have it, I had cut out the pupil of the right eye.

No man knew better than President Lincoln how to turn what he knew to be an accident to good account. He began to laugh, and kept on laughing until he got into his carriage, and then he said: "Colonel, come down tomorrow and I will give you the order for breechloaders." Mr. Lincoln visited us once or twice later, and spoke of "that remarkable shot," as a good joke – a lucky hit!

The aforementioned story resembles, in part, Berdan's exploits as a marksman at Weehawken a month earlier on August 7th. Differing facts suggest that both incidents did occur, and the similarity is coincidental. The August event was dated by *HARPERS WEEKLY* and the September exposition was chronicled by the *NEW YORK TIMES* newspaper:

> THE SharpShooters
> Colonel Berdan had a review this afternoon of his regiment of SharpShooters, and an exhibition of their efficiency. It was attended by the President, Secretaries Cameron and Seward, the Prince de Joinville, [the President's] private Secretary Nicolay, General McClellan and staff, General Mansfield and staff, and a large number of ladies and gentlemen.
>
> Something like four hundred shots were fired, at a distance of 630 yards. The target was two figure of Zouaves, the size of life. The men used thirty-five pound rifles, firing by platoons from a rifle pit, at rest, and with globe sights. The firing was nothing extraordinary, only one-fourth of the shots hitting the target. Colonel Berdan fired offhand, and hit the head of one of the targets.

Nothing extraordinary? Only a quarter of the shots hitting the target? Which account shall we believe, Historian Stevens, or that of the correspondent of the *NEW YORK TIMES?* Meanwhile, all efforts were made by governmental officials to hasten the assembly of soldiers at Washington. On September 12, Secretary of War, Simon Cameron, instructed the governors to send forward their newly-formed SharpShooters directly to the Camp of Instruction in Washington. He also informed them that special uniforms would be furnished.

Quite unexpectedly, some of Berdan's SharpShooters were pressed into battle on September 21. As all companies had not yet arrived in Washington, D.C., only Company C (Michigan SharpShooters under Captain Benjamin Duesler) and Company E (New Hampshire SharpShooters under Captain Amos Jones), armed with heavy target rifles were ready to experience battle.

Historian Stevens stated:

> Leaving camp under orders to join General Smith's expedition on the 21st of September, they marched to Fort

ATTENTION,

RIFLEMEN.

The subscriber has been authorized to raise a company of

SHARP SHOOTERS

to be attached to a Regiment now being formed for the war. The company will be composed of 1 Captain; 1 First Lieutenant; 1 Second Lieutenant; 1 First Sergeant; 4 Sergeants; 8 Corporals; 2 Musicians; 1 Wagoner; 82 privates; 101 aggregate.

The men going in this company will be entitled to Government pay including State additional, will have transportation expenses paid, be furnished with good rations and the best arms in the service. It is desirable to have the men between

18 and 36 Years

age of medium height, all good marksmen, and be ready to move to head qaarters within 10 days from this date. All communications on the subject may be addressed to me at

OXFORD FURNACE, WARREN CO., N. J.,

and the following persons will give any necessary information relative to the organization, viz:

Jos. J. Henry, and Hon. David Smith, Oxford Furnace, N. J. Abraham Depue, and Jacob Sharp, Belvidere. Caleb Swayze, Hope. Marshal Hunt and Hon Isaac Wildrick, Blairstown. Opdycke Cummings, Vienna. Robt. Rusling, Hackettstown. Jacob W. Davis, Andersontown. D. M. Wyckoff, Port Colden. Joseph Vliet, Esq., Washington. Hon. Chas. Sitgreaves, Phillipsburg. Hon. E. C. Moore, Newton.

CHAS. SCRANTON.

OXFORD FURNACE, Sept. 17th, 1861.

Printed at Sellers' CHEAP Job Printing Office, Belvidere, N. J.

Above: *A recruiting poster believed to have been used to attract potential SharpShooters from New Jersey. Dated September 1861 which coincided with Berdan's marksmanship Trials in the northern states. As it turned out no companies were formed due to lack of interest.*

Smith, near Chain Bridge. Then they marched to Lewinsville, where they took part on September 27th, in an attack on a small force of the enemy, who had been on a foraging expedition, destroying and capturing a great portion of supplies, and defeating their cavalry. Here it was that the first shots of the Berdan SharpShooters were fired at the secessionists, with good effect while the affair lasted.

The march had been a hurried one and the soldiers were considerably fatigued, but obeyed the orders to advance with alacrity, performing the part assigned them in a manner that attracted the notice of the commanding general.

Having disposed of the enemy in their front, who made a hasty retreat, they moved forward in connection with the infantry in the direction of Falls Church, and again encountered the enemy at Munson's Hill. Here they became engaged in a night fight, after midnight on September 29th. It was a very unpleasant affair to the SharpShooters, and they were extremely lucky to find, after daylight, that they had but one man wounded.

Berdan offered to send a battle-tested SharpShooter to tell President Lincoln of the battlefield exploits:

September 23, 1861
His Excellency – Abraham Lincoln
President of the United States
Sir:
The bearer, one of my SharpShooters, shot a rebel on Saturday. His account of the affair is quite interesting. If you would like to see him, he will come at your pleasure.

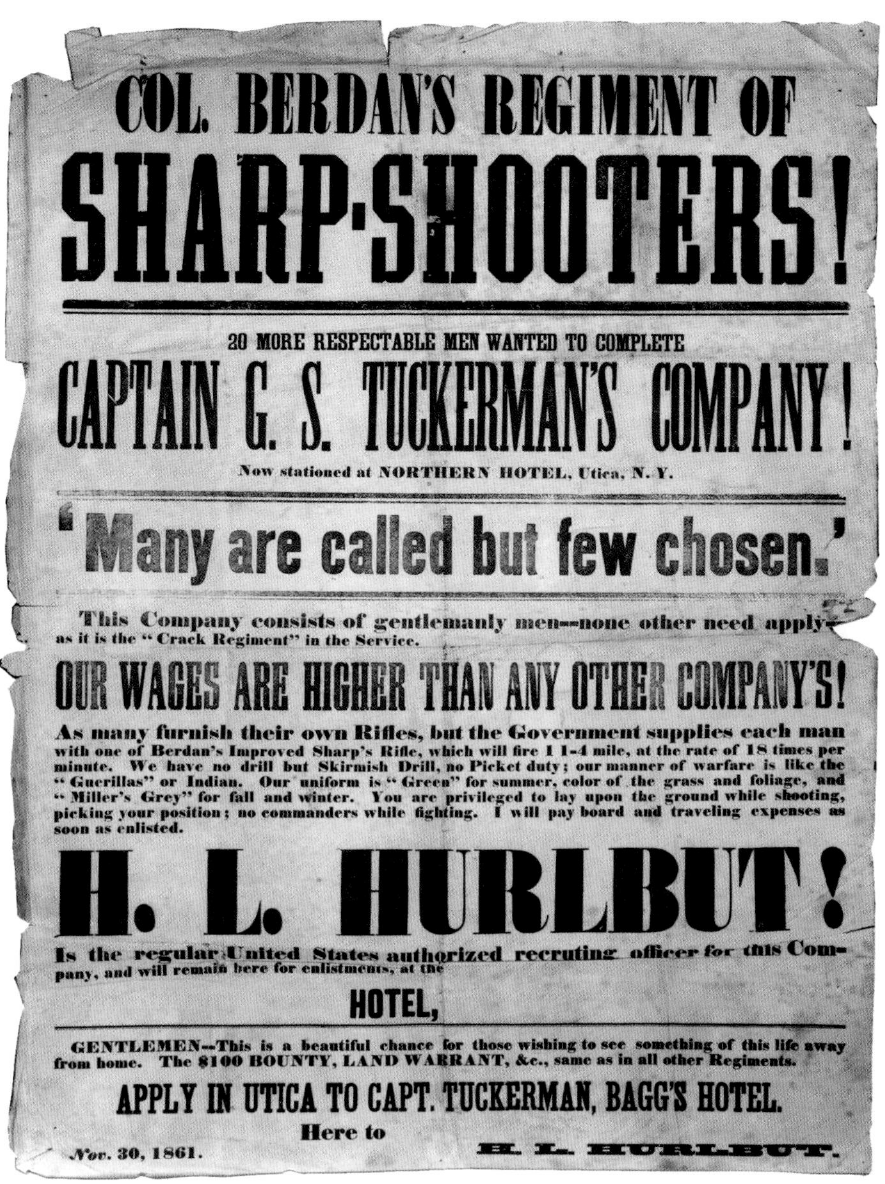

Above: *A very rare and authentic recruitment poster for a company of skilled marksmen from New York for* Colonel Berdan's Regiment of SharpShooters! *It measures 18 by 25 inches, and is dated November 30,1861.*

Remaining companies of Berdan's SharpShooters began arriving at the Camp of Instruction after September 24. Lieutenant Colonel William Y. W. Ripley would later speak of this time:

On the 24th of September the regiment proceeded under orders from the War Department to Washington. We arrived at the late hour on the night of the 25th and were assigned quarters at the Soldiers' Rest, so well known to the troops who arrived at Washington at this time. On the 26th they were ordered to a permanent Camp of Instruction, well out in the country, and near the residence and grounds of Mr. Corcoran, a wealthy resident of Washington (he was accused of supposed secessionist proclivities). Here they were, for the first time, in a regularly organized camp, and could begin to feel that they were fairly cut off, at last, from the custom and habits of civil life.

The field and staff [officers] were made up, as follows:

Colonel — Hiram Berdan
Lieutenant Colonel — Frederick Mears
Major — W.S. Roland
Adjutant — Floyd A. Willet
Quartermaster — William H. Beebe
Surgeon — Guy C. Marshall
Assistant Surgeon — Dr. John W. Brennan
Chaplain — Reverand Dr. Coit

Only one of the field officers had a military education, or military experience. Lieutenant Colonel Mears was an officer of the Regular Army, a thorough drill master and strict disciplinarian. Under his efficient command the regiment soon began to show a marked and daily improvement that augured well for its future usefulness. The officers of the regimental staff were, each in his own department, able and painstaking men.

Above: *Colonel Henry A.V. Post, a pre-war business acquaintance of Hiram Berdan ,commanded the 2nd Regiment of U.S SharpShooters.*

The thought of SharpShooters without firearms was unthinkable, yet the truth was that Berdan's men had few serviceable arms. Their weapons consisted of the heavy-barreled, muzzleloading target rifles that some of the troops had brought with them, and a few antiquated Hall rifles that the V.S. SharpShooters had been issued for guard duty. Berdan complained, as well he should, to his immediate Commander in nearby Camp Benton (a temporary cantonment area not unlike Berdan's Camp of Instruction). General Lander wrote to Berdan and suggested that he order Model 1855 Harper's Ferry rifles and issue them to his men. Berdan answered with anger and informed the General that the men would have none of it. Therefore, the issue of arms for the SharpShooters went unresolved.

Over the next few months, all of the recruited companies of Berdan's First Regiment of U.S. SharpShooters, nearly a thousand hand-picked marksmen, assembled at Colonel Hiram Berdan's Camp of Instruction. They represented five of the "Loyal Northern States":

Company	
A – New York	Captain Caspar Trepp
B – New York	Captain Stephen Martin
C – Michigan	Captain Benjamin Duesler
D – New York	Captain George Tuckerman
E – New Hampshire	Captain Amos Jones
F – Vermont	Captain Edmund Weston
G – Wisconsin	Captain Edward Drew
H – New York	Captain George Hastings
I – Michigan	Captain A.M. Willett
K – Michigan	Captain S.J. Mather

Company D and Company K did not arrive until January and March, respectively, in the following year. Nonetheless, on September 28, 1861, Colonel Berdan informed the Secretary of War of the status of his First Regiment, and stated that a Second Regiment would be assembled shortly:

> I have the honor to inform you that my First Regiment of SharpShooters is now full. Three companies have been sent forward, temporarily, for picket duty, by order of Major General McClellan. The remaining companies will be forwarded with a Lieutenant Colonel in a few days.
>
> I have been ordered to remain in camp to organize my Second Regiment, and I have good reason to believe that it will be full in two weeks from this date. So great is the desire on the part of the good rifle shots throughout the Loyal States to join the service, that I am compelled from a sense of duty to ask that I may be ordered to muster all that I can get during the next ninety days. If they be fully up to the requirements I have adopted for my Corps, I will organize them into regiments. I will report to Major General McClellan when they are ready for the field.
>
> H. Berdan
> Colonel Commanding
> U.S. SharpShooters

Simon Cameron's answer to Colonel Berdan on October 3rd. gave him the authority to muster his 2nd Regiment of SharpShooters:

> I cheerfully grant your application to be allowed to muster and organize into companies and regiments, all the men that you can obtain during the next ninety days, and who, on examination, may be found equal to the regiments that you have already adopted for your Corps.

When finally recruited and assembled, the 2nd Regiment of U.S. SharpShooters was commanded by Colonel Henry A. V. Post, a pre-war business acquaintance of Hiram Berdan. After arriving at the Camp of Instruction, the 2nd Regiment settled in on Meridian Hill, numbering slightly less than 800 marksmen.

Company	
A – Minnesota	Captain Francis Peteler
B – Michigan	Captain Andrew Stuart
C – Pennsylvania	Captain John Dewey
D – Maine	Captain James Fessenden
E – Vermont	Captain Homer Stoughton

F – New Hampshire	Captain Henry Caldwell
G – New Hampshire	Captain Wm. McPherson
H – Vermont	Captain Gilbert Hart

Two companies of SharpShooters originally recruited from Massachusetts for the 2nd Regiment of U.S. SharpShooters were kept independent, and never officially were a part of Berdan's unit. They briefly trained alongside Berdan's men, and became known as The Andrews SharpShooters, named after Governor Andrews of Massachusetts. A Madison, Wisconsin newspaper printed the following in their November 6th issue:

> News arrived of the fighting of the Massachusetts Company of Berdan's U.S.S.S. who did terrible execution in picking off the enemy with their long range Minie's.

Captain Rudolf Aschmann, later commander of Company F of the 1st Regiment, described these first months in camp:

> The tents were arranged in ten long, parallel rows. One row each was to serve one company. At the upper end of the streets formed by the tents, about 35 steps removed from the others, the officers' tents were put up, one each for one captain or two lieutenants. In between these and the enlisted men's tents, the mess kitchens were set up. A large field next to the camp was turned into a parade ground. Colonel Berdan and his staff took up headquarters in a nearby dwelling.
>
> Drill was rigorous, guard duty had to be performed, and each man had to do his own laundry. Tents and camp streets had to be kept clean and neat at all times.
>
> The government tried to keep us well supplied with all that was needed. The rations that were brought in from the city consisted of one and a quarter pound of fresh or corned beef, or three-quarters of a pound of bacon, and one and a third pound of bread, daily for each man. For each 100 men we received fifteen pounds of beans, or ten pounds of rice, eight pounds of roasted and ground coffee, or one and a half pounds of tea, and 15 pounds of sugar. Vinegar, salt, syrup, soap, and candles were distributed twice a week. Occasionally we had potatoes and other vegetables, instead of peas or rice. There was a good supply of straw for preparing adequate sleeping places, so we had no reason, whatever, for complaining.
>
> The Colonel of our regiment, H. Berdan, was not well liked by the rank and file, and often made a fool of himself with his clumsy demeanor. He had no military experience, since he had never been associated with the military. He owed his position only to the influence of high-ranking personages and the favor of the President, with whom he had been on good terms for a long time.

Above: *Lieutenant Colonel Frederick Mears was a serving Army officer who had the necessary experience to train Berdan's raw recruits.*

Training green recruits for the rigors of war was almost as difficult a task as training the equally green officers to lead them. Initially this important task fell onto the shoulders of the Regular Army Officer, Lieutenant Colonel Frederick Mears.

Aschmann would later describe him as:

> ...an excellent military man who did his best to train the still inexperienced officers and troops, to become able soldiers.
>
> Mears had been assigned to our regiment mainly to cover up for Berdan's incompetence and to turn us fast into efficient soldiers. Most of the rank and file idolized him, for he combined expert knowledge with salutary strictness and fatherly solicitude for the men. Under his guidance the regiment was successfully drilled in basic training, skirmishing and guard duty.

Basic training of the Federal soldier in 1861 consisted of learning the manual of arms, following orders, learning parade drill and marching. Therefore, Lieutenant Colonel Mears began his instruction of officers and enlisted men in individual and company drill. As the days grew shorter and the weather colder, Berdan's SharpShooters busied themselves learning military discipline. The following schedule illustrates the daily routine at the Camp of Instruction:

1st Regiment of Berdan's U.S. SharpShooters
Regimental Order No.1

The following will be the order of the daily camp duty:

6:30 A.M.	Reveille, and Company streets to be policed.
7:00 A.M.	Breakfast.
7:30 A.M.	Sick call.
8:00 A.M.	First call for guard mounting.
8:30 A.M.	Guard mounting.
9:00 A.M.	Company drill, and squad drill for new recruits.
11:00 A.M.	Recall.
12:00 P.M.	Dinner.
2:00 P.M.	Company drill, and squad drill for new recruits.
3:30 P.M.	Recall.
4:00 P.M.	First call for dress parade.
5:00 P.M.	Retreat.
5:15 P.M.	Supper.
7:30 P.M.	Tattoo
8:00 P.M.	Taps, lights out, and all quiet

Mears, accompanied by the very few other officers and non-commissioned officers who had prior military experience, did their best to instruct the raw recruits in the elements of skirmishing. *HARDEE'S TACTICS (left)* was the secular bible used to turn farmers, schoolboys, and businessmen into soldiers.

Because of their proven skills as marksmen, Berdan's SharpShooters were later to be utilized as skirmishers, the first elements to encounter the enemy in movement, or in stationary defensive positions. Depending upon terrain, skirmishers would usually be placed up to 500 yards in front of the main body of infantry, their primary purpose to suppress enemy fire as much as possible. They would harass the enemy with carefully aimed and selected fire of their own. The following aspects of skirmishing were to become the trademark of the U.S. SharpShooters:

In skirmish drill, the officers and non-commissioned officers impressed upon each man the idea of his own individuality, and the responsibility that rests upon him. Skirmishers had to economize their strength, preserve their presence of mind, husband their ammunition, and profit by all the advantages which the ground offered for cover. They had to cultivate the feeling that they could not be beaten, and that, when compelled to give ground, a new position was to be gained from which the action would be renewed.

As skirmishers, Berdan's SharpShooters learned that advancing enemy infantrymen would approach at a rate of 70 yards per minute *"common time,"* 86 yards per minute *"quick time,"* and a deadly 109 yards per minute *"double-quick time."* However, trained marksmen, in concealed defensive positions, held distinct advantages over the advancing enemy. They made poor targets, and they could load and fire without much movement. They could aim every shot, with a high probability of a first round hit, and they would not be blinded by smoke from friendly muskets or cannon.

Advancing enemy soldiers, on the other hand, saw smoke from musket fire, but rarely saw a distinct target. They had to fire and reload on the move. They were frequently weary from prolonged marches, heavy packs, muddy fields and temperature extremes. And they were frequently demoralized by seeing the long distance to be traversed, the deaths of fellow soldiers advancing with them, and the smell, smoke and sound of death in front of them.

First Sergeant Wyman S. White of Company F (New Hampshire), 2nd U.S.S.S. later recalled:

> Skirmish drill is an open order drill. Men form in line in two ranks, then at the order, deploy by fours. Two files off both ranks would take distances twenty feet apart, then at the order, deploy in line. Each man on the left of the four would take distance five places to the left of number one in the front rank, he standing fast. Number one in the rear rank and number two in the rear rank taking distances five paces to the left of the number one in the front rank. The squads of fours taking distance still further to the left and deploying to the distance of five paces apart until the whole company or regiment was in a single line, five paces space between each man. Thus deployed, 350 men would make a line a mile long. We took our orders from the call of the bugle, as no man's voice could reach the length of the line.

All of these things would be taught to every SharpShooter, although it would take the experience of actual battle for them to fully understand Lieutenant Colonel Mears' military instruction.

In the late fall, the daily schedule was changed to include marksmanship training. Commencing promptly at 10:20 A.M., target shooting lasted about an hour and a quarter. Afternoon target practice started at 3:45 P.M., and lasted until 5 P.M. Approaching winter darkness would not allow ample visibility much past this hour. Unfortunately, the only arms available for marksmanship were the wide array of target and sporting rifles which were the personal property of some of the enlisted men. There was no uniformity in type, size or caliber, making standardized marksmanship drill extremely difficult. But these men were already accomplished marksmen, proven by the recruitment tests that they had passed weeks or months earlier. To a man, they loved to shoot, making target practice the high point of their day in camp. Historian Stevens would later state:

> Prize shooting was occasionally allowed, and usually created a healthy excitement among the men, as well as visitors who were sure to be there. One of the most important of these matches was held Thanksgiving afternoon, between members of the target-rifle companies C, E and F.

> Each man fired two shots off-hand at 40 rods, with the winner to receive five dollars, presented by the Colonel. The day being fine there was a large attendance of public men and others who came from town to see the SharpShooters shoot. The judges were Captain Giroux of Company C and Sergeant Stevens of Company G. They awarded the prize to a Vermonter named Al Brown, his shots measuring four and a quarter inches from the center. H.J. Peck of the same company, a prominent marksman, was a close second in the match, almost a tie.
>
> Colonel Berdan opened the proceedings by firing two specimen shots, making a string of five and nine-sixteenths inches. Later on, other officers tried their skill, and among them Captain Drew, who, borrowing a rifle, lay on his back and resting the muzzle of the piece on the toe of his boot, fired four shots within the ten inch ring. This manner of shooting was somewhat novel, if not exactly original and became quite popular years after the war, when Creedmoor was established.

Camp life was not altogether difficult for the newly recruited troops, as can be seen in the revised daily schedule, which was put into effect from Monday through Saturday:

5:45 A.M.	Reveille
6:30 A.M.	Breakfast
7:00 A.M.	Sick call
7:00 A.M.	Drill -company movements
8:00 A.M.	Recall
8:10 A.M.	First call for guard mounting
8:15 A.M.	Guard mounting
9:00 A.M.	Drill -skirmishing
10:15 A.M.	Recall
10:20 A.M.	Target practice
11:45 A.M.	Recall
12 noon	Dinner
12:45 P.M.	Drill skirmishing
2:30 P.M.	Recall
3:45 P.M.	Target practice
5:00 P.M.	Recall
5:15 P.M.	First call for parade
5:30 P.M.	Retreat
6:00 P.M.	Supper
9:00 P.M.	Tattoo
9:10 P.M.	Taps, lights out and all quiet in Camp

U.S.S.S. Regimental Order No.2 stated:

> This command will parade every Sunday morning, fully uniformed and equipped, without rifles, and be prepared at 7:30 A.M. for inspection. Men's clothes, equipment, quarters, cookhouses and pans will undergo a thorough inspection by the Commanding Officer. There will be no drill or target practice on the Sabbath. The only duties to be performed will pertain to the ordinary routine of duty at camp.
>
> H. Berdan

An article in a local Madison, Wisconsin newspaper, dated October 19, 1861, referred to Berdan's Camp of Instruction as *"Camp Burnside,"* and stated that arms for the regiment had not yet arrived. The article went on to state that "the volunteers were quite anxious for war." This sounds like the innocent murmurings of youth, anxious for glory, but ignorant of the pain that actual warfare brings. None among them could envision the many long winter months that were in front of them. Some would die of sickness in the damp, bone-chilling days ahead, long before the SharpShooters would be marched into battle.

On October 22, Colonel Berdan informed his commanding officer of the first delivery of overcoats for his SharpShooters. These coats were not the recognizable SharpShooter green, but were actually gray, with green trimming and with hard rubber buttons. Actual field experience in the months that followed forced the men to abandon these overcoats, lest their gray color cause them to be mistaken for Confederates.

On October 28, the War Department put a halt to Berdan's recruiting effort, and ordered all remaining troops to the official SharpShooter Camp of Instruction outside of Washington, D.C.:

> I think we have a sufficient number of SharpShooters enlisted to meet the wants of the Army. Close the camp near New York [Weehawken, New Jersey], and such recruits as are in camp should be brought here [Washington, D.C.], and go into service at once.

The dullness and boredom of camp life were punctuated by infrequent visits from curious government officials. Captain Aschmann remembered:

> The regiment was reviewed in the fall by General McDowell, and visited at various times by those noted war governors of the west and east: Randall of Wisconsin; Blair of Michigan; Ramsey of Minnesota; Berry of New Hampshire; and Sprague of Rhode Island. Also by Senators Wilkinson (Minnesota), Doolittle (Wisconsin), Chandler (Michigan), and Harris (New York), who were looking after the welfare of the volunteers from their respective states.

On November 2, the *NEW YORK DAILY TRIBUNE* published a very interesting account of the U.S. SharpShooters, written by one of its field correspondents. The article gives valuable insight into the early makeup of the Berdan SharpShooter organization:

> UNITED STATES SharpShooters
>
> More than three weeks ago Colonel Berdan notified the Secretary of War that his First Regiment of SharpShooters was full, and received order to remain at Camp Burnside to receive and assign the additional companies as they came in from their respective states. We are now encamped on Seventh Street, two miles from the Capitol, in the loveliest spot in the environs of Washington. From our tent doors we can overlook the river, the city, and the shores of Virginia opposite, over which a bluish haze hangs lazily all these sunny days, softening down the harsh features of the landscape into a picture as Claude would have faithfully reproduced.

Above: *First Lieutenant Charles A. Stevens recorded life in the camp during the initial training period.*

Our men are drilling six or eight hours daily, and becoming as proficient in the movements of skirmishers as they are in the use of their rifles. If the grand advance of the army is only delayed a season longer, we shall be prepared to take the field in a most gratifying condition of discipline, and be so much better prepared to give a good account of ourselves.

We have one of the best drill-masters in the army in Lieutenant Colonel Frederick Mears, who was assigned from the regular service to our regiment by General McClellan himself, as one particularly fitted for the post. He devotes his whole energy to the task of molding the splendid material of the regiment into the shape of true soldiers.

The SharpShooters are not ordinary men. They are of more than ordinary intelligence, and when properly instructed on the peculiar skirmish drill of the SharpShooter, will make as effective a corps as the Ellsworths, themselves.

The Michigan and Massachusetts companies brought with them their own ponderous target rifles, averaging 30 pounds in weight, though some run as high as 60 and 70 pounds. When the President saw our shooting, he ordered the work on the Government carbines [at the Sharps Rifle Manufacturing Company in Hartford, Connecticut] be immediately discontinued, and our rifles finished. These are the finest guns in the world, and cost $45 each.

In November, several issues of a local Madison, Wisconsin newspaper mentioned additional facts about the SharpShooters:

U.S.S.S. arrivals have with them their full rig of clothing, which they procured at Weehawken, N.J., and are ahead of us, as we have not drawn ours.

Full skirmish drills are being held, allied by the call of bugles.

Very little target practice has been conducted, since the unit has not yet been issued rifles.

The Wisconsin unit is now the largest SharpShooter Company, now at 107 men.

This quells the rumor that Colonel Berdan roughed up a soldier in the unit. No such incident happened, and it was born of the actions of a drill instructor.

Problems in Camp

Life in Berdan's Camp of Instruction was not without its personality clashes. Living and working in such close confines took its toll on officers and enlisted men alike. On November 8, Captain Caspar Trepp, Commander of Company A, tendered his resignation to Colonel Berdan. This was to be the first recorded displeasure that Trepp would show toward his commander, but was by no means his last:

I have been impelled to take this course entirely in consequence of one of confidence in Major W.S. Rowland as a military man, and as a gentleman. I insinuated to some of the line officers that the Colonel must be equally bad to have such a man as the Major with him.

It was an excited moment, and without the lest knowledge or belief that you had ever been guilty of anything unbecoming an officer and a gentleman. I ask you to accept a full and heartfelt apology.

I had several field positions offered me, and declined them all, for want of respect of the Commanding Officers, and I certainly should not have taken a Captaincy under your command, but for the deserved reputation you have with us. And whose reputation five months acquaintance I have fully corroborated.

C. Trepp

Berdan later wrote the following endorsement onto Trepp's letter:

I do not accept Captain Trepp's resignation, as I had already given Major Rowland the alternative to resign, or to be courtmartialled. He preferred to resign, which settled the difficulty. I send this in justice to myself, as Lieutenant Beckwith [had already told me] what Captain Trepp said of me at the time.

H. Berdan

While Berdan's official date of mustering into Federal service would later be fixed as November 30, 1861, Hiram Berdan, civilian, was not afforded this until June of the following year. It may be remembered that he *"joined for duty"* on June 15, but his official date of rank had to wait until long after the entire regiment was recruited. It bears repeating that Berdan was not a trained military leader, despite the rank he bore. He had been an inventor, a businessman, and a marksman, but had no military training whatever. Actually, this was not so unusual in its time. Volunteer units, formed in the early months of the war, frequently chose their own leaders, whether they had any prior military experience or not. There were simply too few trained officers to go around, so the men under Berdan's direct command had to endure his lack of military knowledge, and, as some would say, his incompetence.

Some officers, like Captain Trepp of Company A, found it difficult to be subordinate to him. Another officer, Major William S. Rowland, Berdan's first Adjutant, not only despised him, but actively sought to discredit him in the eyes of his superiors. The situation degenerated to such an extent that on December 5, Major Rowland sought to bring charges against Berdan, accusing him of assuming rank well in advance of formal military approval.

> Charge:
> Signing a false certificate, relative to his pay.
> Specification:
> In this, that he, at the Camp of Instruction, D.C., on the 13th of November, 1861, did sign a false certificate relative to his pay. Setting forth that he had been mustered into the service of the United States on the 2nd day of August, 1861, by Colonel D.B. Sackett, U.S. Army, at the City of New York. Whereas, in fact and in truth, Berdan was not mustered into service until the 1st of October 1861.

The official regimental records of the 1st U.S.S.S. leave much unsaid about the rift between Rowland and Berdan, and in later years, unit historian Stevens did not even mention it in the Regimental History, published in 1892. Rowland's accusation against his commanding officer was probably without merit, but it was undoubtedly, the only official charge that he could make. Rowland chose unwisely, because receiving a colonel's pay was one of the furthest things from Berdan's mind.

His pre-war business successes had made him independently wealthy, and not in the least dependent upon military subsistence. Nine days after Rowland filed his charges, Berdan wrote this letter of explanation to the Division Adjutant General:

> I have the honor to inform you that the conduct of Major W.S. Rowland was such that I was compelled to require him to resign or stand a Court-Martial for conduct unbecoming an officer and a gentleman. He, wisely, accepted the former. He has since boasted that he did not file his complaint against me until he had his resignation in his pocket. But he would have the satisfaction of putting me to some trouble, and a good deal of public scandal.
>
> At the time I was paid, I had an application pending at the War Department, which resulted since, in an order to pay me from the time I had [mustered in] 750 men, whether I had been with them, or not. This entitles me to back pay.
>
> I trust that you will believe me when I state that I came to expect this from you, and that very few men have worked harder for that, or spent more money than I have [in selecting and assembling the men]. I can give you more evidence, as to the fact that I had no intention, nor did not, in fact, defraud the Government, in this transaction, should you desire.
>
> H. Berdan
> Colonel Commanding

Below: *The Camp of Instruction to the North of Washington DC during the first hard winter months of 1861-62. The tents are neatly pitched in rows in front of Berdan's Headquarters in the house at the center background of the sketch.*

Suffice it to say that Major Rowland left the regiment, embittered, but by virtue of own accord. His position was taken by F.A. Willett, formerly Commanding Officer of Company I. 1st U.S.S.S. Evidently, nothing became of Rowland's accusations, and court-martial proceedings were not pressed against Colonel Berdan. However, leadership problems continued to plague his newly-formed regiment. So much so, that the only U.S. military-trained officer, Lieutenant Colonel Mears, resigned out of sheer frustration. The loss to the regiment of this valuable officer was immeasurable, as there was no one who could take his place in teaching raw recruits military discipline and parade drill.

Berdan continued to fulfill his duties as commanding officer as best he could, despite the problems he had with Rowland, Trepp and Mears (and, no doubt, others). Possibly to divert negative feelings and pessimism, on December 17, he organized a special shooting match and offered a personal prize of five dollars "to the best off-hand shot on a string of two shots at 40 rods distance." The winner shot a string of eight and a half inches on his two shots, a remarkable achievement using a heavy muzzle-loading rifle. This marksmanship record stood for less than two weeks, when another SharpShooter shot a string of three shots, measuring *a paltry six inches!*

A field correspondent with the *NEW YORK EVENING POST* wrote a very informative article about the regiment, and it was published on December 20, 1861:

A VISIT TO THE SharpShooters' CAMP

A day or two ago I visited the camp of Berdan's SharpShooters. It is quite near town, only about a mile from 7th Street. A short drive past the scattering of houses that stand here and there as sentinels on guard at the outposts of the city, take the visitor out in the country. Not a very inviting rural scene, certainly, with its brown fields, its grass sodden with moisture, and with only a few forlorn trees to vary the prospect. The camp of the SharpShooters is beautifully situated on top of a hill, in a grove of cedars that have been judiciously cleared, so that they now stand in slopes. As the carriage made its slow progress up the hill we passed squads of men picturesquely quartered around fires, one of which were cooking great joints of meat and cauldrons of coffee. Reaching the summit, we left our conveyance at the door of the neat brick house in which is the Colonel's headquarters. Here, in very comfortable rooms, lives Colonel Berdan. His wife is with him.

With an increased party, we now began the sightseeing. First, on the great parade ground, back of the camp, we saw skirmish drill by battalion. This, the men did quite well, making a long line where they were deployed at eight paces apart. The orders were all given by the bugle, and it was very pleasant to hear the chief bugler play the few notes that conveyed to the men the idea of what they were to do, and then the other buglers repeated it down the whole line. They rallied by fours and deployed; rallied by sections and deployed; and finally rallied by companies, presenting a solid mass of men on every side, facing outwards. This movement is intended to resist the approach of cavalry, and one could understand how formidable such a defense, bristling with bayonets, would be.

The men are all picked, most of them capital marksmen. They wear a uniform of dark green, overcoats of gray bound with green, and the knapsacks are covered with brown fur, such as hair trunks were formerly made of, so that they had a decidedly sylvan appearance, suggestive of Robin Hood and his merry men. Their band has a corps of buglers, who make really agreeable music on the ordinary bugles, without keys. It was just at sunset; the sky was flushed all over with rosy crimson, and below a silver mist was rising. From our high position the city and the great white Capitol looked pale and shadowy, as if the city of a mirage.

Here, on the bare hill, these men were drawn up, two thousand strong, complete in every respect but one – they are without guns! It was really sad to see them, a noble body of soldiers, without the rifles which should be their pride. As yet, they have only been able, despite the utmost exertions of the Colonel, to obtain fifty muskets for guard duty. It is a wonder that the men retain their spirits under such long delay, and it speaks well for their officers that they are not discouraged.

Good marksmen as they are, they have not been contented to take the ordinary regulation musket. Sharps rifles were promised them by the President, and ordered by General McClellan, but some trouble in the War Department has, thus far, prevented their getting them. Let us hope they will soon have the weapon they are so competent to wield. One company are all Minnesotans, fine stalwart men, practiced in prairie-stalking; another are Tyrolese sharpshots from the Alps.

Above: *The house near the corner of First and T street, Washington, D.C. which Berdan and his wife, Mary, occupied during the SharpShooters training period.*

Winter came to mean days of inactivity and boredom for Berdan's men, as inclement weather often curtailed drill and

Above: *An engraving of Colonel Hiram Berdan [circa 1861-62]. Note the unusual insignia on his cap, the likes of which have not been recorded elsewhere. Later photographs show him with a cap insignia of a wreath surrounding the letters "USSS".*

marksmanship instruction. Poor sanitary conditions throughout the camp began to take a toll on the health of these untrained and, as yet, undisciplined troops. Poorly situated latrines, upstream from the regiment's drinking and bath water, went unchecked, until sickness and disease became epidemic. Newspaper correspondents who flocked about Washington's encampments sought any shred of military news of interest to the readership back home. The SharpShooters' misery became common knowledge, as evidenced by this *NEW YORK TIMES* article of January 15, 1862:

> THE BERDAN SharpShooters
> The condition of two of the regiments now near Washington, of the finest personnel, and fitted to render under proper management the most important service, should receive immediate attention to remedy the neglect that they have experienced. Will it be believed that the two Regiments of Berdan's SharpShooters are still lying in camp, unsupplied with arms? Such is the case. Worse than this, it is doubtful if they can ever be brought to any degree of efficiency.
>
> The muster rolls of the two regiments contain about 1,500 men. Of these, in the last three weeks, sixty-four have died, and about 700 are in the regimental hospitals and on the sick list. Hardly is the pretense of discipline preserved. Officers and men have become disheartened, and it is most likely that when the officers are paid off the present week, large numbers of them will desert. They pass out of the lines with impunity, day and night, with the sentinels never calling for the exhibition of a pass, except for some officer who is near and who insists upon it.
>
> Absence from roll call and parade, passes unnoticed. The forms of drilling are, to some extent, kept up, but there is no heart in it. The idleness and consequent lack of spirit and confidence, doubtless increases the liability to, and invigorates the ravages of disease. A few days ago, six companies of the 1st Regiment could muster at battalion drill, only 180 men. A large portion of this regiment has been lying in this condition fully six months. Both regiments were enlisted as riflemen, and they claim the right to be armed accordingly.
>
> Where the responsibility for this state of things rests, I do not pretend to decide. I believe, however, not Colonel Berdan, or with any officer of the regiments. It is said that there is some gentleman connected with the Ordnance Bureau [sic], who does not believe in Sharps rifles, and such, like new-fangled notions, but thinks the Springfield musket the "ne plus ultra" in the way of arms, and insists that none others shall be furnished them. But whoever may be responsible, the fact is disgraceful that a body of picked men, everyone of whom is a dead shot, whose services in an advance or in an engagement would be invaluable, should be allowed in idleness, to be without arms or any incentive to soldierly conduct, [to fall] prey to disease.

On January 28, 1862, Charles S. Tripler, Surgeon and Medical Director of the Army of the Potomac wrote a scathing report on the plight of Federal troops bivouaced near Washington, D.C. He noted the unsanitary condition of the just-arriving recruits, and their bouts with typhus, pneumonia, measles, and malarious fevers. He cited, as causes, such conditions as:

> ...foul air, bad clothing, imperfect shelters, exposure to cold and moisture, and imperfectly drained and badly policed camps. As a remedy I suggest good shelter, good clothing, good food, good water, dry camp grounds, and an abundant supply of pure air.

Specifically regarding Berdan's men, he said:

> The Berdan SharpShooters are in a bad sanitary condition, and not improving. Their camp is badly located, and I shall visit this regiment personally. This regiment is suffering from measles, and lately severe lung complications have accompanied the disease. A fresh and dry camp is decidedly necessary for the command. If a suitable ground is selected and the tents put up in the way I have suggested, then I should look for favorable results.

On February 6, Army Surgeon Tripler gave the following statistics on the U.S.S.S. regimental strength, and the numbers reported sick. While these figures are appalling, they are a far cry from the 700 listed as hospitalized or sick by the *NEW YORK TIMES* correspondent twenty-two days earlier:

1st U.S.S.S. (745 men)	71 sick	9%
2nd U.S.S.S. (720 men)	132 sick	18%

The *BOSTON DAILY EVENING TRANSCRIPT* printed the following, overly-simplistic "cure" for the SharpShooter's problems:

> COLONEL BERDAN'S REGIMENT
> The difficulties in Col. Berdan's Regiment will be settled by a removal of the Colonel, the arming of the men with Colt's rifles and revolvers, and then sending them to the front.

Years later, Colonel Wm. Y. W. Ripley would write about these sad, disconsolate days:

> The winter was an unusually severe one, and the enemy maintained a blockade of the Potomac. The supply of wood was often short, and some suffering was the result. Measles, small pox, and other forms of camp diseases appeared.

California Joe

Without a doubt, the most colorful Berdan SharpShooter was Truman Head, better known as "California Joe." This grizzled forty-two year old California Gold Rush pioneer enlisted in Company C (Michigan), of the 1st Regiment of Berdan's U.S. SharpShooters in September 1861. Actually, he was assigned to this unit after he passed Berdan's strict marksmanship test at the SharpShooters' rendezvous at Weehawken, New Jersey. He stood but 5 ft 7 in tall, had a light complexion, blue eyes, and shoulder length brown hair. His unit, along with Company E, being the only ones fully armed (sporting and target rifles!), were sent to join a foray into Confederate-held Virginia on September 27, 1861. The two day excursion

Above: *One of the most familiar images of the SharpShooters, Private Truman Head, nicknamed California Joe, lies "Waiting for Rebs."*

yielded no great military victory, yet was the first taste of blood for Berdan's SharpShooters. A month later, "California Joe" privately purchased a NM1859 Sharps military rifle with saber bayonet from a sales representative of the Sharps Rifle Company. His .52 in caliber breechloading rifle had target style, double-set triggers, and must have been the envy of every SharpShooter (most of whom were unarmed). He probably convinced them that this type of firearm was the one to have, as it was both sturdy and accurate. Both regiments eventually were armed with a similar rifle, but with a special rear sight and angular bayonet.

Regimental Historian Stevens spoke highly of the folk-hero of the SharpShooters:

> Joe was one of those splendid characters that made him a hero, in spite of himself. Entirely free from brag and bluster, Joe was an unassuming man, past middle age, short in stature, light in weight, and a true gentleman in every sense of the word. He was always a special favorite with the entire command.

"California Joe," sometimes called "Old Californy," fought with the regiment through McClellan's Peninsula Campaign of 1862. A photograph of "Joe," entitled Waiting for Rebs, was made into an engraving and adorned a popular article in *HARPER'S WEEKLY* of August 2, 1862.

Failing health affected this aging veteran's eyes, ending his brief career as a Berdan SharpShooter: he was honorably discharged on November 3, 1862. He returned to California, and finally passed away on November 24, 1875. He is buried at the National Cemetery of the Presidio, near San Francisco, but his name will always be synonymous with that of "Berdan SharpShooter."

Truman Head has sometimes been confused with another frontiersman who bore the same name, "California Joe," Moses Embree Milner. While Milner was a friend of "Wild Bill" Hickok and a scout for General Custer, he was never a Berdan SharpShooter.

Command by Bugle

During the entire winter of 1861–62, particular attention was paid to skirmish drill, in which the men became extremely proficient. All orders were given by he sound of the bugle, and the whole regiment deployed as skirmishers could be as easily maneuvered as a single company could be brought in line of battle. The bugle corps was under the charge of Calvin Morse, of Company F. As Chief Bugler, and under his careful instruction, the regiment attained an unusual degree of excellence:

> All camp calls were also sounded on the bugle, and the men found them pleasant little devices for translating curt and often rough English into music. They were bugled to break-

fast and to dinner, bugled to guard mounting, and bugled to battle. Brigades moved and cavalry charged to the sound of the bugle. The men often found fanciful resemblances in the notes of the music to the words intended to be conveyed.

Left: The SharpShooters maneuvered to bugle calls throughout the war.

Unit historian Stevens, later would recount:

> Our calls were all made by the bugle. Each company had two buglers, and a regimental band was formed under the instruction of Chief Bugler Calvin Morse. They became sufficiently proficient to make very fair dress parade music. Only occasionally would the boys get out of wind, and then there was a great gap in the notes. The bugles were also used in skirmish drill, in accordance with the commands of the officer commanding.
>
> About nine o'clock we had guard mounting. Drills, company or regimental, occurred twice a day, and therein the SharpShooters made a fine appearance. We had a proficient instructor, and apt and careful company officers. Among them Captain Drew, who was thoroughly conversant with tactics before entering service. He was popular throughout the entire1st Regiment.
>
> Toward the close of the afternoon, before retreat, and weather permitting, dress parade was held. This was a popular feature of camp life, witnessed generally by many spectators, and really a grand performance. Here reports were made as to the condition of the companies, whether they were all present and accounted for. Orders were read by the Adjutant, and inspections and reviews frequently occurred.
>
> Sunday morning inspections included dress, general appearance, packed knapsacks, etc. During the forenoon, church call brought the entire regiment, excepting those on duty, to the parade ground, where the Chaplain officiated. In bad weather these duties and services were dispensed with.
>
> Besides target shooting, other diversions were indulged, in order to train the men in the arduous duty of active service, particularly marching, destined to be often long and fatiguing. Therefore, football, jumping, racing, wrestling, boxing and fencing were prominent, which seemed to keep up a good feeling among the men, and between the companies.

Camp Life

Army regulation stated that the commanding officer of a volunteer company, a captain, could not be mustered into service until his entire unit was recruited, formed and mustered. Likewise, the commanding officer of a volunteer regiment, a colonel, could not be officially mustered into service until each of his compliment of men making up the regiment were assembled. Surprising as it seems, as late as February 1862, Hiram Berdan was still listed officially as a civilian, and not yet mustered into Federal service. On February 10th, he petitioned the Adjutant General:

> I have the honor to inform you that I had 563 men and officers of my 1st Regiment at this Camp on the 25th day of September, 1861. Besides the Massachusetts Company [Andrews' SharpShooters], 100 strong and raised for this regiment [are now] at this time at Poolesville. My order was to raise a regiment of 750 men and officers. The last company arrived on the 7th of October.
>
> I have the honor, General, to ask that you will order me to be mustered into the U.S. service as a Colonel of my 1st Regiment of U.S. SharpShooters.
>
> H. Berdan

Many more months would pass until Berdan would officially be welcomed as commander, even though his date of muster would be retroactive to 1861. He did have friends in high places, as evidenced by this official letter from the Commander-in-Chief to Major General McClellan. Note that President Lincoln requests, not only that Berdan be officially mustered into the service, but that he be given the rank of Brigadier General:

> Executive Mansion
> Washington
> February 26,1862
>
> Major General McClellan
> My Dear Sir:
> I understand that there are two full, and one inceptive regiments of SharpShooters, mostly raised under the influence of Colonel Berdan. Yet, Colonel Berdan has no position, and the Corps has no commander of the whole. Such commander is, perhaps, needed, and if General McClellan will write below that he approves it, I will appoint Colonel Berdan a Brigadier General to take charge of them.
>
> A. Lincoln

Berdan, it seems, pulled out all the stops in his quest for official rank and position. The Secretary of the Interior, Caleb B. Smith, and Congressman C.B. Sedgwick were asked by Berdan to intercede with McClellan, on his behalf. Berdan wore the rank of Colonel on his shoulders, but was not given official permission to be mustered into Federal service until nearly three months later. He was not to be promoted to Brigadier General until many years after the war would end.

Uniforms and Field Equipment of the SharpShooters

Distinctive Uniforms for the SharpShooters

When one pictures a Berdan SharpShooter, one thinks of a marksman clad in green, armed with a Sharps breechloading rifle. While this is a correct assumption for most of the war, the SharpShooter's uniform began quite differently. As early as June 14, 1861, Colonel Berdan envisioned himself commanding an elite unit of the finest marksmen that the northern states could muster. They were to be clad, he believed:

> ...In loose fitting heavy, dark blue flannel sack coats with metal buttons, black fringe around the bottom, and with black velvet collars. Their heads were to be covered with soft crown hats of felt, ornamented with small black feathers. The uniform would have a single-breasted vest of the same heavy cloth, and loose fitting trousers.

This is hardly the image one visualizes when picturing a Berdan SharpShooter. As the Colonel busied himself enlisting his regiment, he changed his mind about the uniform that they would have. On July 20th he mentioned uniforms of green cloth for the first time, believing that the previously chosen blue would have been:

> ...too conspicuous in the field. The greenness, would better correspond in the leafy season with the colors of the foliage. The green coat will be made double-breasted, with short flannel up, black cloth collar, and black buttons. There will be no vest. Each SharpShooter will have a dark gray overcoat with an integral cape lined with rubber cloth. It will have black metal buttons. and will be long enough to cover the knees. Each marksman will also be issued two pairs of gray pantaloons, of strong Russia twilled linen. A felt hat to be the same shade gray as the overcoat, but each man was to be issued a green cloth cap, according to the shape proscribed by Army regulation.

Contrary to common belief, Berdan SharpShooters were not the first soldiers to be clad in green. As far back as the American Revolutionary War, Hessian Jaegers were uniformed in green. Likewise, some British army rifle regiments in the 1790s wore green, possibly influenced by the uniforms of contemporary Austrian mounted troops. In 1800, the British Rifle Corps was formed, and later the 95th British Regiment, both clad in green. In fact, in Europe, the wearing of green uniforms came to signify either riflemen or light infantry. Whether Berdan knew of this is unknown. We do know, however, that he desired uniforms to help his SharpShooters blend into the summer foliage.

Evidently the originators of a Confederate militia company, known as The Woodis Rifles, had the same idea as Berdan. Their uniform consisted of "hunting-green sack coats, with black velvet facings, gilt buttons, and gold lace." Likewise, the Confederate 6th Battalion of Virginia Volunteers, known as The Alexandria Rifles, also wore green uniforms, but these were trimmed in black lace.

On September 6th, a New York newspaper printed an article about the departure of two companies of Berdan SharpShooters to the seat of war. It went on to say that their uniforms were peculiarly appropriate for their positions as marksmen, as their uniforms consisted of green frock coats, gray pantaloons, and green caps. The uniform color was, the article said, to accord with the colors of nature, as much as possible, and intended to be worn in the summer. In winter, the article continued, the uniform would consist entirely of a gray pattern.

The folly of having Union troops dressed in uniforms of gray cloth soon became evident. In the early months of the war, the familiar blue for Federal troops, and gray for Confederates, had not yet become standardized. In fact, SharpShooter Colonel William Y. W. Ripley stated:

> Certain gray overcoats and soft hats of the same rebellious hue were promptly exchanged for others of a color in which they were less apt to be shot by mistake by their own friends.

On October 15th, Berdan stated that each of his officers were also to have *"uniforms of green cloth."* There was to be *"green cord on the pantaloons, and each would wear a green cap."* A week later, Berdan wrote to his commander, shedding light on the initial procurement of uniforms for his enlisted SharpShooters:

> Camp of Instruction
> Washington
> October 22, 1861
>
> General McClellan:
> Colonel Fenton contracted with the Seamless Clothing Manufacturing Company in New York, to supply my 1st Regiment with gray overcoats, gutta-percha buttons, and with green trimmings. The dark buttons and trimmings I deemed important for my Corps.
>
> The manufacturer stated to me at the time that he had several hundred overcoats on hand, trimmed with red metal buttons, which he wished me to take. I declined, and after much delay we received some 300 or 400 [coats], trimmed as per [my] contract. I have now received the balance of the order, trimmed with red metal buttons. We are very much in need of overcoats and would like to keep those we have until this mistake has been remedied.
>
> H. Berdan

Some of the uniforms were delivered and on hand by late October, according to an account by a Wisconsin SharpShooter:

> The new arrivals have with them their full rig of clothing, which they procured at Weehawken, New Jersey. They are ahead of us, as we have not drawn ours.

Upon his visit to the SharpShooters' Camp of Instruction in Washington, D.C., a field correspondent with the *NEW YORK EVENING POST* wrote:

> The men wear a uniform of dark green, with overcoats of gray bound with green.

The Smithsonian Institution's Museum of American Military History now possesses the original sealed pattern uniform of the Berdan SharpShooters. It was originally in the Army of the Potomac's Quartermaster Department, as it was the sample to which all Berdan SharpShooter uniforms would be compared.

The green enlisted man's coat has brass buttons with officer's infantry branch insignia on each. This is a bit of an enigma, because in 1854, the U.S. War Department declared that henceforth, all enlisted men would wear plain eagle shield buttons. However, officers could continue to wear branch insignia on their buttons. All contemporary references state that Berdan SharpShooter coats had black, hard rubber buttons with Eagle insignia on them.

The sealed pattern uniform also contains SharpShooter trousers of green wool, and an army forage cap of green felt, with a leather head band strap.

Captain C.A. Stevens, who wrote the Berdan SharpShooter Regimental History in 1892, described their early Civil War uniforms as being:

> ...of fine material, consisting of a dark green coat, and cap with black plume, light blue trousers, afterwards exchanged for green ones, and leather leggings. They presented a striking contrast to the blue of the infantry. By our dress we were known far and wide, and the appellation of "green coats" was soon acquired. When fully uniformed and equipped, the SharpShooters made a very handsome appearance.
>
> We wore for a time, principally on outpost duty or in bad weather, gray round hats with wide black visors. But, after our first appearance before the enemy the following spring, they were discarded, as endangering fire from the rear. Certain gray felt seamless overcoats were likewise abandoned, although they were good rain shedders, [as they became] wet, [they became] stiff as a board.

Captain Aschmann described their uniforms like this:

> We had simple green coats which were quite wearable even as civilian clothes, green and blue pants of woolen cloth, a widebrimmed felt hat as protection against the rain as well as the scorching rays of the sun, broad-soled comfortable shoes, flannel shirts, and woolen socks.

About officer's uniforms, Aschmann said:

> Though made with more care and of finer cloth, the officer's uniforms were not much different from those of the soldiers, and just as simple by comparison. The insignia were no glittering epaulets, only a narrow band edged with gold braid and fastened on the shoulder, showing different badges of rank. For daily use, or so-caller lesser tenue, we had a blue flannel jacket which was worn in the field even by officers.

Were these *"daily use jackets"* that Aschmann referred to 4-button sack coats? A number of images of Berdan SharpShooters wearing these coats are pictured in this book. It is quite probable that they were blue flannel, rather than SharpShooter green.

Private Wyman S. White, Company F (New Hampshire), 2nd V.S.S.S., described his arrival at Berdan's Camp of Instruction in December 1861:

> Members of Berdan's 1st Regiment of SharpShooters came down from their camp to escort us up to our camp adjoining theirs. They came to meet us, not to greet us, as might have been expected. A more indignant company of men I never saw. They were dressed in green pants and gray felt overcoats, and wore gray helmets [soft-brimmed hats], and wore tan colored leggings coming up to the knee. The buttons on their coats were of black rubber with the U.S. coat of arms stamped on them. They were a unique looking body of men. They had wreaths on their helmets (sic) and the figures 1st U.S.S.S. We asked them what the letters indicated, and their reply was: "Unfortunate Soldiers Sadly Sold." They then poured into our ears of the meaness of Colonel Berdan. They did not hesitate to call him an imposter and a fraud, and said that he did not keep one of his promises that was made when the men enlisted.
>
> Later we drew all regulation clothing, consisting of two whole suits of clothes [whether green or dark blue he did not say], woolen blanket, overcoat, rubber blanket, underclothing, writing material, needle book, shaving tools, etc.

After a skirmish at Big Bethel in early 1862, Captain William Y. W. Ripley stated that *"the fighting taught them the lesson that the gray overcoats and soft hats had to go, lest they be shot by their own troops."*

The SharpShooter uniform of the day, he said, consisted of coats, blouses, pants and caps of green cloth. They were augmented by leather leggings (spats) which buckled high near the knee, and were worn by officers and enlisted men, alike. Evidently, the black ostrich feather (plume), the heavy russet leather leggings, the blue trousers, and the gray winter overcoats were discarded soon after hostilities resumed in the spring of 1862.

Throughout the war, the SharpShooters continued to be resupplied with fresh, new, green uniforms. Numerous refer-

Opposite page: *Don Troiani's painting of a SharpShooter in action accurately records fine details of his equipment.*

***Above:** Two SharpShooters depicted by Don Troiani showing a variety of different clothing and equipment including the Colt Revolving Rifles that were originally issued.*

ences to these troops in many diverse letters, texts and diaries mention their unique clothing. As late in the war as September 17, 1863, Historian Stevens mentions that the SharpShooters were issued *"a large amount of green clothing, regulation blue overcoats and blankets."* Dozens of wartime photographs of Berdan SharpShooters (many of which are shown in this book) show the men's uniforms in various stages of disrepair. To study the uniforms of the American Civil War, one must understand that the common soldier lived in his clothes 24 hours a day, 7 days a week. They frequently became wet during the rain, when crossing rivers and streams, and after the morning dew. They became dirty, odorous, torn and mildewed. Since resupply was often scant, it is easy to understand that the soldiers would take what they could from the slain. The SharpShooters were no different, and between resupply issues, they would take whatever uniforms or accoutrements were handy, green or otherwise.

The majority of uniform components for the Berdan SharpShooters were standard regulation, including:

- Bootees (shoes), leather ($2.20)
- Cap, forage (green) ($1.95)
- Drawers, flannel or knit cotton ($1.00)
- Frock coat, enlisted (green)
- Gloves, cold weather
- Great coat, cold weather (gray)
- Leggings, leather
- Poncho, painted or rubber
- Sack coat, flannel (blue) ($3.25)
- Shirt, flannel ($1.57)
- Shirt, knit ($1.42)
- Stockings ($.35)
- Trousers (green)($4.25)
- Trouser suspenders

Above: *Carved wooden pipe owned by Sergeant Frank Tilson of the 2nd U.S. SharpShooters who was wounded no less than nine times including at Gettysburg.*

The SharpShooters were issued standard Federal infantry accoutrements, including:

- Ammunition box, (Sharps pattern) leather, with sling & plate
- Bayonet, angular with leather scabbard
- Blanket, wool ($3.60), rubber lined ($2.55)
- Canteen, wood or tin ($.45)
- Cap pouch, leather
- Cooking kit
- Cup, tin
- Haversack ($.67)
- Knapsack, leather, tanned with hair on outside ($2.15)
- Knife, fork & spoon
- Rifle sling, leather
- Shelter half ($4.60)
- Waist belt, leather & brass plate

The common SharpShooter might also have the following personal items:

- Candles, tallow or adamantine
- Hair comb
- Housewife, sewing kit
- Identification tag or pin
- Rations for one day (bacon, peas or beans, sugar, hardtack, coffee beans, salt)
- Shaving equipment
- Soap
- Tobacco
- Writing implements (pencil or quill & ink. and paper)

SharpShooter Knapsacks

The knapsacks issued to the Berdan SharpShooters were of a Prussian design, and consisted of leather tanned with the hair exposed on the outside. Historian Stevens stated that these knapsacks were *"heavier than the regulation knapsack, fitted the back well, and were roomy and highly appreciated by the men."* Depending on the action, the SharpShooters often went into battle without the encumbrance of their packs, leaving them with the regimental supply wagons.

One such surviving example was formerly the property of Private Leonard Small of Company D (Maine). 2nd U.S.S.S. It is made of brown calfskin, tanned with the hair left on. It is linen lined, except for the sides which are a heavy wood composition board (inside). The knapsack is edged in brown leather. All straps are brown bridle leather, and the belt hooks,

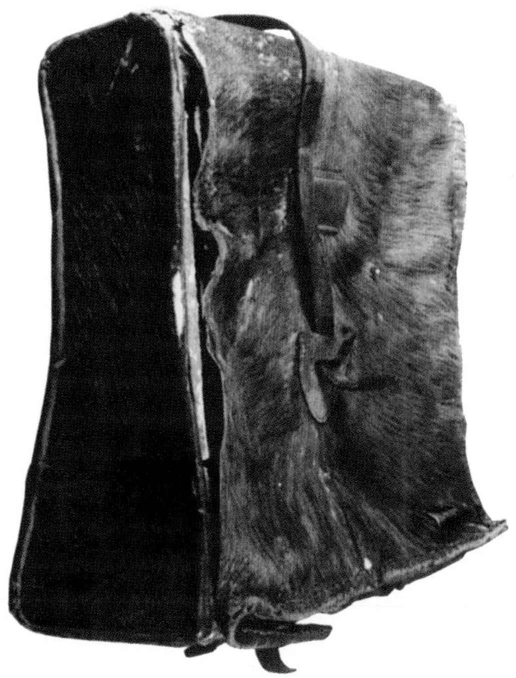
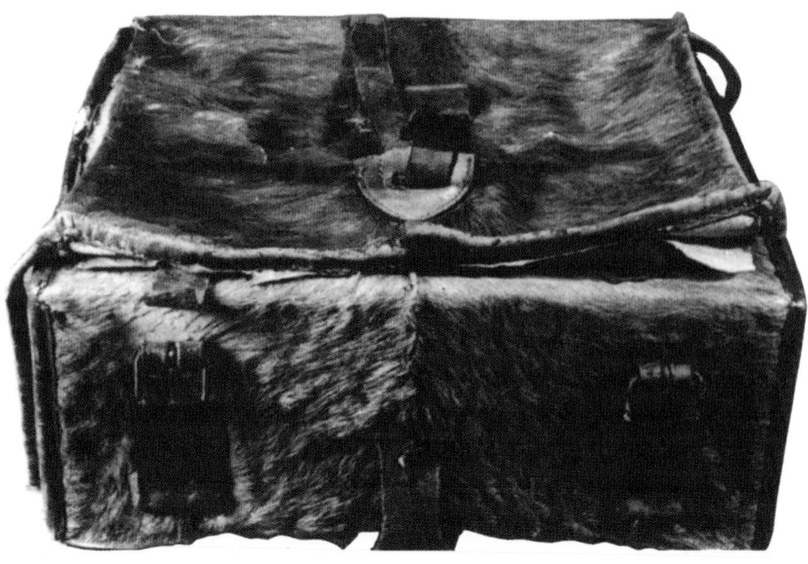

***Above:** A knapsack belonging to Private John S.Geer of Company C, 2nd U.S. SharpShooters. Framed in pine, it measures 14 inches high, 12 3/4 wide and 5 3/4 deep at the base, 4¼ deep at the top. It has straps and buckles to secure the blanket roll and cooking kit.*

tabs and G rings are made of brass. The roller buckles are iron and "Japanned." The body of the knapsack measures approximately 14 in tall, 12 3/4 in wide. and 4 1/4 in deep at the top and 5 3/4 in deep at the bottom. Leather straps hold the tin cooking kit on the exterior of the knapsack. Historian Stevens stated that:

> ...one sergeant's knapsack weighed 28 pounds, the heaviest in the regiment. The next two heaviest weighed 22 pounds and 17 pounds, respectively.
>
> In light marching order, the knapsack (if carried at all) had little more within or on top than a rolled blanket, sometimes extra rations, and the balance of sixty rounds of ammunition that couldn't go in a forty-round cartridge box. At other times, the knapsack varied all the way from a new outfit (generally with new troops), to the smallest possible kit or supply of extras (principally underclothes, poncho or rubber blanket, and woolen blanket, as the overcoats [had been] turned in. These, all told, with the nine or ten pound gun, forty rounds [of ammunition], canteen of water (pretty weighty), haversack (packed with hard bread, coffee, sugar, and pork, boiled or raw) added 40 pounds with all accoutrements... The average weight of a [SharpShooter] knapsack would not exceed, well packed, 15 pounds.

Regimental Flags

The Regimental flag of the 1st U.S. SharpShooters listed each of the campaigns and battles in which they had been engaged and was made of blue silk. These flags were carried in the field and suffered greatly from the elements and from battle. As they wore out they were retired and replaced with new ones. A reconstruction of the missing letters in the surviving standard reveals the following engagements:

Fair Oaks	Mine Run
Williamsburg	Kelly's Ford
Hanover Courthouse	Auburn
Great Bethel	Gettysburg
Gaines Mill	The Cedars
Savage Station	Fredericksburg
White Oak Swamp	Antietam
2nd Bull Run	Malvern Hill
Bloody Angle	Charles City Cross Roads
Chancellorsville	Chickahominy
Wilderness	Mechanicsville
Wapping Heights	Yorktown
Blackford's Ford	

At least one other 1st U.S.S.S. Regimental flag is known, although it is in relic condition. In his Regimental History of the SharpShooters, Stevens says this about the colors flown at Auburn on October 13, 1863:

> The torn and ragged regimental colors received three more bullet holes through them.

At the Skirmish at Locust Grove on November 27, 1863, Stevens said:

> The regimental colors were waved on high in response [to the assault by the enemy to their front]. The Color Sergeant, E.R. Blakeslee, of Michigan, was afterwards promoted for his coolness and bravery on this and other occasions.

At the Battle of the Wilderness on May 5, 1864, Stevens remembered:

> The [SharpShooter] troops rallying, rushed forward and drove the enemy back through the brush, the flag of the First SharpShooters being conspicuously waved outside the works on the heels of the retreating rebs by the brave color-bearer, Sergeant Blakeslee of Company C. Color Sergeant J. Madison Tarbell of Company E, 2nd Regiment, stood with

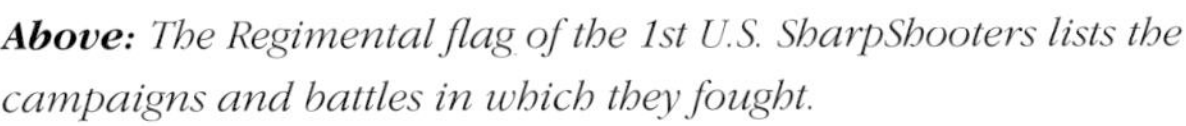

Above: *The Regimental flag of the 1st U.S. SharpShooters lists the campaigns and battles in which they fought.*
.***Left:*** *The National Colors of the 2nd U.S. SharpShooters are now kept at the West Point Military Academy Museum collection.*

> his colors planted on the breastworks until he received a shot through the arm and had to give up, though he hung on to the flag.

At the Battle of Deep Run on August 15, 1864, Stevens recalled:

> During this sharp disadvantageous skirmish, to the SharpShooters the regimental colors were gallantly pressed forward on to the concealed enemy in charge of Corporal Andrew Kirkham.

These colors, believed to be the last ones used by the regiment, were turned over to the War Department on March 17, 1865, and are now part of the West Point Military Academy Museum collection.

The Uniform of the SharpShooters

Two examples of the nine-button frock coat that was adopted by Berdan's SharpShooters. On the right a Sergeant's coat and an enlisted man's on the left.

These forest green coats are of the official single-breasted style with nine buttons on the front and two at waist level on the back – at the top of the rear vents. They feature a stand-up collar and two-button cuffs, both the collar and cuffs bear piping of lighter emerald green. The one on the left is believed to be a prototype of the design that was accepted by the Federal Quartermaster as a pattern for all subsequent coats. The buttons on this coat are unusual as they are brass and of an infantry officer's pattern. The right hand example has the more usual rubber buttons designed to avoid the light glinting on them, picking the men out as targets. At bottom left is a pair of sealed pattern trousers made of dark forest green wool cloth with loose-fitting legs without cuffs, dual pockets, buttons to secure the fly front and suspenders.

Left: *The official sealed pattern forage cap was made of forest green felt, with a leather headband and chinstrap. The label indicates that it was made by "Geo Hoff & Co., Philadelphia." and is size No4 =7⅛ inches.*

Above: *Two views of a Berdan SharpShooter forage cap made of dark green felt and fitted with small hard rubber buttons. On the crown of the cap are metallic insignia of an eagle, the letter "D"[Company D, Maine] and the number "2"[2nd U.S. SharpShooters] as issued to Private Leonard Small.*

Right: *Don Troiani's fine painting of an officer in the U.S. SharpShooters. The gold bars on his shoulder boards indicate that he is a First Lieutenant.*

Above: *Examples of First Lieutenant's shoulder boards [left] woven and [right] with gold bars which may have been pinned to plain boards when the officer was promoted from Second Lieutenant.*

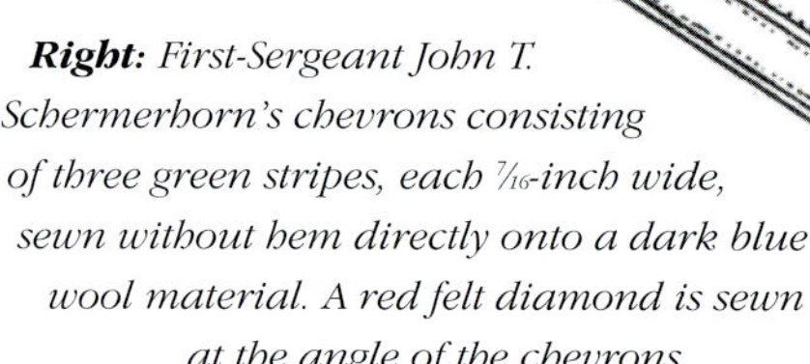

Right: *First-Sergeant John T. Schermerhorn's chevrons consisting of three green stripes, each 7/16-inch wide, sewn without hem directly onto a dark blue wool material. A red felt diamond is sewn at the angle of the chevrons.*

Below: *Detail of the inscription of First-Sergeant Schermerhorn's presentation sword which reads:*

PRESENTED TO
1st Sgt.John T.
Schermerhorn
1st REGT U.S.S.S.
BY THE MEN OF
CO. H.N.Y.V.

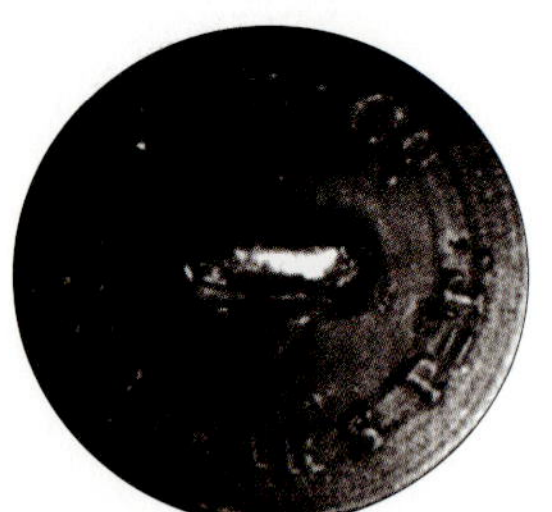

Above : *Enlisted men's hard rubber button left and officer's style center. On the right is the rear showing the cast letters of the makers name: "N.R. Co. GOODYEAR'S P=T."*

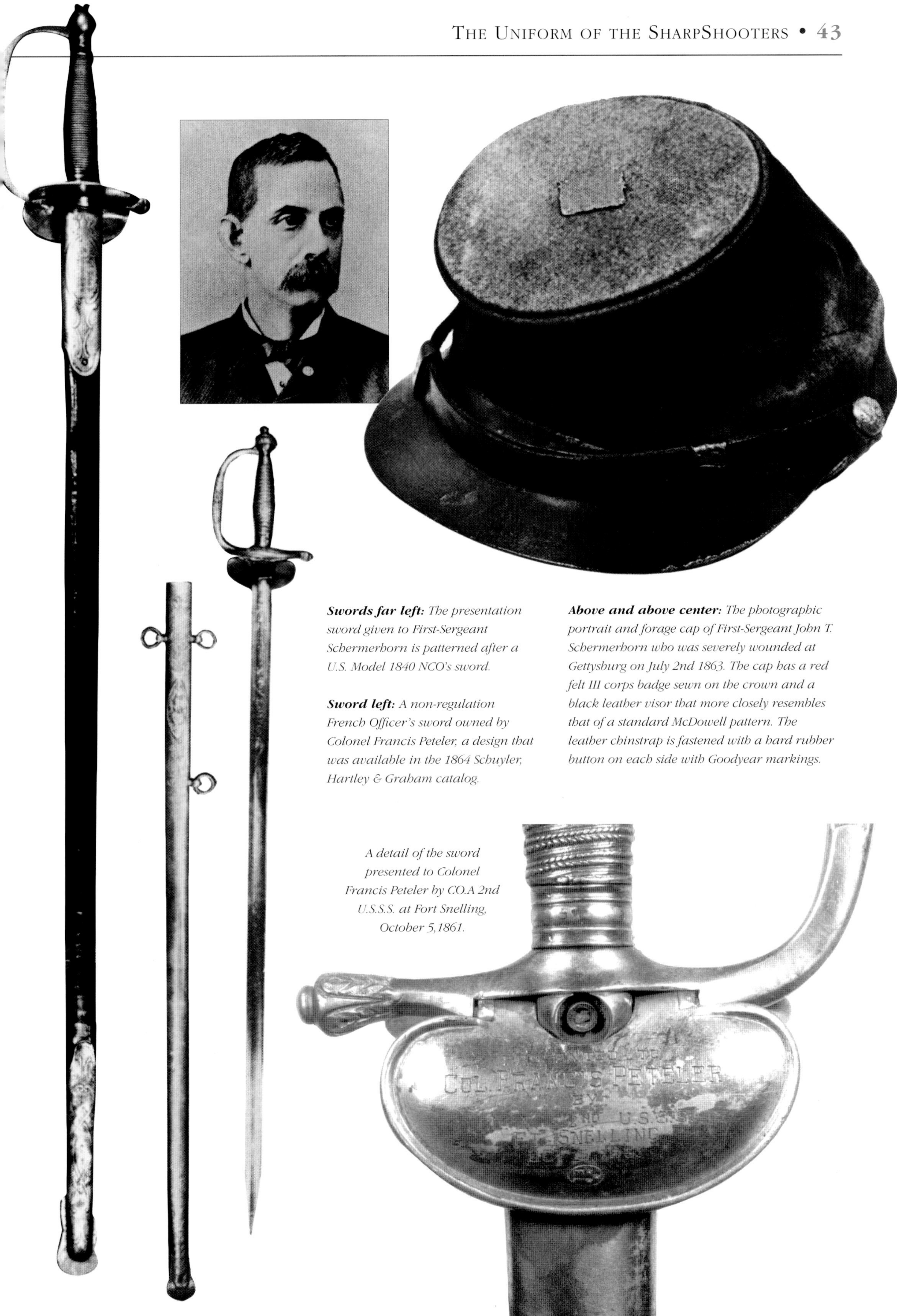

Swords far left: *The presentation sword given to First-Sergeant Schermerhorn is patterned after a U.S. Model 1840 NCO's sword.*

Sword left: *A non-regulation French Officer's sword owned by Colonel Francis Peteler, a design that was available in the 1864 Schuyler, Hartley & Graham catalog.*

Above and above center: *The photographic portrait and forage cap of First-Sergeant John T. Schermerhorn who was severely wounded at Gettysburg on July 2nd 1863. The cap has a red felt III corps badge sewn on the crown and a black leather visor that more closely resembles that of a standard McDowell pattern. The leather chinstrap is fastened with a hard rubber button on each side with Goodyear markings.*

A detail of the sword presented to Colonel Francis Peteler by CO.A 2nd U.S.S.S. at Fort Snelling, October 5,1861.

Firearms of the U.S. SharpShooters

Muzzleloading Target Rifles

Hiram Berdan's intention was to recruit the finest marksmen from each of the northern states, arrange them in companies, and have them fight as SharpShooters. Berdan, himself, was said to have been one of the best shots in America in the fifteen years leading up to the Civil War. The National Museum at Gettysburg still has numerous trophies and other awards won by Berdan, and donated by his heirs after his death. He took this talent for marksmanship, and convinced the War Department that he could recruit and train men to be military SharpShooters. One would pass Berdan's initial marksmanship test if he could:

> At 200 yards, put 10 consecutive shots in a target, the average distance not to exceed five inches from the center of the bullseye. Or, in other words, the string measurement of the 10 shots could not exceed 50 inches.

Berdan said:

> When on the battlefield, such a Corps would be relied upon, firing at rest, to hit a man every time at one-eighth mile, hit him two out of three times at a quarter mile, and three out of five times at a half mile.

At the trials, each man was free to use any rifle with telescopic or target globe sights while firing at 200 yards. The shooter could stand at 100 yards, if he fired a gun with open sights. He could fire at rest, supporting his rifle on any object he chose, as long as the butt was in contact with the shooter's shoulder. As early as mid-June 1861, Berdan envisioned his men armed with:

> ...well known target rifles, with cast steel barrels, swedged balls, false muzzles, and either globe or telescopic sights.

A month later, Berdan was to say:

> In my judgment, the best sights for this service are the plain, open type, consisting of a notch sight [on the barrel], a silver pin at the muzzle, and a windage globe sight at the breech. The open sight would be convenient in obscure places, while the globe sight would be used with good light.

The men were encouraged to supply their own rifles, as they were promised a bounty of $60 if they would bring their weapons with them when mustered into service. This was a promise that would never be kept.

Marksmanship trials took place in numerous locations in nearly every northern state. It was said that the best shooting was done by Charles H. Townsend, at Camp Randall, Wisconsin. He fired five shots at the 200 yard target, with a total measurement (center of bull to the center of each shot) of only three and three-quarter inches. This is remarkable shooting, even by today's standards with sophisticated high-powered target rifles. Such accuracy in 1861, utilizing muzzleloading target rifles with black powder loads, illustrates the degree of marksmanship skill that was possessed. Townsend was not alone in his shooting ability, as the average target shot by men who passed Berdan's test was a mere two inches per shot, or a ten-shot string of twenty inches. This was well under the allowable 50 inches per string.

Precision-made American target rifles of the 1850s and '60s were fully capable of this accuracy. They were hand-crafted by skilled gunsmiths, utilizing only the straightest of heavy octagonal barrels. They were percussion muzzleloaders, and most were equipped with false muzzles which would facilitate loading the ball without damaging the actual muzzle. The guns were not especially portable, as they weighed from fifteen to nearly thirty pounds each. One of Berdan's officers, Horace Warner, said this about the arms in July 1861:

> The truth is that I am partial to the American target rifle, believing that there is no other gun that can exceed it in performance if properly handled. I have worked for years, alternately at making and using them, and think that I understand their use and capacity as well as most men in this country. I have a double-barreled cast steel rifle of my own make, which is a combination of a hunting and target rifle. I have the whole rig for target practice, such as globe sights, swedged balls, etc.

In July 1861, Berdan corresponded with the Army Chief of Ordnance, General James Wolfe Ripley, regarding the procurement of quality firearms for his SharpShooters. Ripley, charged with the difficult mission of supplying functional arms to thousands of Federal troops, stressed uniformity, and thought that the new Springfield .58 caliber muzzleloading rifle musket was best for Union infantrymen, *and for Berdan's SharpShooters*. Initially, Berdan agreed with

Above: *The Springfield Model 1861 was an early suggestion by for the Sharpshooters standard issue, made by General Ripley, which never came to fruition.*

Above: *Private Horace Kimble's heavy target rifle is equipped with a tubular sight. These were either provided with lenses or as a simple aiming tube with crosshairs only. He is wearing an M1861 style kepi and an untrimmed nine-button frockcoat.*

Above: *Private Myron Mansfield of Company H (Vermont) 2nd U.S. Sharpshooters. The inscription on the back of the photograph states that the target rifle he is holding was made by the famous New York State gunsmith, Morgan James, of Utica.*

Right: *A typical candidate for recruitment into Berdan's regiment. Probably between 17 and 23 , physically fit, and an accomplished shot. Recruitment tests required each man to prove his skill with a chosen weapon, in this case a heavy percussion target rifle. Many recruits brought their own guns with them. The rifle shown here was probably .44 or .50 caliber,and hand-made by a skilled gunsmith as evidenced by the fine inlays, checkered wrist and polished finish.*

Ripley:

> Every man's skill with a rifle has been tested, and not one who has been admitted did not carefully fit to the requirements. All have superior rifles, but there is such a variation of caliber and weight, that I have concluded to take your suggestion and leave them all at home and take a uniform weapon. I have tried the Springfield rifle musket, and much prefer it over others I have seen, and I would take 750 of them for my regiment. Can you supply this number?

The following week Ripley replied to Berdan that he could supply the arms, as requested. However, a letter from Berdan to Governor Curtin of Pennsylvania revealed that he thought of these muzzleloaders only an interim arm that would be turned in, *"as soon as a 1st class rifle of uniform caliber, adapted to this special arm of the service, can be made."* For unknown reasons, Berdan's SharpShooters never did receive Ripley's Springfield rifle muskets.

Not all of Berdan's recruits were mustered in with rifles brought from home. But two companies were the exception, Michigan's Company C and New Hampshire's Company E of the 1st Regiment. Each man was armed with a different target rifle, and these two companies carried these cumbersome muzzleloaders throughout the war. These very same companies were the first of Berdan's men to see action, being part of General Smith's expedition which left the Washington area on September 21,1861. On the 27th, they utilized their heavy rifles in a small skirmish near Lewinsville, and two days later in a night fight at Munson's Hill, Virginia. Clearly, no SharpShooter enjoyed lugging his heavy target rifle into battle, proving that a lighter, accurate infantry-style rifle was needed for Berdan's command. As one SharpShooter said:

> It was soon found that there were severe objections to the use of these heavy weapons in the field, [which had been] so effective on the target ground. The great weight of some of them was almost prohibitory, for to a soldier burdened with the weight of his knapsack, haversack, canteen, blanket and overcoat, the additional weight of a target rifle was too much to be easily borne.
>
> It was also difficult to provide the proper ammunition for such rifles in the field. And finally, owing to the delicacy of the construction of the sights, hair-triggers, etc., they were constantly liable to be out of order. When thus disabled, they were of even less use than the smoothbore musket.

First Sergeant Wyman S. White of Company F (New Hampshire), 2nd U.S.S.S. stated:

> Heavy target rifles with telescopic sights were used throughout the war for "special sharpshooting." There were not many of them, but they were assigned to those soldiers that were considered the best shots. Each gun had a special wooden case, and when the unit moved, it was carried by a supply wagon. When the man put his telescopic rifle away, he took up his Sharps rifle again, and moved with the troops until a special duty required the use of his long range rifle again. He of times operated as an independent marksman in various parts of the line where he thought he could do the most good.

Breechloading Rifles for the SharpShooters

When they were recruited, the SharpShooters were promised that they would be issued the finest rifles available. Rudolf Aschmann, an officer with Company A, 1st U.S.S.S., mentions that the famous Sharps breechloading rifle was first demonstrated to the men while still at their rendezvous at Weehawken, New Jersey. "This firearm," he said, "had a hair trigger and open sights, and was found to be the most efficient of all. However, its price was so high, $45 apiece, that the authorities in Washington wanted no part in it." Ultimately, the Sharps rifle would become a deadly instrument of destruction in the trained marksmen's hands, but many months would elapse before this could come about.

Above: *The Hall Model 1841 issued to the SharpShooters in early 1861 . Although the Hall was groundbreaking in its day, being a Breech Loader, by the outbreak of war it was antiquated and hardly suitable for a crack regiment.*

As fall of 1861 approached, Berdan's SharpShooters were, for the most part, unarmed. In fact, they had only a few hundred heavy target rifles, and a few dozen antiquated, percussion, Hall breechloading rifles that had been issued for guard duty. This was a sorry plight for the most skilled marksmen in the Union Army at this time. But, nonetheless, the situation worsened.

In September 1861, Berdan's commanding officer made the mistake of trying to order the SharpShooters to arm themselves with outdated, muzzleloading Harper's Ferry rifles. This order was not accepted well by the men, as it represented a broken promise. In anger, Berdan wrote back:

> Camp of Instruction, Washington
> September 25, 1861
>
> Brigadier General Landers
> Commanding Brigade
> Camp Benton
>
> General:
> Your letter of the 20th instant, ordering me to requisition Harper's Ferry rifles and ammunition for all that have arrived in my command, and to send all the men that had been mustered into service, and remain myself at this camp to receive the remainder of my companies, reached me yesterday. I feel confident that the men would suffer any punishment that might be inflicted for disobedience of orders, before they would go into the field with any such weapon. They have the same contempt for those common guns that a house painter would have for a whitewash brush. They say that they did not come here to use any such gun, and that they will lay in jail until the war is over before they will use them.
>
> They are willing to use the common Sharps rifles until the new guns can be made. I am trying to get some of these, and think that I shall be able to obtain 600 or 700 the first of next week. The men are anxious to have them, and then go forward as we are. It will take me four to five days, yet, to get all that my men require, in the way of uniforms, knapsacks, leggings, transports, etc. etc.
>
> H. Berdan

Evidently, General Landers rescinded his order, and the SharpShooters were not required to carry the inferior weapons.

The following is one of the earliest references to Sharps breechloading, single-shot rifles for Colonel Berdan's marksmen. On September 21, 1861, Berdan telegraphed Richard S. Lawrence of the Sharps Rifle Manufacturing Company in Hartford, Connecticut:

> When will the sample rifle be here without fail. Answer immediately.

Based on a notation in the Sharps factory records that referred to a Sharps arm weighing about twenty pounds, f it seems clear that the sample rifle sent for evaluation to Berdan's men was a heavy barrel sporting arm, not a military rifle, as one would expect. A contemporary article in the *DETROIT FREE PRESS* stated:

> The guns... at a cost of sixty or seventy dollars each, are Sharps improved target rifles, with globe sights, rifle stock, octagon barrel, double triggers, patched balls, etc.

In September, numerous representatives from a host of firearms companies descended upon the Federal troops I encamped near Washington, D.C., hoping to interest commanders in their respective breechloaders. Extemporaneous shooting trials were frequently held, with the promise of contracts of large sales of weapons for the many, as yet unarmed regiments. It is known that agents from the Sharps Rifle Manufacturing Company, of Hartford, Connecticut, demonstrated their Breech Loading, single-shot rifle to the Berdan SharpShooters at this time, successfully convincing them that the Sharps New Model 1859 rifle would make the best all-around arm for sharpshooting. An excellent reference to what later became the accepted rifle for Berdan SharpShooters is found in a letter from Colonel Berdan, dated September 27, 1861:

> Superior rifles will be furnished here, with Sharps improved breech gate [not the older, slant breech Sharps], cast steel barrels, patch falls [patch box], double triggers, and rifle

Above: *California Joe in April 1862 with the Sharps rifle that he had privately purchased a year earlier. It is thought that the regimental armorer must have refitted his rifle with double-set triggers and a new lever.*

stock, all in the best manner, made to order. In my judgment, [these are to be] greatly superior to any guns you can bring for this branch of the service.

It is clear that Berdan and his men considered the Sharps breechloading rifle to be the one that they had been seeking. One of the SharpShooters, believed to be California Joe (Truman Head of Company C, 1st Regiment U.S.S.S.), purchased a sample NM1859 Sharps .52 in caliber rifle from a sales representative in late September. Berdan sent him to meet with the Secretary of War, hoping that this would convince him to order this type of weapon for both regiments:

Camp of Instruction
Berdan's U.S. SharpShooters
Washington
October 22, 1861

Hon. Simon Cameron
Secretary of War

Sir:
The bearer has a sample gun, one of Sharps improved pattern, and a new bayonet, which I think will interest you. I have selected this gun as the most suitable weapon to be placed in the hands of my SharpShooters that I know of.

In fact, any of the ordinary weapons would make my men little better than the common infantry. As my men are getting in very good drill, no time should be lost in arming and sending them forward.

Mr. J.C. Palmer, President of the Sharps [Rifle] Mfg. Co., informs me that he can furnish 3,000 of these guns, commencing to give us 100 a day after 20 days, on receipt of the order, and without any interference with the present government order for carbines.

We have about 200 heavy target rifles, which is as many as I care to have of these heavy guns. We are exceedingly anxious to have these improved breechloaders with long bayonets. The price is $43, but this includes fly lock, double triggers, and the long bayonet with sheath. The additional charge of fifty cents over the ordinary gun is certainly very reasonable for the extra work.

The men, as well as myself, feel that with these weapons, we can not only make a name for ourselves, but be of vast service to the country.

H. Berdan

No surviving record exists of Secretary of War Cameron's reply, if any, to Berdan, The fact remains that no Sharps firearms were ordered for the SharpShooters at this time. The rifle mentioned in the letter was very likely one equipped with a bayonet lug beneath the barrel, and the long bayonet was none other than the standard sword-type bayonet, as manufactured for Sharps by Collins & Company, of nearby Hartford. This may be the exact gun held by California Joe in the famous picture entitled Watching for Rebs. About him, Historian Stevens later recalled:

There was but one Sharps rifle in the regiment at the time, which was the personal property of Truman Head, better known as Old Californy, or California Joe. He gave most convincing proof of his skill as a marksman. This particular Sharps rifle was purchased while at Camp of Instruction, and had a sabre [sword type] bayonet and single trigger.

The rifle seen in the picture, Watching for Rebs, has a double-set trigger, without locking arrangement for the lever, but with a bayonet lug for the sword bayonet. The bayonet can be plainly seen at Truman's waist. This picture was taken in September 1862, nearly a year after Truman Head privately purchased the rifle. In all probability, the company armorer refitted the rifle with a double-set trigger, common to all SharpShooter Sharps rifles.

As the chilly fall days dragged on, the men complained that the breechloading rifles had not arrived. A Madison, Wisconsin newspaper of November 7th, carried the following terse remarks:

SharpShooter rifles have still not arrived. The men occasionally borrow rifled muskets, and steal away to shoot them. Others are fearful that the promised arms may never arrive, and they could be issued muzzleloaders, instead.

Berdan, meanwhile, sent a request for 2,000 Sharps rifles through to Chief of Ordnance James W. Ripley. Despite the fact that General McClellan had earlier approved the procurement, it was denied. Secretary of War Simon Cameron was then approached, and he agreed to write directly to Ripley, requesting that he order the Sharps rifles for Berdan. Again Ripley refused.

Colt Revolving Rifles

On November 12th, the Wisconsin newspaper reported:

A new firearm was tested here [Berdan's Camp of Instruction in Washington, D.C.] yesterday by Colonel Berdan, which is called Colt's 5-shooter. It looks like a musket, and has a bayonet attached. The barrel is bright, and it is pronounced by our Colonel to be a superior weapon. Many, however, wish to have the Sharps patent, and it is probable that both kinds will be used by this regiment.

Colonel Henry A. V. Post, Commander of the 2nd Regiment of SharpShooters, agreed to take *Colt Army New Model Rifled Muskets* (this is the official, 1861-era Colt term for what today would be called Colt Model 1855 military, five-shot, revolving

Above: *Left hand side view of the Colt Army Rifled Musket-New Model.*

COLT ARMY RIFLED MUSKETS – NEW MODEL

barrel:	*37 1/2 inch round ,with 3 1/8 inch octagonal section near the breech*
barrel Markings:	*none*
bayonet:	*angular type, with a serial # matching the rifled musket*
calibre:	*.56 inch*
cartouche:	*none*
cartridge:	*Colt .56 caliber skin cartridge*
catalog price:	*$52.50 with angular bayonet*
cleaning rod:	*iron with swelled button head*
contract price:	*$45 with angular bayonet*
cylinder:	*fluted ,with 5 chambers*
cylinder pin:	*removable,enters frame from the rear*
frame:	*solid*
forestock:	*full length oiled walnut, secured by 2 barrel bands [clamping type]*
front site:	*small blade mounted on base, which was machined to accept angular bayonet*
furniture:	*all exposed metal parts blued, except for case-hardened hammer and loading lever and bright barrel*
grooves:	*7 grooves, gain twist*
hammer:	*exposed, side-hung*
loading lever:	*creeping type*
modern designation:	*Colt-Root Model 1855 sidehammer, revolving rifle musket with creeping lever ramrod*
overall length:	*55 inches*
quantity produced:	*1000 for U.S. SharpShooters; unknown quantity for others*
rear sight:	*Colt folding leaf type, graduated for 100, 300 and 600 yards*
serial number range:	*shared with all Colt military rifles in .56,.58 and .64 calibers from 1-9310 (however, some sporting rifles and .56 carbines are intermixed in this range)*
sling swivels:	*on rear barrel band and on stock*
stock:	*walnut with oiled finish*
top strap marking:	*COL.COLT HARTFORD CT. U.S.A.*
weight:	*10lbs/8oz*
year produced:	*late 1861- early 1862*

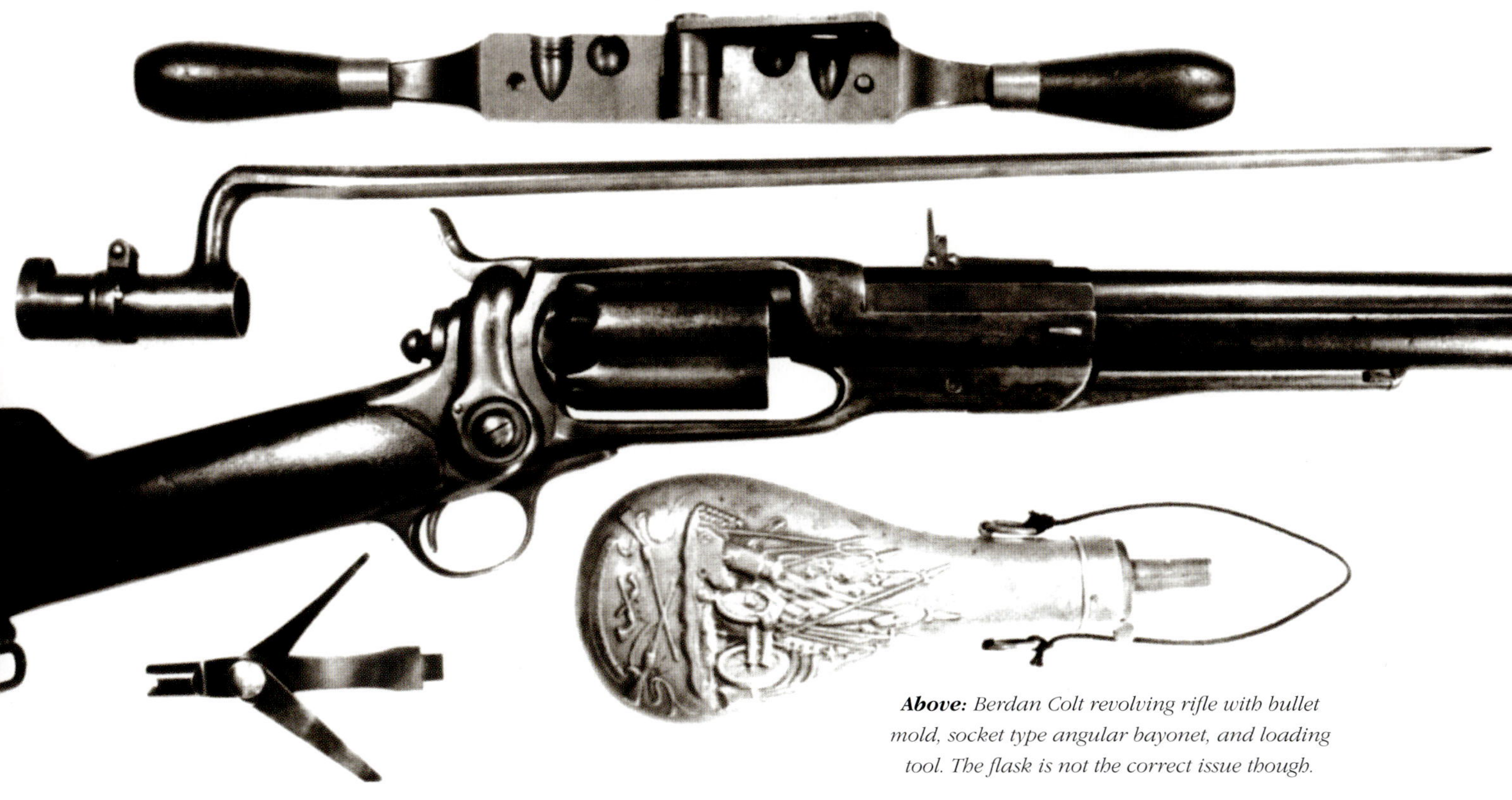

***Above:** Berdan Colt revolving rifle with bullet mold, socket type angular bayonet, and loading tool. The flask is not the correct issue though.*

***Above:** An unidentified SharpShooter with a Colt revolving rifle. Despite the initial enthusiasm, after use in the field, the weapon was not liked by the men.*

rifles with 37½ in barrels) for his regiment, but only as a last resort. Berdan, however, wanted to hold out for the Sharps firearms, but urged all parties to proceed with procuring the Colt firearms. Major General McClellan again got involved, and wrote directly to Ripley, requesting that he order them:

Headquarters of the Army
Washington, D.C.
November 23, 1861

General James W. Ripley
Chief of Ordnance

General:
Colonel Colt of Hartford, Connecticut, offers to sell 1,000 of his repeating rifles (according to the model that has been submitted to Colonel Kingsbury) at $45 each. You will please purchase these arms, if they can be had at the price stated. They are intended for Colonel Berdan's regiment.
George B. McClellan
Major General

A week later, after Ripley refused to act on this request, McClellan again wrote to Secretary of War, Simon Cameron, imploring him to influence the obstinate Chief of Ordnance. President Lincoln was shown the letter, and wrote a personal approval, adding that Chief of Ordnance Ripley "let it be executed, at once," Upon receiving the order for the 1,000 Colt Model 1855 revolving rifles, at a delivery price of $45 apiece, Colonel Colt dispatched his treasurer, Hugh Harbison, to Washington. The order would amount to at least $45,000, and Colt, shrewd businessman, had too much at stake to leave anything to chance:

Willard's Hotel
Washington, D.C.
December 7. 1861

Sam Colt
Colt Pat. Fire-Arms Mfg. Co.

My dear Colonel:
I arrived here last evening after a long and tiresome ride. This morning I went out to see Colonel Berdan. When I arrived, I found he was in the city. On my return I called at General Marcy's office [McClellan's Chief of Staff], and while there, I met Colonel Berdan and made arrangements to meet him at Willard's. I did not see General Marcy. I met the Colonel according to our agreement, and had a long interview with him. He feels very anxious about the rifles, but says that he must have them no matter what the consequences are.

To show you what has been done, I enclose a copy of a letter which General Marcy addressed to the Secretary of War, and also a copy of the endorsement of the President on said letter, which will speak for themselves. General McClellan has agreed to take hold of the matter, himself, today, if time will permit. Secretary Cameron referred the letter to his Assistant Secretary, and General Ripley was sent for. After they had an interview together, they called upon General McClellan, and proposed to him that Colonel Berdan's regiment be armed with the Springfield rifles, to which the General consented.

Below: *An interesting example of a converted civilian version of the Colt rifle with tubular sight and double-set triggers. The fancy trigger guard differentiates it from the military version.*

It is possible that this weapon was a private purchase, adapted for military [sharpshooting] use.

Colonel Berdan says that the only reason he can give for the General's action is that General McClellan was not familiar with the arrangement between Marcy and Berdan. He then called upon General McClellan and had an interview with him. He told him that the rifles were positively promised to him by Chief of Staff Marcy, and that he, Colonel Berdan, had promised Colt's rifles to his men, and that the President had also approved the action.

General McClellan then said that the rifles must be procured, and that he would call upon the Secretary of War, himself, and arrange the matter, if possible. Colonel Berdan says that Ripley is determined that the rifles shall not be ordered, and General Marcy and himself are determined that they shall be ordered.

So the matter stands, at present. Colonel Berdan desires me to say to you that he has been fighting this matter for the past six weeks, with all the energy that he could muster, and he is determined not to give it up until he obtains what he wants. Should General McClellan fail to secure the order, he, Berdan, intends to still go further. The Colonel wanted to know if you would furnish him the rifles without an order from the Ordnance or War Department, provided he procured an order from General McClellan for the liberty of arming his regiment with Colt's rifles. Said rifles to be paid for within 30 or 60 days, and in case they are not paid for, he, Berdan, will agree to return them to you in good order, if you require it.

He will furnish you personal security for the fulfillment of said agreement, in order that he may carry out his own and General Marcy's wishes, but hopes it will not be necessary to enter into such an agreement. I told him that I shall submit the matter to you, for consideration. The Colonel further states that with the letters which he has in his possession, he can obtain an appropriation from Congress to pay for them. And that if he is compelled to take the latter course, he will make it for a much larger number, as he really wants 2,400, in lieu of the 1,000. But, in order to do this, the rifles must be on the spot.

He has shown the sample to every member of Congress, both branches, and he has visited his regiment and there has been quite a number of them out to see him and his men. His regiment has a target shooting every Saturday, and he gave me a very pressing invitation to go out and spend the day with him and see it, but money matters prevented. I have agreed to see him on Monday or Tuesday.

Hugh Harbison

As it was, the Colt factory would have to wait for nearly two months to pass before General Ripley agreed to order these 1,000 Colt rifles for Berdan's troops. The fear, uncertainty, and anger that the SharpShooters felt at this time, without firearms, was illustrated by the following petition from several U.S. SharpShooters to their Congressmen:

> Washington. D.C.
> December 1861
>
> We, the undersigned members of Company A, 2nd Regiment of Berdan's SharpShooters, from Minnesota, respectfully petition our representatives in Congress, that inasmuch as we were mustered into the U.S. service at Fort Snelling on October 3, 1861, as SharpShooters, and that we have been in Washington since October 11th without arms, and that it was represented that we should be furnished with superior rifles which we have not been issued. We would respectfully ask you to intercede with the proper department for the privilege to furnish our own guns, with the following condition: That the government will allow us the price of the guns that they [promised to] furnish us, and the men would pay the difference in [obtaining] Sharps improved target rifles.
>
> (signed by eight men)

SharpShooter Colonel William Ripley later wrote:

> It became known that the promises made to them at the time of enlistment, that the government would pay them for their rifles at a rate of sixty dollars each, was unauthorized, and would not be fulfilled. Also, that the representations made to them with respects to telescopic breechloaders were likewise unauthorized. Discontent became general, and demoralizing began to show itself in an alarming form.

In an effort to quell the brewing dissatisfaction, Colonel Berdan arranged daily marksmanship instruction and target shooting for all of the men, utilizing the few target rifles that were on hand. Occasionally, on weekends, special marksmanship competitions were staged. One contest took place on November 28, 1861, when several of Berdan's officers offered a small prize. The terms were that the shooters were to fire only two shots apiece, off-hand, at targets placed at two hundred yards. The winner would be the marksman with the shortest string. First prize was won by Al Brown, of Company F, his two shots measuring a scant four and a quarter inches, or each shot only two and an eighth inches from the center of the target!

On December 7th, another regimental shooting match took place, with first prize going to a Michigan SharpShooter. His string of three shots, fired off-hand at two hundred yards, measured a scant six inches!

Spencer Repeating Rifles

Sales representatives continued to visit Federal units that were camped near Washington through the cold winter months. One representative brought an untried, breechloading, repeating rifle to Berdan's Camp of Instruction in late December. The rifle was unique, insomuch as it fired self-contained, metallic cartridges, rather than loose ball and powder. It was heavy, weighing nearly ten pounds. Actually, it weighed more than eleven pounds fully loaded with seven .52 caliber cartridges in the buttstock magazine, and another in the chamber. The firepower that it was professed to deliver captured the imaginations of SharpShooters who would occupy skirmisher positions in warfare. Unfortunately, only this inventor's sample arm existed, and there was no factory yet built to manufacture the hundreds that Berdan would need to arm his troops.

Berdan, avid shooter that he was, eagerly inspected the revolutionary weapon, and then near-tragedy struck while firing the rifle:

Headquarters
First Reg't Berdan's U.S. SharpShooters
Camp of Instruction
Washington
December 26, 1861

Colonel Thomas A. Scott
Assistant Secretary of War

Colonel:
While trying the Spencer gun yesterday, the butt of one of the cartridges burst, and some powder blew through the slot in the gate, into my face and eye, destroying the entire sight for the moment. The surgeon thinks, however, that he will be able to save it.

I am unable to go out today, and write to ask if the agent or manufacturer of the Spencer gun is now in the city. If so, will you be kind enough to request him to call on me, that we may see if it is not possible to guard against similar accidents with the new guns. The bearer, Mr. Doherty, will take any note or message you may desire to send.

H. Berdan Colonel Commanding U.S.S.S.

No response from Thomas Scott exists, and no further mention of the Spencer repeater was made by Berdan's SharpShooters until mid-1863. Only one other early reference exists, and that is from a Madison, Wisconsin newspaper dated January 2, 1862, quoting a SharpShooter:

> We are not armed yet, but probably will be, as soon as they can be made. We are to have Spencer's magazine rifle, which proved a strong shooter on trial, and will, no doubt, be an effective weapon in the field. It shoots eight times without reloading, and needs little cleaning.

The Berdan SharpShooters might well have ascended to even greater glory had they received the Spencer repeaters instead of their single-shot Sharps rifles.

Armed at Last

In late January 1862, Chief of Ordnance Ripley finally ordered the "1,000 Colt Army Rifled Muskets – New Model" for Berdan's SharpShooters:

Above: *The Spencer 7-shot rifle was another unsuccessful contender for the SharpShooters standard issue arm. It fired a .52 caliber rimfire straight copper cartridge.*

TELEGRAM

Ordnance Office, Washington
January 27,1862

H. Harbison
Hartford, Connecticut

Send to Colonel Ramsay, Washington Arsenal, one thousand Colt's repeating rifles and appendages, and one hundred thousand cartridges for the same.
J.W. Ripley
Brigadier General

For the record, the 1,000 Colt revolving rifles which had been ordered on January 27th, had an official purchase date of the following day. The $45 cost for each gun was far below the posted broadside price of $52.50. The contract price for each arm also included angular bayonet, and cone wrench & screwdriver. One Colt .56 caliber bullet mold (casting one round and one elongated bullet) was included with every ten rifles. The Colt factory also shipped *one military company bullet mold* (casting six elongated bullets) *with every-one hundred revolving rifles*.

During the Civil War, Colt military rifles were packed 20, to a box. Unfortunately, the exact size of the boxes for Berdan's shipment was not stated in any known order or correspondence. Also, while not stated in the contract, it is believed that Ripley's mention of appendages, did not include a powder flask for each rifled musket, as ones with plain dispensers sold for $1.50, while those with Colt's patented dispenser sold for $1.75.

Ironically, the same day General Ripley ordered the 1,000 Colt rifles for Berdan, he also ordered 1,000 Sharps NM1859 rifles:

TELEGRAM

Ordnance Office
Washington
January 27, 1862

J.C. Palmer – President
Sharps Rifle Company
Hartford, Connecticut

Send 1,000 Sharps rifles with accoutrements and 100,000 cartridges to Washington Arsenal for Berdan's SharpShooters. More by mail. Send as soon as possible,
J.W. Ripley
Brigadier General

The following day, Palmer wrote to General Ripley, informing him that the rifles for the SharpShooters would be ready in about twenty to twenty-five days. Furthermore, that work was in "full power" on the carbines for the Ordnance Department. However, by early February, Ripley grew concerned that Berdan's order for 1,000 rifles would severely impact on the existing order for Sharps carbines. He wrote to Palmer on February 4th, expressing these concerns. Before receiving Palmer's reply, Ripley ordered an additional 1,000 Sharps rifles, identical to those already ordered. It stated that *"these, too, were intended for Berdan's men."*

Palmer's reply to General Ripley's February 4th telegram was mailed on the 6th. In it, Palmer stated that *"making the 1,000 rifles for Berdan would be the same as if they were making 1,000 carbines, more or less."* On February 12th, Palmer again wrote to Ripley, explaining that *"the military order for rifles and appendages did not cover cartridge boxes, bayonet sheaths, and cap pouches."* He stated that *"the Sharps Company could supply them to the government for three dollars per set."* While Palmer did not elaborate, it is known that his factory was not in the leather goods business. It is likely that he went to Emerson Gaylord of Chicopee, Massachusetts, for these accoutrements, and then resold them to the Ordnance Department.

The Sharps cartridge box is a rare and desirable item for present-day collectors. It should not be confused with the cavalry carbine box for Sharps linen cartridges, which is a rectangular box, with twenty holes bored in the wood block. The Sharps infantry-style cartridge box is patterned after the M1855 standard .58 caliber cartridge box, but proportionally smaller. The metal tin inserts hold two packets of Sharps cartridges on the bottom, and twenty loose rounds on the top. Each unopened packet contained ten .52 caliber linen cartridges and percussion caps.

Right: *Studio portrait of a young Berdan SharpShooter holding his NM1859 Sharps rifle with the breechblock open .He wears a SharpShooter black ostrich feather in his non-regulation hat. The pistol in his belt is probably a studio prop.*

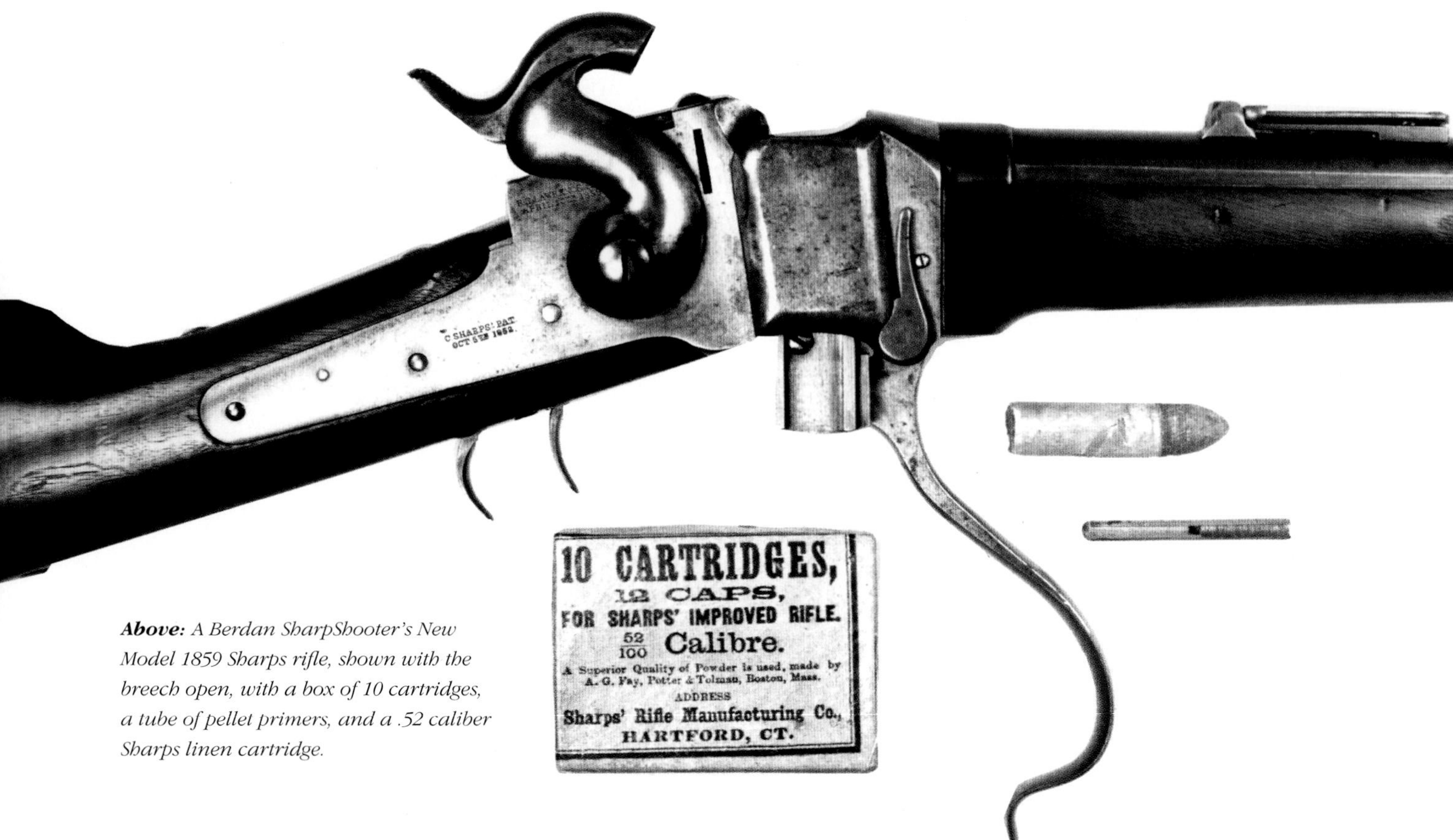

Above: *A Berdan SharpShooter's New Model 1859 Sharps rifle, shown with the breech open, with a box of 10 cartridges, a tube of pellet primers, and a .52 caliber Sharps linen cartridge.*

On February 15th, Palmer wrote to Ripley, stating that the initial 1,000 rifles for the SharpShooters would be delayed until the existing run of 1,000 Sharps carbines was completed. Besides, he said, "the party engaged to make the bayonets is behind time." He was referring to Collins & Company, in nearby Hartford. Bayonets for the Sharps NM1859 military rifles for Berdan's SharpShooters were marked C & Co. on the socket. By February 28th, no Sharps rifles had arrived, so Ripley again wrote to the Sharps factory, asking why they had been delayed. *"I scarcely need to repeat,"* he said, *"that the 2,000 rifles which have been ordered for the SharpShooters are very much needed, and feel that you will use every exertion to have them finished at the earliest possible day."* Four days later, Palmer informed Ripley by letter that *"the first order for 1,000 rifles would go forward by the 20th, and the remaining 1,000 by April 20th."*

By March 6th, the SharpShooters were anxious and upset that marching orders were imminent, but no firearms were as yet on hand. Berdan's letter to the Sharps Rifle Company expressed this serious concern:

Capitol Structure
Washington, D.C.
March 6, 1862

Mr. Palmer
Sharps Rifle Company
Hartford, Conn.

Dear Sir:

You wrote to me on the 20th of January that you would deliver 1,000 guns in 20 to 25 days. This had been in answer to a dispatch from me, in which I asked you not to deceive me as to the time the guns would be delivered. Instead of receiving the guns as promised, I received a note from you on the 24th, stating that the first 250 guns would be delivered in a few days, and the balance in amounts of 400 per week.

Ten days have now elapsed and neither my men nor myself are willing to wait any longer with these promises and delays, especially when we were informed by the Ordnance Department that no order for carbines was, in any way, to interfere with these guns being made at once. I have heard at the department that you have not only delivered many hundreds of carbines since you received this order, but have written to the department, ordering many hundreds more before the guns for my corps are delivered.

I strongly suspect that you are employing a large portion of your force on carbines, which you distinctly promised me that you would not do. You told me, when here, that if you receive the order, you would put your entire force on my guns, and work night and day until they were completed. The order would have allowed you to do this, and I shall be glad to learn that my fears are unfounded, and that the first 1,000, at least, will be forthcoming. Such must be the case, if you expect the government to take the guns from my corps, if I have anything to say about it. For I am told that both of my regiments would be in the forward movement, and if we have to take Colt's guns, we will most likely keep them. Now, my dear sir, I must ask you to give me, by return mail, the exact time, if possible, when the 250 guns will be here. Also, when the balance of the first thousand will be here, that we may be able to decide that course the interest of the service demands.

H. Berdan

There is no evidence to suggest that Palmer replied to Berdan's very bold letter.

Meanwhile, on March 10, 1862, Palmer wrote to Ripley, explaining that the reason for the delay rested squarely on the modifications that Colonel Berdan ordered to the basic NM1859 Sharps rifle with sword bayonet and single trigger. Berdan, evidently, had changed the order, requesting angular bayonets, double-set triggers, and modified sights. Unfortunately, no official military correspondence exists reflecting Berdan's communication with Palmer on these modifications. Nevertheless, Palmer made the changes, believing that Berdan spoke with the authority to do so. Palmer explained:

> Colonel Berdan has no cause to complain on this account or any other that I know of, but the real occasion for delay has been in consequence of his insisting on having different sights, bayonets, and double triggers put on to the rifles, which he was well informed would cause the delay by me.

Chief of Ordnance Ripley was clearly vexed when he discovered the reasons for the delay. In a heated return letter to the Sharps factory on March 12th, he said:

> By the authority of the Secretary of War, I have to inform you that Colonel Berdan was not authorized to give you any instructions in relation to making the rifles. Whatever variations you have made at this instance, or by his directions, from the regular rifle ordered by this department, and whatever may be the effect of those variations, either in quality, cost, or time of delivery, must be at your risk, and must be borne by you as to the consequences.

Whether Palmer replied to Ripley is not known. The physical evidence (i.e., surviving specimens of Berdan Sharps rifles) tells us that Berdan's request for double-set triggers, angular bayonets and special sights was carried out by the Sharps factory. The workmen continued to work on the 2,000 special NM1859 rifles for the SharpShooters. Weeks passed, and with warm weather approaching, the Federal Army would soon begin the spring offensive. It was this awesome reality which caused apprehension among the unarmed SharpShooters.

Meanwhile, the 1,000 Colt revolving rifles which had been promised to Berdan's SharpShooters took many weeks to be shipped, warehoused, inventoried, and distributed. In fact, the first rifles appear to have been issued in late February 1862. Most, however, were not issued to Berdan's SharpShooters until shortly after the men left in late March 1862, to initiate McClellan's infamous Peninsula Campaign. Lieutenant Colonel William Ripley later recalled:

> On the 20th of March, the regiment received orders to report to Major General Fitz John Porter, whose division then lay at Alexandria, Virginia, awaiting transportation to Fort Monroe, to join the army under McClellan. At this time the regiment was without arms of any kind, except for the few target rifles remaining in the hands of their owners, and a few old smoothbore muskets that had been used during the winter for guard duty. The War Department... sent the revolving rifles of the Colt pattern to camp, to issue to the men, with promise of exchanging for Sharps rifles at a later day.
>
> They were five-chambered breechloaders, very pretty to look at, but upon examination and test, they were found

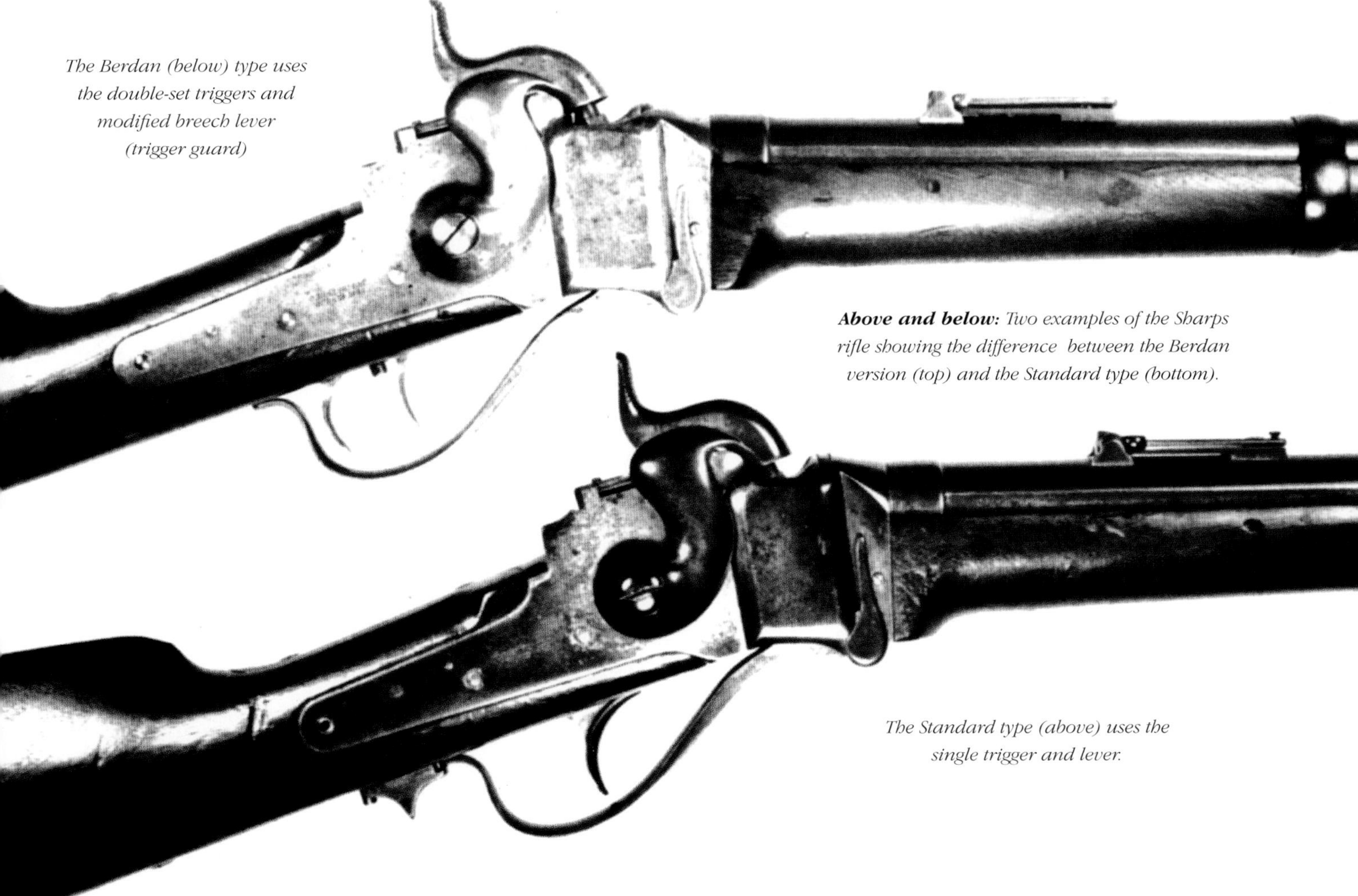

The Berdan (below) type uses the double-set triggers and modified breech lever (trigger guard)

Above and below: *Two examples of the Sharps rifle showing the difference between the Berdan version (top) and the Standard type (bottom).*

The Standard type (above) uses the single trigger and lever.

inaccurate and unreliable, prone to get out of order, and even dangerous to the user. They were not satisfactory to the men, who knew what they wanted, and were fully confident of their ability to use such guns as they had been led, by repeated promises to expect, to good advantage. When news came... that the campaign was about to open in good earnest, they took up these toys. Company F, Vermont, 1st U.S.S.S. was the first in the regiment to receive their arms.

A personal letter from Private Theodore Preston, Company B, 2nd U.S.S.S., describes these troubled times to his brother:

Last Wednesday, we had an order read on dress parade to be in readiness to march Saturday morning. So we all got our knapsacks packed, and all things ready for a march. The officers flew around wonderful smartly. They thought that they saw themselves over the [Potomac] river, in the smoke of battle, all mighty heroes. But in the meantime, amid all the preparation for marching, some of the privates were scratching their noodle over a large sheet of paper, framing petitions to their respective [Congressional] representatives, stating how we are to be armed, and how we are armed, and the danger a person is in that fires one of the [Colt] guns, and the threats that were made to get us to take the guns, and the promises that were made us after we had them. That we were promised Sharps [rifles] as soon as they could be made, and... now that we had learned the [Colt] manual of arms, we were to be rushed into battle with these poor guns, stating our dissatisfaction with the proceedings and praying them to do something for us. There were seven petitions sent in to as many Representatives.

The result of all this was that these Representatives went to headquarters to see General McClellan, but he was absent and the Adjutant General suspended the [marching] order, temporarily, until McClellan should return and consider the matter, and confer with the Representatives. Then the Representatives came up here to see us and the guns. They said that they would do all for us that they could. They saw Colonel Berdan and had a talk with him. And you may guess that he was mad. He could hardly contain himself when he heard what had been done. It was very humiliating to him to think that he had been outgeneraled by the privates. When the commanding officers of this regiment found out what had been done, they were ready to split every private's head open. They called a meeting of the officers in the evening, and had a hot time of it. Colonel [Post], Lieutenant Colonel [Francis Peteler], Major [Amos B. Jones], and Adjutant [Lewis Parmelee] tried their prettiest to get the captains to resign. Two captains and one lieutenant did resign, and when they found that the others would not, they abused them as bad as they knew how.

...Perhaps a slight description of the [Colt] gun would not be out of the way. To commence with, it is too light for

Right: *A fully armed and equipped Berdan SharpShooter in April 1862 ready to embark on McClellan's Peninsular Campaign. This private is wearing his SharpShooter green M1861 forage cap and black ostrich feather,and green nine-button frock coat with contrasting emerald green color piping about the collar and sleeves. He is wearing a pair of leather "leggins" over his "bootees" (shoes).*

the size and weight of the lead [bullet]. Second, when the ball leaves the cylinder and enters the barrel, there are small shavings of lead [that] escape from between the cylinder and barrel, and fly six or eight feet, endangering a person. Yes, I have often seen the boys picking out these pieces of lead from one another's necks and faces. Not long ago, a fellow in G Company was firing one when three barrels [shots within the cylinder] went off at once, cutting away his forefinger and thumb. The Major was firing one not long since, when it burst. All very true. But still they say that it is a safe gun, and as good as they make. But if [the] Sharps [rifle] is poorer, we want it. For we think we are capable of judging a gun, yet. If we are soldiers, give us Sharps [rifles], and we will run all the risk. For some unaccountable reason, they will persist in our using and keeping these guns. But they have got a pill now that will set them a thinking. If they won't do anything for us, why our Representatives will. And I think they will have as much influence as our officers.

The officers are crestfallen to think that the privates should out-wind them at last. Perhaps we are not through with it yet, but we are prepared for anything that comes up. What can't be cured, must be endured. If they do out-wind us... we may never get Sharps [rifles], nor another gun.

Soon thereafter, all one thousand Colt revolving rifles were distributed to the 1st and 2nd Regiments of Berdan's U.S. SharpShooters, with the exception of the two companies that retained their heavy muzzleloading target rifles: Michigan's Company C and New Hampshire's Company E, of the 1st Regiment. The regiments fielded at least 1,500 SharpShooters at this time, although many men in each company did not need or receive the Colt firearms, such as cooks, teamsters, musicians, those confined, and the like. A Madison, Wisconsin newspaper dated March 28, 1862, stated that the SharpShooters that were still unarmed carried picks, spades and axes! Regimental historian Stevens later recounted their thoughts about the 5-shooters:

It was thought, at first, that these Colts would not shoot true, but this proved not exactly the case. They were pretty good line shooters, although there was some danger of all the chambers exploding at once. The shooting qualities of this arm were tested in several instances before getting into action, and some good shots were noted. Andrew J. Pierce, of Company G, Wisconsin, while on the way down the Potomac, made a trial shot of the five chambers in the presence of the regimental officers, at a buoy bobbing up in the river some 400 yards distant. The result was thus announced by Colonel Berdan, who, with the other officers, were intently watching with their field glasses: "There, that will do, sir. You have struck the buoy twice, and t'was well done."

After numerous skirmishes on the Peninsula, the temperamental Colt revolving rifles proved their worth to many of the SharpShooters:

Advancing ahead, they met the Confederate fire with their five-shooters in a manner that evidently surprised the foe, who little expected such rapid firing. The revolving chambers of the Colts were soon heated up, and right here a most favorable opportunity was presented to test these heretofore doubtful arms. The boys were compelled to admit that they were not so bad after all, having done good work with them.

Above: *An example of a Sharps NM 1859 breech loading rifle, as issued to Berdan's SharpShooters. Original guns like this are hard to find.*

Sharps NM1859 Breechloading Rifles

Work progressed in Hartford on the 2,000 Sharps rifles for Berdan's SharpShooters. On April 7th, Springfield Armory Commander, George T. Balch, ordered his best civilian sub-inspector, John Taylor, to proceed from his assignment at the Colt factory, taking as many inspectors with him as he needed, to the nearby Sharps factory. He was ordered to take charge of the government inspection process, and to get the completed rifles for Berdan on their way without delay. On April 9th, Palmer, reporting from the Sharps Rifle Mfg. Co., informed Chief of Ordnance Ripley that all 2,000 barrel and receiver assemblies were finished and already inspected by the recently arrived Ordnance Department civilian inspectors. Furthermore, the first 200 completed rifles were ready for delivery. Palmer stated that ordnance inspector Taylor was now in charge of the final inspection procedure, assisted by inspectors Hartwell and Chapman. He said that the government employees were capable of approving up to 200 rifles a day, and would work overtime, including Sundays, until the entire order was completed and inspected.

The following day, General Ripley wrote to Palmer, telling him that "the first 1,000 rifles, when completed, should be shipped to Fort Monroe." "The second thousand," he went on to say, "along with all accoutrements and 200,000 Sharps cartridges, should be sent to the Washington Arsenal. The Sharps factory shipped the first 100 completed rifles on April 11th, to Fort Monroe, and sent the remainder of the 1,000 in lots of 100, as they were finished and inspected. One of John Taylor's surviving Ordnance Records indicates that he shipped 100 rifles each on April 11th, 14th, 16th, 19th, 21st, and 23rd. Sharps factory records indicate that deliveries of the first 500 rifles were completed on April 21st, consistent with Taylor's account. Other shipments of 500 rifles were completed on May 2nd, May 14th, and May 24th. The final cost of each rifle, complete with angular bayonet, was $42.50.

Palmer, at the Sharps factory, responded to the Chief of Ordnance that *"1,000 sets of accoutrements had already been shipped to Washington Arsenal on March 18th, and the remaining 1,000 sets and 200,000 cartridges and primers had been sent on April 1st, nearly two weeks earlier."*

The first shipment of 600 Sharps rifles was delivered to Berdan's 1st Regiment of U.S. SharpShooters on May 8, 1862:

> On the 8th the [1st] Regiment [of Berdan SharpShooters] received the [first of their] long-awaited Sharps rifles, now needed more than ever, as the Colts were found defective in many respects, and they gladly turned in their five-shooters.

Berdan realized that Samuel Colt would not like to hear that the SharpShooters were forsaking his revolving rifles for single-shot Sharps arms. Therefore, with utmost diplomacy, Colonel Berdan wrote to the Colt factory on May 8th, explaining the changeover:

> We are, today, exchanging our Colt revolving rifles for the Sharpes [sic] rifles, and it occurs to me that to do this without explanation may be a cause of great injustice to your valuable arm. The change is made in accordance with a promise made to the men when they were enlisted, that they should have the Sharps rifles. All our reputation, thus far, has been made with the Colts and the target rifles [heavy-barreled muzzleloaders], and the former have proved themselves a very superior weapon, especially for skirmishers. Several [other] regiments have applied for these arms, but I am determined to keep them in my Corps, if possible.

Evidently Berdan did not retain the Colt rifles for his regiments. Some SharpShooters who were armed with their tried-and-true target rifles refused to give them up for the Sharps rifles, and carried them through the remainder of their enlistment. Many of the nearly-new Colt revolving rifles were collected and shipped to other regiments that needed them. These arms may have been the ones that were later issued to the 2nd, 3rd, and 4th Michigan Cavalry, which carried this type of Colt firearm until 1864.

When the Sharps rifles finally arrived on May 8th, there was no ammunition provided. In haste, Ripley gave assurance that 200,000 Sharps cartridges were en route, having been sent from Washington Arsenal on April 27th.Although the 1st U.S. SharpShooters received their new Sharps rifles, Colonel Post's 2nd Regiment did not. On May 19th, he angrily wrote to the Ordnance Department, stating:

> When can I get the 550 that I require, with the necessary ammunition? I hear that the 1st Regiment has 400, over and above what they require.

On the 24th, Chief of Ordnance Ripley telegraphed Post, informing him that 550 Sharps rifles would be sent to him

Above and right: *A number of private ammunition manufacturers like Johnson & Dow, A. G. Fay, Potter & Tolman, made .52 caliber combustible linen cartridges for Sharps rifles.This is a typical packet containing 10 cartridges and 12 percussion caps.*

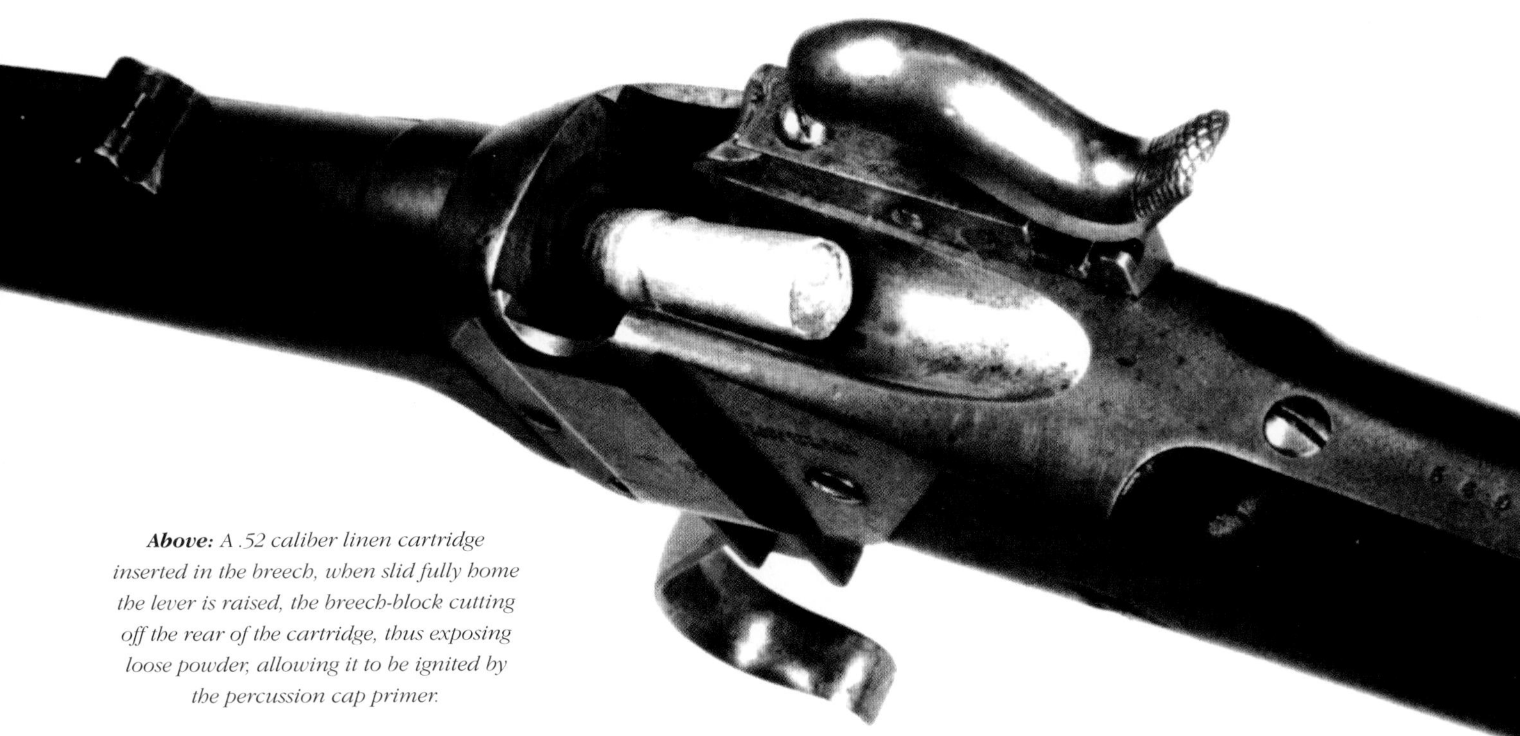

Above: *A .52 caliber linen cartridge inserted in the breech, when slid fully home the lever is raised, the breech-block cutting off the rear of the cartridge, thus exposing loose powder, allowing it to be ignited by the percussion cap primer.*

from the Washington Arsenal, along with necessary ammunition and accoutrements. The breechloaders finally arrived for the 2nd Regiment on the 1st of June, while they were camped near Fredericksburg, Virginia. Then they too, turned in their Colt revolving rifles.

There is no doubt that Berdan's men liked their new Sharps rifles. Historian Stevens stated:

> On receiving the new arms, the men were impatient to get again within shooting distance of the enemy. These rifles shot both linen and skin cartridges of .52 caliber. We also had primers – little round, flat, coppered things – which were inserted below the hammer. But the regular army cap was more generally used, as the [wafer] primers were not always a sure thing.

Stevens was referring to the Sharps self-contained, pellet priming mechanism. It was activated simply by emptying a brass tube containing the a packet of copper clad disc wafers, each containing a small amount of fulminate, into an opening at the underside of the primer mechanism. The soldier actuated the device by merely cocking the hammer, and pulling the trigger. As the hammer fell, it moved a small slide forward, thrusting a single disc primer outward, which was caught between the inside face of the hammer and the top of the nipple. The crushed primer exploded, spewing flame through the nipple cone into the chamber, igniting the base of the prepared paper or linen Sharps .52 caliber cartridge. These disc primers were most appreciated in cold weather, as the shooter did not need to fumble with small, loose percussion caps.

After using the Sharps rifles in thick fighting, one SharpShooter wrote:

> We had orders to take all the cover possible. Being armed with breechloaders, we could lie low, and without changing position, reload and fire ten shots a minute. A regiment of SharpShooters in line could play havoc with an approaching column, as was afterwards demonstrated. The superiority of breechloaders over muzzle loaders was plainly manifest.

The increased firepower that the breechloading Sharps afforded also meant that the SharpShooter needed to carry more ammunition. While the basic combat load for the typical Federal infantryman was forty rounds, Berdan SharpShooters carried sixty, and sometimes more. Frequently, they ran out of ammunition, and if more could not be brought up from the regimental ammunition wagons, then the SharpShooters were forced to retire from the field. It appears that this first occurred during the fighting at Malvern Hill on July 1, 1862.

> On one occasion, Private Silas W. Howard of Company E, 1st Regiment, was badly wounded by enemy musket fire. It occurred on September 16, 1862, at the Battle of Antietam. Howard was shot several times, and was not expected to survive, as he had a severe chest wound. He took out the fire block [breech block] of his Sharps rifle, and threw it far away so no rebel could find it to make use of the rifle against us. He had the presence of mind to realize how valuable his Sharps breechloader would be to the enemy, and he had the strength left to dispose of the key component that would render it useless.

Berdan's Rifles Re-issued to Other Units

Both regiments of Berdan SharpShooters suffered heavy casualties during the campaigns of 1862. Men were killed on the battlefield, wounded and then evacuated to hospitals in the rear, were captured by the enemy, died of disease or of their wounds, deserted, or were simply absent without leave. The original 1,700+ SharpShooters enlisted in 1861, yielded a scant 723 present for duty in March 1863, just prior to the

Chancellorsville Campaign. The individual companies were so decimated that Lieutenant Colonel Trepp suggested that both regiments be combined into one, to make a more effective fighting force. However, this consolidation never occurred.

What, then, became of the 2,000 Sharps rifles that had been specially built for the SharpShooters? The surplus, rifles which had not been issued directly to the two regiments of Berdan SharpShooters were retained by the Ordnance Department, and re-issued to other units.

Berdan confirmed this in a letter to his superiors, dated September16,1862. In it he stated that the new, as yet unissued Sharps rifles that had been held for his new recruits, and the surplus rifles belonging to those already wounded or killed in action, *"had been issued to other regiments." "These,"* he went on to say, *"are leaving me not a single Sharps rifle for my men returning from hospitals, or for my recruits."*

While convalescing in Washington, Berdan succeeded in recovering 300 of his rifles from a Michigan regiment, plus an additional 197 which had been turned in to Fort Monroe. He lamented that there were rifles still out, all in the hands of the Pennsylvania Bucktails (13th Pennsylvania Reserves of the 42nd Pennsylvania Volunteer Infantry). He went on to say exactly how this came about:

> Before marching from Harrison's Landing, I received orders to turn in all extra arms for transportation. I turned in about 100 that belonged to men in hospitals. These guns were given to some Bucktails that just returned from Richmond, without arms. The Assistant Secretary of War, Mr. Watson, gave the Bucktails enough to arm the regiment. I request that General McClellan order these guns to be returned at once, and give the Bucktails Springfield rifles, instead.

Berdan never did recover these rifles. However the issue became moot, as his regiments of SharpShooters never again regained their original strength to justify issuance of additional arms. Despite fifty new recruits that had just arrived, all of the SharpShooter companies remained under strength for the rest of the war. The Regimental Historian of the Bucktails confirms that the Sharps rifles were issued on August 10, 1862, and were carried until the unit was rearmed with Spencer repeating rifles two years later. They believed that the Sharps rifles, *"fitted with extra hair [double-set] triggers,"* were superior arms.

In all the pages of research material that this author has viewed concerning the Berdan SharpShooters, not one word against the Sharps rifle was found. It was a weapon well suited to these remarkable troops, remaining with them from their date of issue in May 1862, until the enlistments expired in 1864 and 1865. It was common practice for soldiers departing the service to take their arms with them. In the case of the Sharps rifles, it could be done legally by paying a flat $6.00 fee, as established by Federal Ordnance Department Circular No.13. Sharps rifles that were not taken by the departing SharpShooters, legally or illegally, were turned in, cleaned at any of several arsenals, and held in storage. Years later they were sold at government ordnance property auctions for a few dollars apiece.

Above: *Close-up of the socket portion of a Berdan Sharps bayonet. Note the marking: C&Co., denoting manufacture by Collins & Company.*

The Matter of Bayonets

Most of Berdan SharpShooters enlisted because they were assured that they would be treated as *"elite troops," "as trained marksmen,"* and not as *"common infantry."* They accepted their dangerous role as skirmishers, placed hundreds of yards forward of the main body of troops, where they could do the most harm against an advancing enemy. This they took as their responsibility, but they abhorred the thought of being used in mass frontal assaults, as regular infantry would be utilized. What finer way to assure that this would not come about than to divest themselves of the infantryman's bayonet! No commander, it was supposed, would order troops forward without fixed bayonets.

It should be recalled that when the SharpShooters were issued their Sharps rifles in May 1862, each firearm was delivered with an angular, infantry-style bayonet, useful not only for its intended purpose, but as a digging tool, as a holder for meat over a fire, and, if bent correctly, as a fireside pot hook. As the SharpShooters wanted no part in frontal assaults, many of their bayonets were utilized for these latter purposes, or were simply discarded. Their commander, Hiram Berdan, was no field officer and it would hardly be expected that he would be capable of leading a frontal charge upon enemy positions, with or without bayonets. He, no doubt, played some role in making sure that his SharpShooters had *"no bayonets to affix."* This fact became a part of the original charges and specifications against Colonel Berdan at his court-martial of March 2, 1863. Specification 4 of the 2nd charge, so stated:

> In this that said Colonel Hiram Berdan did, at Camp near Falmouth. Virginia, on or about December 19th, 1862, at an inspection of his regiment by Lieutenant Colonel Batram, Inspector General of the 5th Army Corps, on being asked why some of his companies were not supplied with bayonets, did answer that they had drawn their rifles, which had no bayonets. Furthermore, that there were no bayonets to issue with the rifles at the time. When the real reason was that said Colonel Berdan had given those companies the privilege of taking the rifles without bayonets. And that the rifles were new, when drawn, and provided with bayonets

> packed in the same boxes with the rifles. And that said Colonel Berdan knew that the reason given by him in answer to the inquiry was false.

Colonel Berdan pleaded *"NOT GUILTY"* to all charges and specifications, and the nearly month-long trial began. On March 7th, Major George Hastings of the 1st U.S.S.S. testified that the "guns without bayonets" that the Inspector General had seen had, indeed, been issued as such. The guns had belonged to "the sick and discharged men, who had thrown away their bayonets." Later Captain James H. Baker of C Company stated that the bayonets had been issued when the rifles were new, but when they were re-issued to new recruits or to SharpShooters returning from the hospital, there were none on hand. He went on to say that Colonel Berdan gave them permission to use their Sharps rifles without bayonets.

Even though Colonel Berdan did not testify in his own defense, the prosecuting officer failed to convince the Court of his guilt. The result was that Berdan was found "NOT GUILTY" on all charges, on March 27th. However, upon reviewing the proceedings, Brigadier General Whipple went on record that he did not agree with the verdict on many of the charges against the Colonel, and that the specification regarding the bayonet issue, "had been clearly proved." Nonetheless, he confirmed the decision of the Court, and dismissed the charges.

After the verdict, Berdan felt it prudent to write to Chief of Ordnance Ripley, requesting a re-issue of bayonets for his regiments. At this time, regimental records indicate that there were only 247 bayonets for the 426 rifles Berdan had on hand. This situation was corrected soon afterward, as unit records show that 248 angular bayonets for the SharpShooters' Sharps rifles were delivered in June, just prior to the Battle of Gettysburg.

It is not likely that Colonel Berdan would hear of the exploits of Colonel John T. Wilder and his Lightning Brigade at Hoover's Gap, armed with the effective Spencer repeaters. It is much more likely that he would have heard of the successful use of them by a brash and bold Brigadier General at the East Cavalry Battlefield at Gettysburg, July 3, 1863, namely George Armstrong Custer. His men were armed, in part, with Spencer repeating rifles, and it was his 2nd Brigade of Michigan Cavalry that held off the vastly superior forces of J.E.B. Stuart's Confederate Cavalry. Berdan was at Gettysburg, with the Army of the Potomac, as it licked its wounds in the weeks that followed that epic battle. News of Custer's success with Spencer repeaters very likely prompted Berdan's renewed interest in these rifles for his SharpShooters.

Berdan applied directly to Captain D.W. Flagler, Ordnance Officer of Meade's Army of the Potomac, in late July, requesting Spencer rifles for his command. Flagler telegraphed Chief of Ordnance Ripley concerning Berdan's request, and was told that Berdan should, indeed, initiate the paperwork necessary to order the Spencers. In his return request to General Ripley, Flagler stated:

> Colonel Berdan told me yesterday that he would require about 4,000 of the Spencer rifles, as he has been authorized to raise a brigade of SharpShooters. The remnants of eight of the picked regiments of this army are to be transferred to it, and officers were going home immediately to fill up these regiments with recruits and drafted men. He wished me to tell you in order that he might empower these men to tell recruits that he would give them Spencer rifles.
>
> Judging from a conversation which I had with the Chief of Staff at these Headquarters today, I do not think that the brigade will be raised, or that the rifles will be called for.

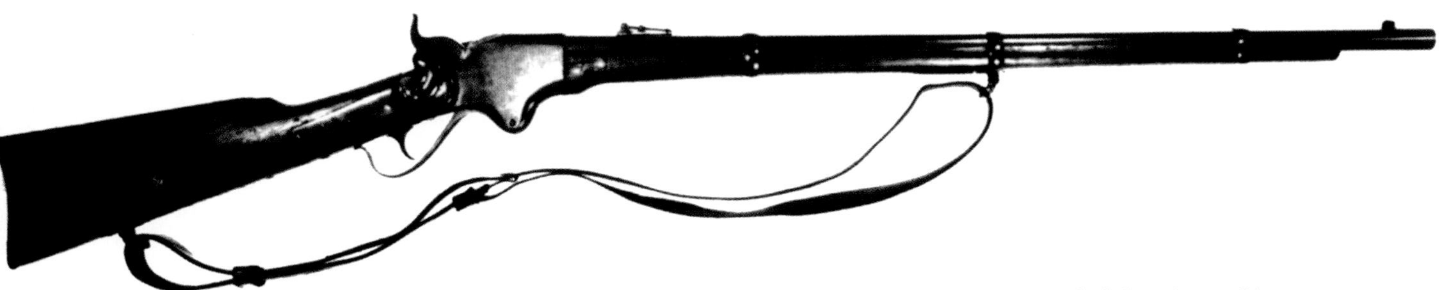

***Above:** The Spencer rifle that created its own success eluded Berdan and his unit.*

Spencer Rifles Again

Colonel Berdan had tried, unsuccessfully, to arm his SharpShooters with Spencer repeaters in December 1861. The entire matter was dropped, and the marksmen grew to like their Sharps single-shot breechloading rifles. Because of numerous business problems, the Spencer Repeating Rifle Company was unable to produce and deliver its first M1860 Army rifles until December 1862, more than a year after the SharpShooters had first seen them. It took many months for the Ordnance Department to warehouse and ship the 7,500 Spencer rifles to the troops for which they were destined. In fact, it was not until May 1863, that the first unit utilized them in actual warfare, forever endearing them to soldiers lucky, enough to be issued one.

Berdan's men never did receive Spencer repeaters. Shortly after his discussions with Flagler, the Colonel went on to convalesce in Washington, never to return to his command. This ended any further effort to obtain the Spencer repeating firearms.

What is a Berdan Sharps Rifle?

A serious study of surviving examples of Sharps rifles issued to Berdan SharpShooters was conducted by respected historian Wiley Sword. Building on his valuable research, this author continued the search for authenticated SharpShooter weapons and for contemporary records of the arms.

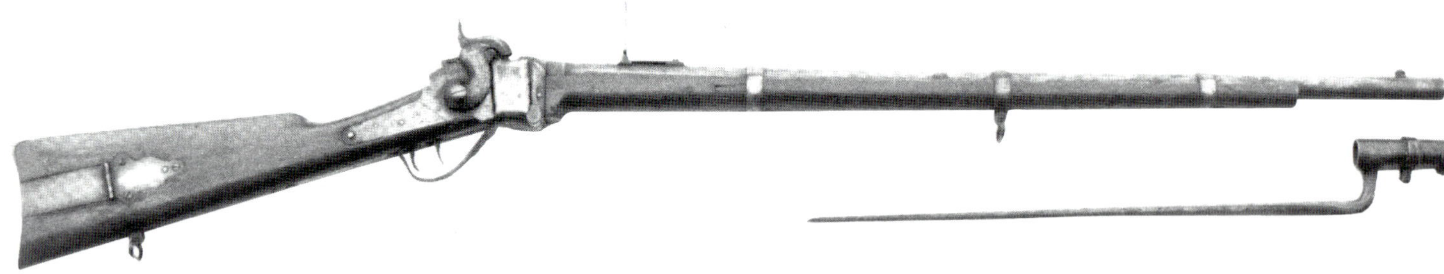

Above: *Another Example of a Berdan Sharp rifle , this time with angular socket bayonet*

Right: *A close-up of California Joe's Sharps Berdan rifle which he had adapted to use a sword bayonet (shown on his left hip).*

It appears that two thousand Sharps New Model 1859 rifles were ordered for Berdan's 1st and 2nd Regiments of U.S. SharpShooters by the Federal Ordnance Department on January 27, 1862. The completed and inspected arms were received on April 21st, May 2nd, May 14th, and May 24th, 1862. Together with appendages (angular bayonets, screw-drivers, brushes & thongs), the arms cost $42.50 each.

To date, the lowest serial number of an authenticated Berdan Sharps rifle is 54374, the highest 57567. A total of 43 rifles have been identified which bear all of the characteristics of true Berdan Sharps rifles, including: double-set triggers; JT inspector's cartouche on the left wrist of the stock; and the absence of a bayonet lug beneath the barrel, near the muzzle. The serial number range of authenticated Berdan Sharps rifles covered approximately 3,300 arms. Not all of the firearms within this range (54374 to 57567) were Berdan rifles, as eighteen Sharps NM1859 carbines, and five single-trigger, Sharps NM1859 rifles were also located in this range. It could not be determined whether the single-trigger rifles were originally double-set trigger rifles, or if they came from the factory that way. In a worst-case scenario, the types of arms noted within the 3,300 range were:

43 double-set trigger rifles	65 per cent
5 single trigger rifles	8 per cent
18 carbines	27 per cent
66 Sharps firearms examined	100 per cent

In this example, 65 per cent of the range of 3,300 arms is equal to 2,145 rifles. This extrapolation yields only 145 arms more than the actual number of 2,000 Berdan rifles delivered by the Sharps factory. Since 65 per cent is too great, 61 per cent would be closer to the actual percentage of Berdan Sharps rifles within the known serial number range. Therefore, a revised estimate would be that within the known range of Berdan Sharps rifles were about 300 single-trigger Sharps rifles (9 per cent), and 1,000 carbines (30 per cent).

Prior to the Berdan SharpShooter order (January 27, 1862), the Federal Ordnance Department ordered 100 Sharps rifles with sword bayonets, 36 in barrels, and single triggers (September 12, 1861), and a large number of carbines. After the Berdan order, the government ordered many thousands of Sharps carbines, but did not order Sharps rifles again until March 1863 (these were probably NM1863 rifles).

The exact number of Sharps NM1859 rifles sold to private individuals or to individual units is not known. The percentage of rifles fitted for sword, verses angular bayonets is also unknown. Noted Sharps authority Frank Sellers states that the range of NM1859 rifles covers approximately 36000 to 60000. He stated that within that range, there were 6,989 rifles produced. We know that 4,800 NM1859 Sharps rifles were sold to the Federal military:

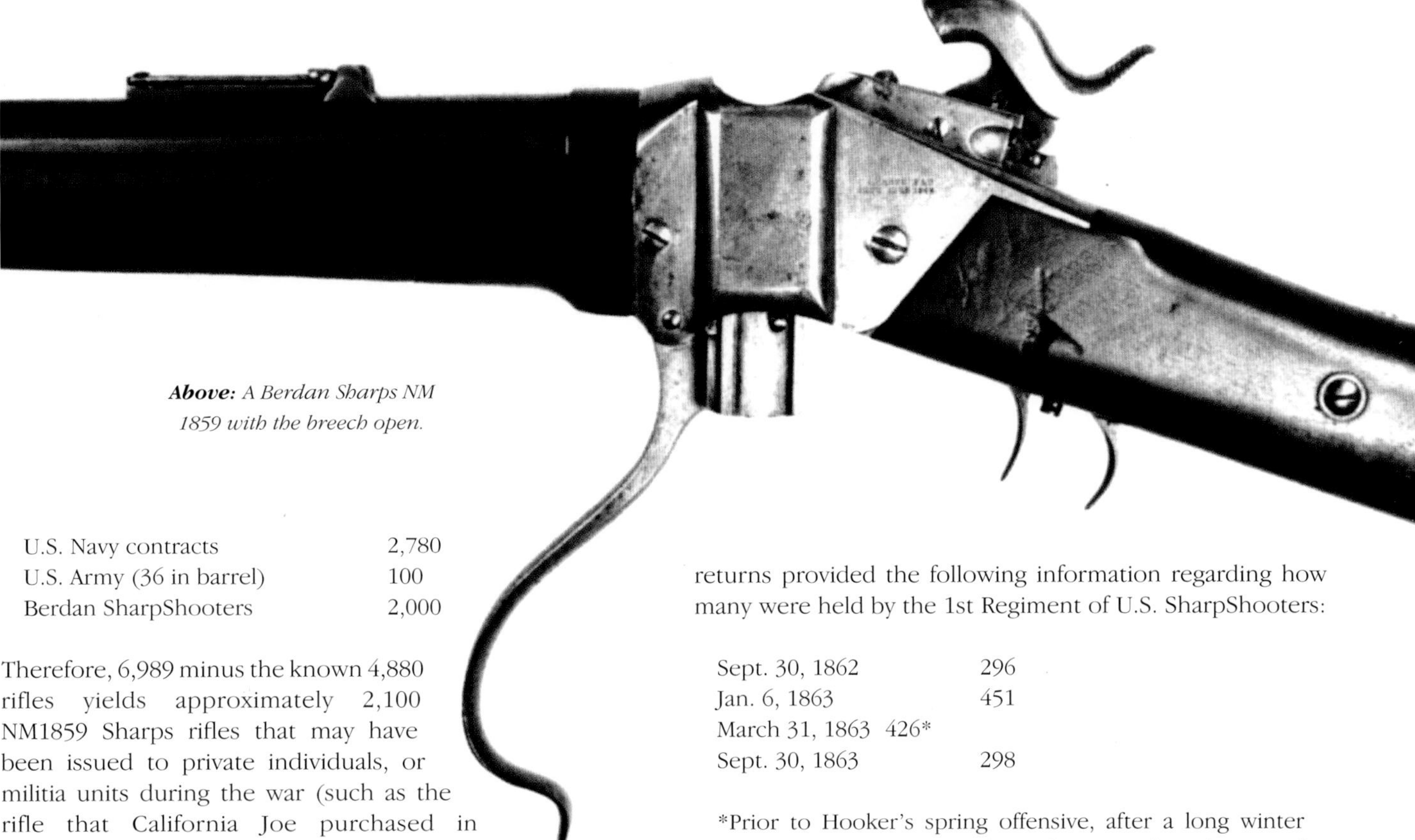

Above: *A Berdan Sharps NM 1859 with the breech open.*

U.S. Navy contracts	2,780
U.S. Army (36 in barrel)	100
Berdan SharpShooters	2,000

Therefore, 6,989 minus the known 4,880 rifles yields approximately 2,100 NM1859 Sharps rifles that may have been issued to private individuals, or militia units during the war (such as the rifle that California Joe purchased in September 1861). The actual number may be quite smaller, since the range would contain condemned arms, unusable receivers, and samples. Some serial-numbered receivers were probably set aside for future projects. This example excludes New Model 1863 Sharps rifles that were ordered and delivered to the Federal Ordnance Department in 1863 and 1865.

Were all 2,000 Sharps rifles ordered by General Ripley issued to the Berdan SharpShooters? When first enlisted, the SharpShooters numbered slightly more than 1,700 men in two regiments. After a full month of fighting, the number was considerably smaller, especially considering the men who had died from disease during the winter of 1861–62, those who had deserted, and those who would not have carried rifles (cooks, teamsters, etc.). In May 1862, possibly only 1,500 SharpShooters had been issued rifles. Colonel Post, Commander of the 2nd Regiment of SharpShooters, had complained to General Ripley that the 1st Regiment had on hand "400 Sharps rifles, above and beyond what they required." The 1st Regiment may have been issued 1,300 rifles, even if they could field only 900 for front line duty. The 400 excess would be the number referred to by Post. The 2nd Regiment probably fielded only 600 front line troops at this time, and it is known that the Ordnance Department issued Colonel Post 550 new Sharps rifles. The excess rifles may have been held by the Ordnance Department, for future replacements for damaged or lost weapons.

Not all Sharps rifles were issued to SharpShooters on the firing line. Extra arms would have been retained by regimental supply sergeants, and a smaller number held by armorers, awaiting repair. Quarterly regimental ordnance returns provided the following information regarding how many were held by the 1st Regiment of U.S. SharpShooters:

Sept. 30, 1862	296
Jan. 6, 1863	451
March 31, 1863	426*
Sept. 30, 1863	298

*Prior to Hooker's spring offensive, after a long winter encampment and plenty of time for resupply and repair of all firearms. The figure does not include 29 Sharps rifles held by the regimental armorer.

The rigors of warfare must have taken their toll on the rifles issued to the SharpShooters. Rain, heat, humidity, snow, mud, and dust left the rifles scratched, pitted and broken, despite the care that the men would have given them. Both of the regimental armorers were probably kept quite busy replacing parts and repairing what couldn't be replaced. A list of spare parts in the 1st Regimental Armorer's possession on September 30, 1863, included:

16 triggers
20 middle barrel bands
4 hammers
78 barrel band springs
23 levers
10 lock plates
4 receivers
38 nipple cones
30 mainsprings
7 front sight studs

Above: *The Sharps pattern , infantry-style cartridge box was specially fabricated for the SharpShooters. Evidence indicates that they were made by leather goods contractor , Emerson Gaylord of Chicopee, Massachusetts. The box was designed to be worn on the waistbelt.*

The armorer also had in his possession nine complete Sharps rifles, presumably, to exchange for unserviceable ones that were turned in for major repair.

Sharps Rifle Cartridge Box

This is the type of infantry-style cartridge box that was issued to Berdan's SharpShooters in 1862. The body measures 7¼" by 1⅜" by 4⅝". The two wooden blocks measure 3⅜" by 1¼" by 4$\frac{11}{16}$", and each box is bored with ten holes. Each hole measures between 0.56" and 0.59" in diameter, and is 1½" deep. The top two tins each measure 3⅜" by 1⅜" by 1⅝". The bottom two tins each measure 3⅜" by 1⅜" by 4$\frac{9}{16}$".

This is a very rare example of a Sharps cartridge box as issued to Berdan's SharpShooters with their Sharps NM1859 breechloading rifles in 1862.

It is shown from the front (above) with U.S.seal; and the back (below) showing the belt loops.

Heavy Target Rifles

Above: *Taken from The U.S. Cartridge Collection catalog of the early 1900s this telescopic, percussion, muzzleloading target rifle was made by R.A. Moore, gunmaker of Courtland Street, New York City. Rifles of this kind were favored by some SharpShooter units even after issue of the Sharps rifle.*

Above: *A Morgan James percussion target rifle with a 33½ inch length heavy octagonal barrel of .44 caliber. The telescopic sight measures 37 inches in length. It cost one hundred dollars in 1860.*

Right: *This complete SharpShooter's rifle in its original box shows the variety of implements that were necessary to keep it functional in the field. A muzzleloader like this one, complete with accessories and box, could weigh as much as fifty pounds. Normally carried in the regimental supply wagon and not readily portable in action.*

Above: *A gun thought to have seen action at Hare's Farm ,Virginia when Private James Ragin, Company G [Wisconsin],1st U.S. SharpShooters used it to scare off a rebel SharpShooter at a distance of 300 yards.*

LANGDON'S ADVICE,

TO CAPT. SAUNDERS SHARP SHOOTERS.

1st. In taking the Gun from the Box, put the left hand under the centre of the barrel, the right hand at the small part of the stock, lift it up, in all cases the breech first.

2d. If the Gun has remained some time without being used, wipe with a dry swab, and snap one or two Caps to clean the oil.

3d. In loading for war purposes use an oiled patch, to prevent the barrel from rusting near the chamber.

4th. When the Gun is fired every day, it need not be wiped out with a swab wet by the mouth, but a little oil.

5th. (And last) Trust in GOD, keep the sight straight, and POWDER DRY.

Boston, Mass. Sept. [illegible]

No. ....

Right: *Some basic advice to rookie SharpShooters which hardly seems necessary as many of the recruits were seasoned shooters.*

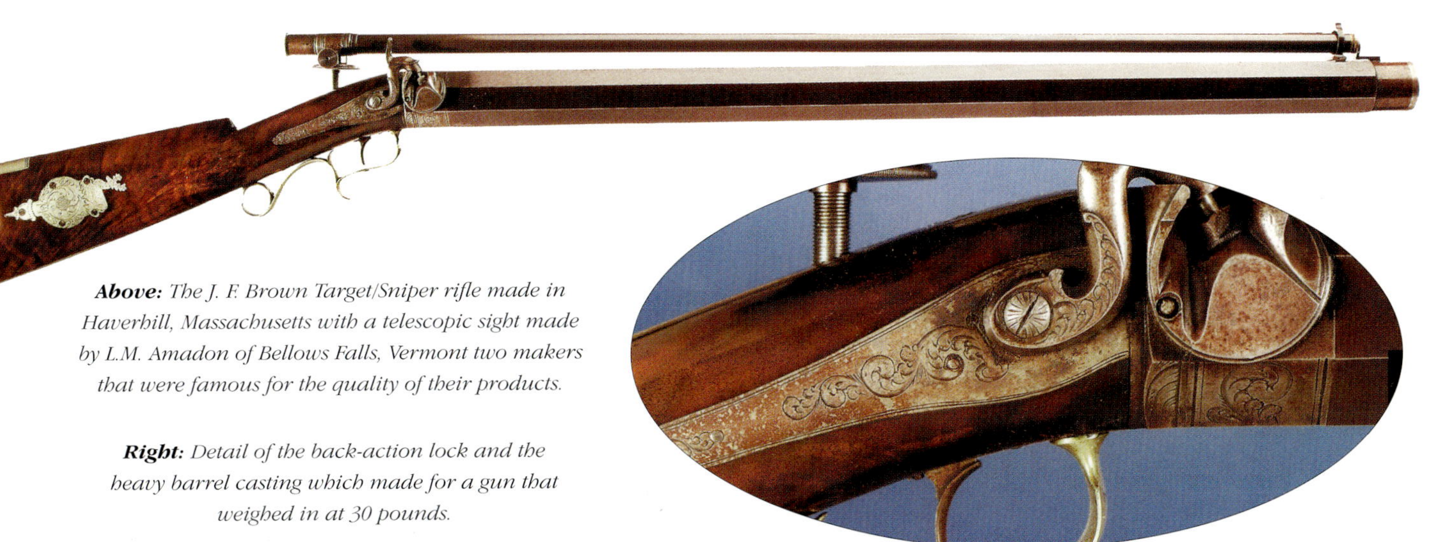

Above: *The J. F. Brown Target/Sniper rifle made in Haverhill, Massachusetts with a telescopic sight made by L.M. Amadon of Bellows Falls, Vermont two makers that were famous for the quality of their products.*

Right: *Detail of the back-action lock and the heavy barrel casting which made for a gun that weighed in at 30 pounds.*

Above: *In its original box, dated September 3, 1861 is a rifle made by Cyrus Baldwin Holden of Worcester, Massachusetts. It has a 34 inch heavy octagonal barrel of .42 caliber. Measuring 50 inches overall and weighing 23 pounds.*

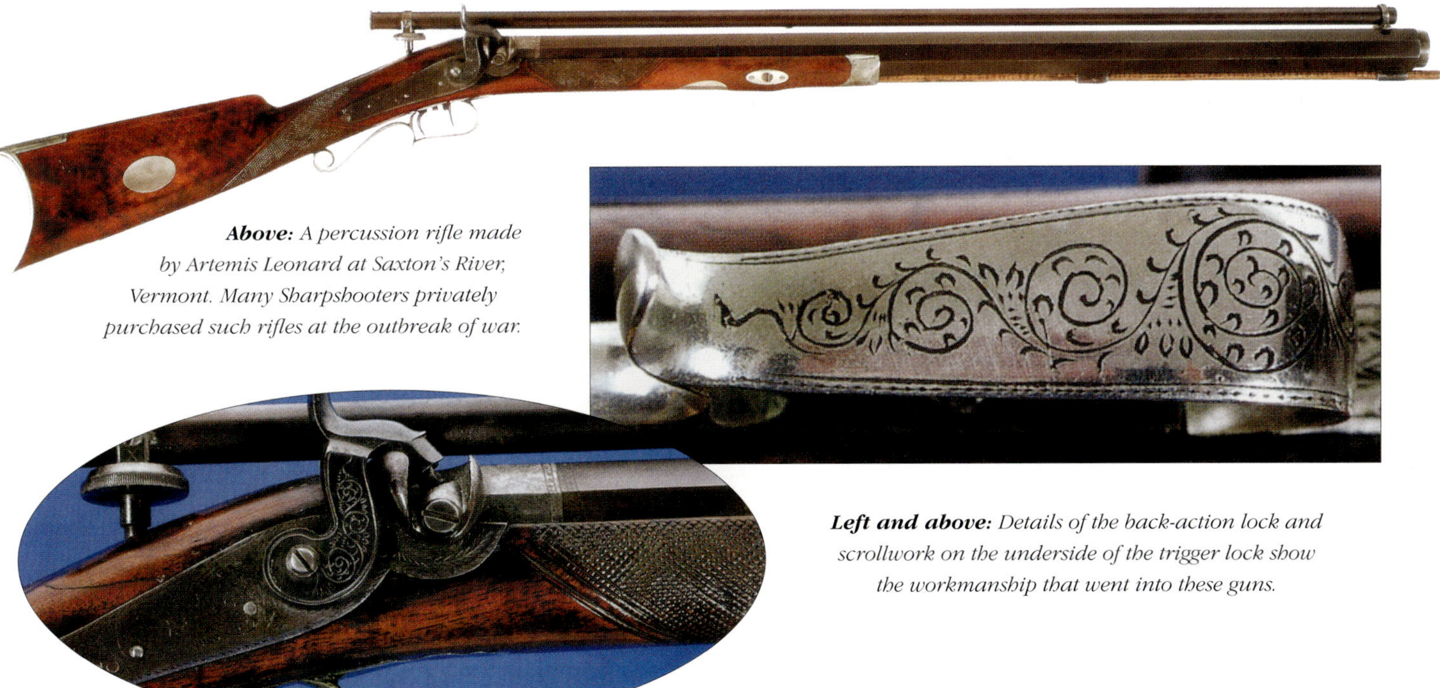

Above: *A percussion rifle made by Artemis Leonard at Saxton's River, Vermont. Many Sharpshooters privately purchased such rifles at the outbreak of war.*

Left and above: *Details of the back-action lock and scrollwork on the underside of the trigger lock show the workmanship that went into these guns.*

SharpShooters in Action

Trial by Fire: The SharpShooters' First Battle

On March 20, 1862, months of campside boredom came to an end for Berdan's SharpShooters. On this date they received orders to report to General Fitz John Porter, whose division was encamped near Alexandria, Virginia. This movement was part of General McClellan's spring offensive for his Army of the Potomac, in preparation of the Peninsula Campaign against the Confederates. Unfortunately, the SharpShooters were still without weapons, except for heavy target rifles brought from home, or the few Hall muskets that had been issued for guard duty. Berdan's SharpShooters marched first to Alexandria, Virginia, then the unit embarked two days later aboard the steamship Emperor, bound for Fort Monroe. On March 23, the regiment landed at Hampton, Virginia, and awaited orders and supplies.

General Porter's circular of March 25th, fixed ordnance requirements for all infantry troops under his command, including the unarmed SharpShooters:

> CIRCULAR:
> The allowance of transportation will be six wagons per regiment. One wagoneer is to be devoted exclusively to carrying hospital stores. Commanders are directed to keep up their stock of ammunition to 80 rounds per man. 40 rounds are to be carried by the men in full cartridge boxes, and the balance carried in the wagons.

One thousand Colt 5-shot, Mode1 1855 revolving rifles, which had been ordered in January, were finally delivered to Berdan's men. Some were issued just prior to the steamship journey to Fort Monroe, while the remainder were delivered after the boat landed. Nevertheless, all SharpShooters were now armed with Colt revolving rifles, except two companies which still retained their muzzleloading target weapons, and two others armed only with picks, spades and axes.

It was soon realized that the Colt revolving rifles had been delivered without ammunition. This was an untenable situation that was hastily remedied by Chief of Ordnance General Ripley's dispatch to the Colt factory for the immediate shipment of rifle ammunition.

Berdan's SharpShooters were given the order to proceed toward Yorktown, Virginia, in advance of the body of 30,000 unseasoned Federal troops, to act as both skirmishers and scouts. They came under direct fire on April 5, and as Berdan put it, they were ordered to:

> ...guard the road against enemy cavalry; guard the right and left wings against enemy flankers, and watch the movements of the enemy; and to pick off enemy gunners.

General McClellan, Commander of the Army of the Potomac,

Above: *General George B.McClellan, Commander of the Army of the Potomac, with his wife Georgiana. He was frequently chided by Lincoln for his hesitant and indecisive actions in the field.*

was not an offensive tactician. The Siege of Yorktown, therefore, was typical of Federal indecision and stalemate. He halted more than 100,000 troops on April 5, instead of overwhelming the mere 15,000 Confederate troops that opposed them in a frail line of fortifications along the Warwick River. Federal troops, including Berdan SharpShooters, were ordered to construct rifle pits, with which marksmen could harass the Confederate artillerymen. *"The U.S. SharpShooters' skill at long range shooting did great harm to the rebels,"* and as Colonel Ripley was later to recount:

> Gun after gun was silenced and abandoned, until within an hour every embrasure within a range of a thousand yards was silent. The rebel infantry, which at first responded with a vigorous fire, found that exposure of a head meant grave danger, if not death.

Day after day went by with little forward progress for McClellan's troops. Finally, on May 4, The Siege of Yorktown ended, as Confederate defenders, under General Joseph E. Johnston, pulled back toward Richmond. They had successfully delayed McClellan for nearly a month, allowing Confederate strength at Yorktown to swell to nearly 55,000 troops. The Army of the Potomac entered Yorktown, following Johnston's evacuation, and McClellan uttered: *"The success is brilliant."* Despite McClellan's failure, the success that Berdan's skilled marksmen had at Yorktown became typical throughout the war: they fought in advance of the main body of infantry, and they inflicted heavy casualties upon the enemy.

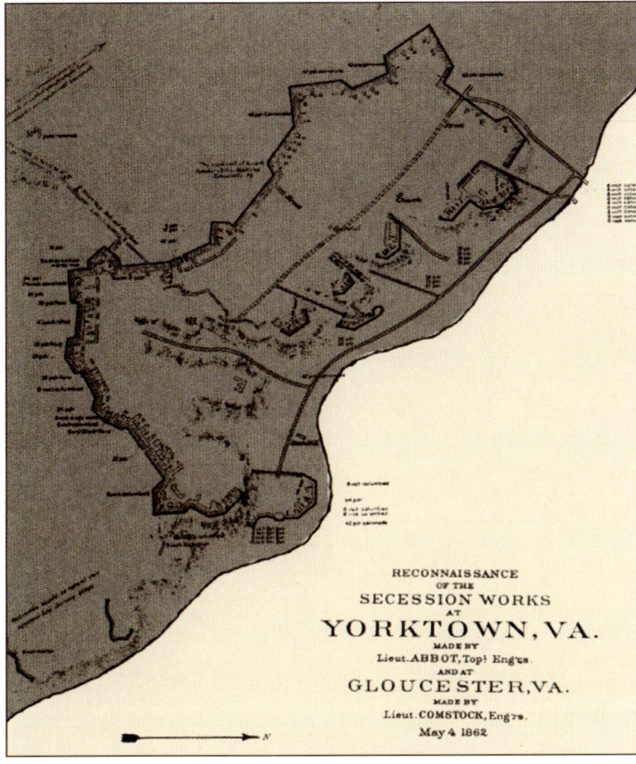

Above: *The Confederate fortifications at Yorktown were well laid out and well gunned with a variety of cannon. The Confederates reshaped many of the original breastworks from the Revolutionary War's Battle of Yorktown, eighty years before.*

The Siege of Yorktown had lasted from April 10th until May 4th, with the 1st U.S. SharpShooters suffering only four casualties. This included the wounding of Private Truman Head, better known as California Joe, "who took a bullet on the band of his Sharps rifle, snapping it into his face."

Following the siege, an officer on General Porter's staff wrote to Colonel Berdan and praised the actions of the SharpShooters at Yorktown:

> The Commanding General instructs me to say to you that he is glad to learn, from the admissions of the enemy themselves, that they begin to fear your SharpShooters. Your men have caused a number of the rebels to bite the dust. The Commanding General is glad to find that your Corps are proving themselves so efficient, and trusts that this intelligence will encourage your men, and give them, if possible, steadier hands and clearer eyes, so that when their trusty rifles are pointed at the foe, there will be one rebel less at every discharge.
>
> Fred T. Locke
> Asst. Adjutant General

On May 8, 1862, the long-awaited Sharps New Model 1859 breechloading rifles were finally delivered to several companies of Berdan's SharpShooters. The following day, Colonel Berdan reported that his personal Colt pistols were stolen, and he immediately telegraphed the factory for replacements:

Below: *This period woodcut portrays Berdan's SharpShooters firing on the Confederate positions of Yorktown in April 1862. The SharpShooter laying on his back is loading what appears to be a target rifle, probably brought from home. The official issue at this time was the unpopular Colts Revolving rifle.*

TELEGRAM
To Colt's Patent Fire-Arms Mfg. Company:
Some thief stole my revolvers from my holsters yesterday on board the Steamer State of Maine. Send me, at once, in care of General T.J. Porter, duplicates of the pistols only.
H. Berdan Colonel

Above: *An early photograph of Berdan taken at the studio of famous Civil War photographer Matthew Brady. He is full Colonel's uniform, but with individual touches like the double breasted coat in green cloth and the two rows of seven buttons are in hard rubber.*

In the weeks that followed the Yorktown engagement, Colonel Berdan's health took a turn for the worse. In a letter to Congressman Sedgwick, an old friend, Berdan wrote of his *"bout with typhoid fever and congestion of the liver."* As late as May 17, he lay in a sickbed, a mere twelve miles from his regiment. He complained to Sedgwick that his men were split apart from the Division, with companies detached to provide skirmishers for other brigades, often without proper supplies. He asked his influential friend to intercede on his behalf and ask the President to promote him to Brigadier General. He also reacquainted his friend with the fact that he had not, as yet, been officially mustered into Federal service, and asked Sedgwick to remind the President about that, too. In actuality, Berdan was still nothing more than a private citizen in spite of the uniform and rank he wore on the field. This must have been demoralizing for a man who worked so diligently to form and train his SharpShooters for war.

Congressman Sedgwick added his endorsement to Berdan's letter and forwarded it to President Lincoln on May 30. Nearly a month passed before Colonel Berdan's wish to be mustered into Federal service was realized. His request for promotion to Brigadier General went unheeded.

The 1st Regiment of U.S. SharpShooters fought at the Battle of Hanover Court House, Virginia, on May 27, 1862. They suffered one enlisted man killed and nine wounded. They fought, not as a complete regiment, but as separate companies on detached service. This angered Major Caspar Trepp of the 1st Regiment of Berdan's U.S. SharpShooters, who on May 31 submitted his resignation (for a second time) to Colonel Berdan (the first one had come on November 8, 1861, while the SharpShooters were still at their Washington Camp of Instruction),

Trepp, a respected leader and outstanding officer, never came to respect Berdan as a commander. In his letter of resignation Trepp cited his displeasure that General Porter would detach companies of SharpShooters from the regiment, and their new brigade commanders would use them as "common infantrymen." This was too much for Trepp to bear, but Berdan flatly rejected his resignation. Trepp, an obedient officer, continued his duties in silence.

On June 11, the Secretary of War received a letter which had been signed by three officers and seventy-six enlisted SharpShooters. The frustrated men complained that promises made to them when they enlisted had not been kept. They stated that Colonel Berdan had assured them that they would receive at least $15 pay per month, that they would not be utilized as regular infantry, that they would not be compelled to perform guard duty, and that they were to be armed with Sharps breechloading rifles. They alleged that none of these promises were kept, except for the rifles, and they sought the Secretary of War's direct intervention. As this Cabinet Official was extremely busy, he took no action himself, but did assign subordinates to investigate the matter further.

In the months of warfare that would follow, the SharpShooters had their wishes met on all matters except pay and guard duty, but this did not put an end to the resentment that the men would have toward Colonel Berdan. The internal problems that the SharpShooters were experiencing were just beginning.

The First Prolonged Action:

The Seven Days Battles

On June 17, 1862, General Thomas J. "Stonewall" Jackson's Army left the Shenandoah Valley, to join Lee's Army of Northern Virginia at Richmond. Eight days later on June 25, General McClellan attacked the Confederate forces at Oak Grove, Virginia, starting what would become known as the Seven Days Battles.

On June 26, several of Berdan's detached companies were placed forward as skirmishers, in advance of Brigadier General George Morell's Division, of General Fitz John Porter's V Corps. Lee attacked McClellan's right wing, but failed to destroy Porter's Corps. This engagement became known as the Battle of Mechanicsville. Fortunately, the SharpShooters suffered no casualties, although Colonel Berdan, himself, came close to being injured.

> Colonel Berdan was ordered to visit the right and left flanks, alternately, to make such changes in the position of the SharpShooter outposts as was thought proper. On the day prior to the Mechanicsville battle he had ridden out to the right and saw the enemy working on a small earthworks. Riding further along, he dismounted to take another look, and as he raised his glass, saw a puff of smoke from some bushes at the creek. The ball passed under his right foot and produced a stinging sensation.

Since many of Berdan's companies were on detached service, he placed the forward-most SharpShooters under the direct command of Lieutenant Colonel William Y.W. Ripley. This reassignment of a commander's responsibility would later prove to be a key element in charges brought against Colonel Berdan.

On June 27, Lee again attacked Porter, and achieved a breakthrough at Gaines Mill, forcing McClellan's Army to retreat towards the James River. Two days later, continuing his attack, Lee engaged McClellan in the Battle of Savage's Station. The following day, at the Battle of Frayser's Farm, Lee was unable to cut off McClellan's retreat. Finally, on July 1, Lee's last effort to halt McClellan's retreat was repulsed at Malvern Hill, ending the Seven Days Battles. The 1st Regiment of U.S.S.S. suffered the following losses during these engagements:

	killed	wounded	missing
Gaines Mill	5	3	3
Glendale	6	5	1
Malvern Hill	4	9	0

Berdan as a Military Leader Questioned Again

The after-action report of the Battle of Gaines Mill was written by Berdan:

> I have the honor to report that I marched the portion of my command not on detached service, late in the afternoon of the 26th ultimo [June 26th], with the 2nd Brigade. We lay on our arms all night, and retired on the morning of the 27th ultimo, and I then posted my men in front of the 2nd Brigade, on the farther side of the woods in which the principal action of the day occurred.
>
> About 1:30 P.M. the enemy advanced in line of battle, the whole length of the woods. My men had good cover, and so rapid was our fire from our breechloading guns, that we repulsed the enemy with great loss. They were also repulsed on our left, but the 9th Massachusetts fell back some 300 yards in disorder, where it reformed. This made it necessary to bring my right back, to prevent being outflanked.
>
> We received and repulsed the enemy a second time, as did the troops on our left. At this charge the 9th Massachusetts fell back altogether. We held the same position during the third charge, repulsing the enemy with great loss, but finding that at this time the lines of the 1st and 3rd Brigades were broken on our left, and that our supports were falling back. We also fell back in good order.
>
> When I arrived on the field in the rear of the woods, I saw no less than 12,000 of our men and officers, each apparently making quick-time for the bridge. Only a few of the enemy's cavalry would have been necessary to create a stampede. In this event, the most of our force would have been inevitably lost. Seeing no effort made to rally the men, I rode through them to the right and left, appealing to the officers to get the men together, and I would go down to the bridge and bring up the rear.
>
> The bridge was full when I reached it, and finding my appeals to the officers and men of no avail, I drew my pistol and threatened to shoot the first officer or man who passed me. Finding these threats of no use, I fired several shots over their heads before I succeeded in checking the rush, which had become almost a panic at this point. I forced them into line, without reference to regiment or rank. I regret that I have not the names of some line officers who were more determined on crossing than the men, if possible. Others saw the importance of forming lines, if only for the appearance of order, to deter the enemy from attacking us, and rendered valuable assistance. In about a half hour we reached the top of the hill with our four battalions, varying from 600 to 2,000. Here I halted them, and compelled the stragglers in front to form. Many a brave officer had responded to my appeals, and gathered large squads of men. Seeing the rebel cavalry forming in line in the field on the left of the woods which they had taken possession of, and having little confidence in the men, I set them to cheering, when the enemy, thinking perhaps that we had been reinforced, retired. Then we crossed the bridge in good order.
>
> ...My men have all been in several engagements, and are almost worn out, but are in good spirits. 1 officer and 7 men killed; 4 officers and 31 men wounded; 13 men missing; 14 men left sick in hospital.
>
> H. Berdan, Colonel
> Commanding U.S. SharpShooters

Near the end of the week-long engagement, tragedy struck. Lieutenant Colonel Ripley was severely wounded by a musket ball while leading the SharpShooters. The wound was a grievous one, the bullet having entering his right thigh, breaking his leg bone. The bullet could not be removed until much later, resulting in his evacuation to Washington for hospital treatment. Unfortunately for the SharpShooters, this fine commander was not to return. Ripley's leadership and command influence over the SharpShooters would always be held in direct contrast to the lack of decisive action by Colonel Berdan.

Serious questions arose as to Berdan's actions under fire. At no time when the fighting ensued at Gaines Mill or Malvern Hill was Colonel Berdan seen at the front. It might be said that since most of his SharpShooter companies were on detached service and were not fighting as a complete regiment, their commander, Hiram Berdan, could have busied himself with other chores. Note, then, the scathing endorsement added to Berdan's after-action report by his direct superior, General Morell:

Above: *In the heat of the action at Gaines Mill Berdan went missing.*

> Colonel Berdan was not in the fight at Gaines Mill. What occurred far to the rear near the bridge I do not know of my own knowledge, but I have every reason to believe this statement is highly exaggerated.
> Geo. W. Morell
> Brigadier General

Historian Stevens would later recount:

> After some maneuvering, the SharpShooters moved forward into a piece of woods to the left. There, they were suddenly greeted with rebel canister. Meanwhile, the firing in the woods was a constant uproar, the bullets speeding back and forth by the thousands. Nothing in words can better describe the terrific strife than those of Colonel Simpson, of the 4th New Jersey (whose regiment, along with the 11th Pennsylvania, were later surrounded and captured after a most gallant struggle). It was Colonel Simpson who said: "The hissing of balls was like that of a myriad of serpents."
>
> SharpShooter Companies C and G were ordered to a position on a side hill, covering the road to the bridges. Here they assisted greatly in checking the stragglers, while falling back. During this exciting period, we found Colonel Berdan, and Colonel Matheson of the 32nd New York, engaged rallying the scattering troops hurrying to the rear. Colonel Berdan said that he had stopped them from crossing the bridge below, and had never worked harder in bringing them into line – these scattered men who had lost their regiments.

Four months later an anonymous letter was published in the *PENN YAN CHRONICLE* newspaper of November 4, 1862. Although we do not know who the author was, we can presume with confidence that it was an officer in Berdan's 1st Regiment of SharpShooters:

> The Colonel turned the command over to Lieutenant Colonel Ripley, and started to the rear, as usual. The Colonel was not seen again that day on the battlefield. He was away in the rear trying to rally stragglers, when he became so excited as to shoot an artillery horse with his revolver. He then endeavored to persuade the [artillery] Lieutenant that it was a shell that hit his horse. He tried to get his story published, but to no avail. At Harrison's Landing the Colonel persuaded a Frank Leslie artist to sketch a view of the battle, showing the Colonel in the act of halting eighteen thousand [sic] panic stricken officers and men. But General Morell sent for him and forbade him to have it published, as it represented an untruth.
>
> The Colonel first said that he went to the rear for ammunition. He dwelt strongly upon what he did at the rear, without first explaining how he came to be there, when his regiment was at the front. He stated that Lieutenant Colonel Ripley begged to be placed in sole command, in order to repair his reputation.

The same letter also stated what was reported to be Berdan's version of the incident:

> If I had insisted on keeping the command, then Ripley would have tendered his resignation. The rebel cavalry appeared on our right, and seemed anxious to charge in our rear. I rallied from fifteen to eighteen thousand men

Above: *Brigadier General George W. Morell who endorsed Berdan's muster into Federal service as a full Colonel, despite scepticism on his battle reports.*

and formed them into eleven lines. It was the most critical moment of the battle, or the war. I forced many officers into the ranks with privates. The [rebel] cavalry, seeing my lines, thought them to be reinforcements, and retired.

General Morell grasped my hand, with tears in his eyes. Colonel, he said, you have saved me from disgrace. You have preserved my Army.

Could Berdan's story, as far-fetched as it sounds, have been true? Some of the meager facts tend to bear out part of Berdan's story. The fact that the SharpShooters were detached might have compelled Berdan to transfer forward control to Lieutenant Colonel Ripley, thus he could have been justified in associating himself with detached companies C and G near the bridge. However, one must agree with General Morell's reluctance to believe that a single officer, with pistol in hand, could rally more than 12,000 officers and men who were fleeing the enemy in panic. If Berdan really accomplished this feat, then he would truly be a hero. Conversely, if he did not, then he could be branded a coward and a liar.

Despite his skepticism and comments on Colonel Berdan's after-action report, General Morell must have accepted Berdan as a leader, because on June 24,1862, he endorsed his muster into Federal service as full Colonel. This, and another endorsement by Division Commander Porter, were attached to President Lincoln's original letter of February 26, 1862, and forwarded to Army of the Potomac Commander McClellan.

I take pleasure in recommending Colonel Berdan for promotion. He has served near me all of the time during the advance of the Army of the Potomac, from Fort Monroe, to this point at Howard's Bridge, Yorktown and Hanover. I can bear witness to his skill and efficiency with which he has performed his duty.

Geo. W. Morell
Brigadier General
Commanding. Division

On the same day, General Porter also added his favorable endorsement:

I cordially recommend the appointment of Colonel Berdan to the position proposed. He has labored, incessantly and successfully, to make the regiment (1st Berdan SharpShooters) efficient and the most useful to the service. Their qualities were proved and appreciated at Yorktown, where Colonel Berdan devoted himself incessantly and under fire to place his men where the greatest injury to the enemy could be inflicted, and the greatest benefit to us arise. He will command, I am confident, a Corps of SharpShooters most successfully and profitably to the service.

F.J. Porter
Brigadier General
Commanding

Following the intense fighting that took place at Malvern Hill on July 1, Berdan's SharpShooters, as well as soldiers on both sides, were exhausted. The Confederate troops fell back to Richmond to tend to their wounded and to regroup their forces. This allowed the equally beleaguered Northern troops time to mend, as well. In the days that followed, detached companies of SharpShooters were released to rejoin Berdan's Regiment. They, and other units of Major General

Above: *An unidentified U.S SharpShooter who looks barely out of his teens with fixed bayonet on his Sharps rifle.*

McClellan's Army of the Potomac, were reviewed by President Lincoln on July 8. It was said that the President "was appalled by the large numbers of dead and wounded."

Encampment meant a time for all soldiers to rest and to prepare for the next engagement. It was also a time when the wounded would recover sufficiently to rejoin their comrades, would be so debilitated that they would be evacuated to hospitals in the rear, or would succumb to their wounds. Eight of Berdan's men died at this encampment.

They were buried low in the shade of the deep wood by their remaining comrades. Parting salutes were fired over their graves. Gray blankets were their only shroud, with a network of branches below and above them, then covered with earth.

Unfortunately, Colonel Berdan's leadership problems with the SharpShooters continued. On July 4, 1862, five company grade officers wrote to Berdan's immediate superior, condemning his actions on the field:

> We have a duty to perform, however unpleasant. We feel it as a duty to ourselves, respectfully, and for the military art and discipline, to call to your notice the acts of our Colonel Commanding, which if not checked or brought to the notice of the Commander of the Division, will result in the total demoralization of this regiment.
>
> **First**: We beg leave to represent that in all of the engagements lately, the Colonel of this regiment was nowhere to be seen in action. He was with the remaining companies, that is, those not on detached service.
>
> **Second**: That the Colonel has not the confidence of any of the subscribing officers, either as a man competent to attend to the welfare of men, and that he has proven himself neither a soldier, officer or gentleman.
>
> **Third**: That in every case of action whenever this command has taken part, he has been found absent from the field. But found always out of danger, thereby endangering the men when in action. At Yorktown, he left the field in the hottest of the engagement and omitted to return. But had the daring to send an orderly with a verbal order for his command to return to camp without first being relieved in a proper manner. In subsequent actions at Hanover Court House he was not to be seen till action was over. And in the late actions of the Chickahominy, he was further from the scene of conflict than in it. He abandoned his command to the gallant Lieutenant Colonel Wm. Y.W. Ripley who fell wounded, thereby leaving the regiment without any field officer.
>
> The instances here noted are insufficient to cause a complaint to be entered, which we now do, humbly, asking that you may take cognizance of the facts and act accordingly.
>
> We would further say that his demeanor toward his line officers, personally, have been anything but gentlemanly since we landed on the Peninsula. If our petition be heard, we shall be proud in continuing in the organization. Otherwise, we believe it will be our duty to respectfully ask a detaching of all companies here represented, to their respective State Brigades.
>
> E. Weston – Captain, Co. F
> Wm. P. Austin – Captain, Co. E
> B. Giroux – Captain, Co. C
> Wm. H. Gibbs – 1st Lt., Co. E
> Wm. Beebe – Lt., Q.M.

Above: *Berdan stood an imposing 6 feet 2 inches tall, according to army records, and he looked every inch an officer despite his uncertain reputation under fire.*

Later, these key officers recanted their accusations, saying that they were mistaken in condemning their Colonel for cowardice. Only a few days later they were to correct their apparent oversight by sending the following to General Morell:

Camp at Harrison's Landing
July 9,1862

General:

Since our memorial of the 3rd instant, requesting your attention to special allegations against Colonel H. Berdan, lst Regt. U.S. SharpShooters. We have learned that in said memorial we did Col. Berdan great injustice, that by order of General Marcy, he had turned the remaining detachment of the SharpShooters over to the command of Lieutenant Colonel Ripley, that he might visit the lines daily. And that in doing anything more than to post the men as he did, it would have been a just cause of offense to Lt-Col. Ripley. Further, that Colonel Berdan was employed, during both engagements referred to, in procuring food and ammunition for the command.

In view of the above, it is but justice to him and to ourselves that said memorial be withdrawn. We are pleased with the opportunity to replace the Colonel in the estimation held prior to the drawing and sending of the memorial.

E. Weston – Captain, Co. F
Wm. P. Austin – Captain, Co. E
B. Giroux – Captain, Co. C
Wm. H. Gibbs – 1st Lt., Co. E
Wm. Beebe – Lt., Q.M.

Despite the seeming change of heart of these unit leaders, a private letter from an anonymous writer praised Berdan's rear-guard actions at Gaines Mill. Whether Berdan, himself, was the writer, may never be known, but his influence is apparent:

We were whipped at Gaines Mill, and our army a rabble. The cavalry appeared on our right and appeared anxious to charge on the bridge in our rear. They could have done it easily. Then the whole army would have been ruined, and the Southern Confederacy a fixed fact. It was the most critical moment of the battle, or of the war. A beaten army, a bridge and morass in the rear, a stampede, add to that a charge by 3,000 cavalry on the bridge, and anyone can see the terrible result.

To Colonel Berdan is due the most of the credit of saving the army. Rallying the men, forming a nucleus, he began to inspire the men with the idea that all was not lost.

Still they wavered. Officers and men were forced into the ranks. Others, assured by the Colonel, assisted him in the terrible struggle not to win the day, but to save the army. At length, eleven lines were formed, and at this critical juncture the [enemy] cavalry appeared on our right. They had not seen our rout, and supposed the lines were reinforcements. They were not decided, and appeared to be calculating the chances. On their decision depended the fate of everything. Colonel Berdan seeing this, ordered an aid to ride to the rear and gallop up, announcing that Richmond was taken. He did so, and the effect was magical. The men cheered, flags were waved, and the cavalry, thinking our whole army was there, halted and we were saved.

General Morell thanked Colonel Berdan, and gave him the credit of having saved the army, as he indeed had done.

It was the turning point. Generals in the front could not have seen it. Luckily, Colonel Berdan was equal to the emergency. It was impossible to portray the effort required to stop the tide of 10,000 retreating men. You can only comprehend that it was done, the cavalry charge averted, the bridge kept, and the army saved.

Unsigned

Above: *Berdan's SharpShooters of Morell's Division skirmishing in the meadow wheatfield , July 1862.*

An obscure letter to the *MADISON GAZETTE* provides a common soldier's insight into this controversy surrounding Berdan. Note the following facts: first, that Berdan was accused of a hasty propensity to turn over his command to Lieutenant Colonel Ripley whenever a battle seemed near; second, that the SharpShooters had gotten rid of all of their bayonets, eliminating the possibility of being ordered to charge enemy positions as regular infantrymen; and third, that Colonel Berdan's true actions at the bridge at Gaines Mill would prove to be an embarrassment, as the "retreating cowards" he encountered had been Pennsylvania and New Jersey troops, lawfully under full command and control of their regimental commander:

Headquarters – McCall's Division
P. V. Reserve
Harrison's Landing on the James River
July 11, 1862

Dear Wife,

Our company is dropping off, day by day, and soon there won't be enough left for a corporal's guard. I don't know as this company is any worse off than any other, but I do think that we have been very unlucky in everything since we came into the service.

It seems as though Colonel Berdan thinks more of giving up the immediate command of his regiment to the Lieutenant Colonel when there is a chance for a fight, as he has always some very pressing business with the quarter-master in the rear, or has to look after ammunition. And after the fight is over, putting all his officers under arrest, and making himself notorious, generally, than in looking to the good of his regiment.

Our company has given up our bayonets, all those that had not been lost, so there will be no danger of our ever being put into line of battle, to charge bayonet again, or to support a battery in an open field. But we will be used as SharpShooters, and get what position and course we can.

In connection with Colonel Berdan going to the rear, I ought to mention further, to pick up stragglers and men that fell out of the ranks while fighting, and are used up with fatigue from standing fire from two to five hours, and ordering them back under the penalty of being shot by him, he, covering them with a cocked pistol all the time.

He tried to turn a whole Pennsylvania regiment that was falling out of a wood into an open field, and called them all cowards and ordered them to halt and turn to face their foe. It embarrassed the regiment some, and the Colonel of the Pennsylvania troops rode up to Berdan and said: "Who the hell are you? I am Colonel Simmons and I command this regiment, by God, sir!" Berdan apologized and left, and in a few moments after that, Colonel Simmons was shot dead.

I hope you will preserve all my letters, for it will be interesting for me to read and see what foolish moves have been made, as well as some of the style and courage put on by officers, as well as privates.

(unsigned)

Controversy over Berdan's command abilities reached higher authorities. On July 13, General Porter condemned Berdan as a leader and withdrew his earlier endorsement of June 24, which recommended his promotion to Brigadier General:

I have withdrawn my recommendations of Colonel Berdan to the position of Brigadier General. My reasons are as follows:

1st. At the battle of Gaines Mill (Chickahominy) Colonel Berdan was not in a sound state of mind.

2nd. At the battle of Malvern Hill, Colonel Berdan was not with his regiment, which was in action during the greater part of the day. This point is being examined into, and if cleared up, will be withdrawn.

3rd. I do not wish to be the means of placing him in a position of controlling the lives of many men.

Another letter from a common SharpShooter was written at this same time, also condemning Berdan as an inadequate military leader. Twenty-two-year-old Private William C. Kent wrote the following letter to his father, with what we can believe as complete candor:

Harrison's Landing, Virginia
July 28, 1862

Father,

On Thursday, June 26, all the forenoon, there was heavy fighting in direction of Mechanicsville, but not more so than we were accustomed to every day. Toward noon, it grew heavier, and while we were eating dinner, the orders came to fall in light marching order. In a few minutes we had started toward the scene of action under Lieutenant Colonel Ripley. And here I want it to bear testimony to the bravery of Colonel Ripley, and to the unlimited cowardice of Colonel Berdan. Though Colonel Ripley is, at times, harsh, in action he is perfectly cool, pleasant, and has the unbounded confidence of the men, that he will do everything just right. Colonel Berdan loses what little coherency there is about him when he is placing the men in position, and takes excellent care to be far in the rear before there is a possibility of being shot.

A brisk firing commenced on our right [the Battle of Gaines Mill], and scattered along until it came opposite to me. Tremendous volley of small arms and the peal of heavy guns were the last things I heard before I went in. We fought pretty much on our own hook, the officers being far to the right, and the human voice was of no account. The rebels rushed down the hill in line of battle, but it wasn't quite so easy rushing across a swamp, waist deep in thick mud. And as they tried it, we fired Sharps rifles at eight rods, firing as fast as we could put in cartridges, the distance being so short that aim was unnecessary. We couldn't help hitting them, and our vigorous fire held them in check for some minutes.

Later, we marched down the road until we came to the woods, which extended a little more to the front on the left of the road than on the right. Here we saw the last of Colonel Berdan for the day. He gave us some incoherent orders which, if obeyed, would have rendered this letter an impossibility, and then muttering something about sending forward ammunition to the rear.

Your affectionate son,
William C. Kent
Company F
1st Regiment U.S.S.S.

Berdan's 1st Regiment of SharpShooters was not engaged in battle for the greater part of July and August, 1862. They remained encamped with Porter's Division, allowing a time to momentarily forget war and to put fear far behind. The company officers organized recreations that stressed marksmanship skills and intra-unit competition. Also during the lull, recruiting parties were assembled and sent north to try to fill depleted ranks. It should be understood that during the Civil War, volunteer units were filled by local recruiting efforts in the home states. As no new battles were thought to be forthcoming, Colonel Berdan petitioned higher headquarters for permission to lead such an element personally.

I have the honor to ask that I may be detailed on recruiting service for my regiment, which now numbers but 436 men fit for duty. My regiment has no state authorities to recruit for it, like the other regiments, and every effort that has been made to recruit for it through my officers has failed. But I am confident that with personal effort, with the assistance I ask for, I could recruit it to the maximum number in a very few days.

I can leave the unit in command of Major Trepp, who is a very competent officer, and plenty of line officers. I am sure with proper authority I can raise two or three regiments in a very short time.

I should be glad if the Commanding Generals would approve my increasing my command to a brigade, to be used generally as light troops, but any portion of which can be temporarily placed on detached service during the sieges, should the interest of the service, in the opinion of the Commanding General require it.

I have Sharps and Colt rifles, enough to arm the entire brigade, and I would spare no expense in raising a brigade, unsurpassed by anything in the service. The 93rd New York Regiment, now here doing guard duty and not brigaded, were raised principally by me, and have applied to be assigned to my command.

Berdan's immediate superior, General Morell, forwarded the letter through, without comment. However, General Porter, the Division Commander, added the following rejection to Berdan's request.

> Having had some experience with the service of the Corps of SharpShooters, I do not feel inclined to encourage the raising of regiments to be educated as these have been. They have not been drilled as light troops for skirmishing purposes, or to be used as heavy infantry. They have no confidence in the support given them, nor in themselves, except when behind a bank of earth and no probability of an enemy getting at them. Many of the men have delicate rifles, without bayonets, and when the regiment is required to go into a contest, they fail because their gun is not designed for such work. Colonel [Berdan] has officers now recruiting.

Berdan remained with his SharpShooters. He did, however, send recruiting parties north. One such group consisted of four U.S.S.S. officers who had been wounded in battle, but were said to be fit enough to travel and recruit. The party consisted of Captains Wilson and Willett, and Lieutenants Bronson and Elmendorf. After several weeks on such duty they wrote to their commander that they had not recruited a single man, owing, they said, to their poor health. Therefore, on August 21, Berdan again petitioned his immediate commander, Major General Morell, asking for permission to journey north, himself. In his letter, he sadly states that his once thousand-man strong regiment now numbered only three hundred fit for duty. For a second time, Berdan's request was denied.

The Fighting Resumes

On August 14, 1862, the Army of the Potomac, under orders of General-in-Chief Halleck, left its summer encampment at Harrison's Landing and marched toward Washington. The SharpShooters of the 1st Regiment, part of V Corps, turned in their knapsacks and marched 70 miles to Newport News, Virginia. Here they embarked on water transports on August 21, arriving at the railhead at Aquia Creek, Virginia. Then they traveled by rail to Falmouth, a distance of only twelve miles, whereupon they marched again, this time westward to Barnett's Ford, then to Bristoe, Virginia.

The SharpShooters of the 1st Regiment were again thrown ahead of Porter's Division as skirmishers, seeing action at Dawkin's Branch, Virginia on August 29. They suffered two dead and two wounded during the day's fighting. The 2nd Regiment had rejoined Berdan's 1st Regiment only a short time before, the first time they had

FORM OF A MEDICAL CERTIFICATE.

Col. Berdan, of the 1st Regiment of U.S.S.S., having applied for a certificate on which to ground an application for leave of absence, I do hereby certify that I have carefully examined this officer, and find that he is suffering from repeated attacks of Haemoptysis, in consequence of a severe contusion of the left side of the chest by a fragment of shell, received on the 30th ulto. in the line of his duty. He cannot do duty with his command without risk to life, & he should leave this city to prevent permanent disability

And that, in consequence thereof, he is, in my opinion, unfit for duty. I further declare my belief that he will not be able to resume his duties in a less period than twenty (20) days

Dated at Washington City D.C. this twenty second day of September, 1862

[illegible signature]
Surgeon, U. S. A.

***Above:** Berdan's medical certificate exempting him from duty on the grounds of hemoptysis after he was wounded in battle.*

been together since leaving the Camp of Instruction in Washington, four months earlier.

The 2nd U.S.S.S., under Colonel Henry A.V. Post, acted as skirmishers, in support of the 17th, 24th and 44th New York Volunteer Infantry units. During the action, members of the Confederate 18th Georgia Infantry, under General Hood, captured the colors of the 24th New York Regiment under fire. Losing the colors was regarded as one of the greatest humiliations that a unit could endure, as they represent the heart and soul of the fighting unit. Realizing the importance of this action, Colonel Post charged his horse forward, caught the fleeing enemy troops, and wrenched the flagstaff from their grasp. Colonel Post was a hero, not only to his SharpShooters, but to the New York Infantrymen, as well. His boldness and decisive action under fire contrasted with Colonel Berdan's lack of decisive action in numerous previous engagements.

Fighting resumed the following day on August 30, at Groveton, Virginia. General Porter's V Corps, to which Berdan's Regiment was attached, suffered heavy casualties, especially after its main forward element was outflanked by Longstreet's artillery. Porter lost more than one third of his force, both killed and wounded. Berdan SharpShooters were again in the forefront of the fighting, as they were sent forward to the skirmish line through several advances.

Colonel Post's 2nd Regiment performed similarly on the Division's opposite flank. It was said that their ranks numbered 600 when the 2nd U.S.S.S. broke camp on August 10, but by the time the fighting ceased on the evening of the 30, they could muster only 127 men fit for duty. A sad affair, indeed, attesting to the carnage of war in mid-19th century America.

Colonel Berdan's Regiment fared even worse. Sixty-five men were killed, wounded, captured or missing, out of only 290 available for duty before the battle. The most notable casualty was that of Hiram Berdan, himself, although much controversy surrounds this whole affair. Berdan was not listed as a casualty on the official regimental list compiled after the Battle of Groveton. Historian Stevens, writing nearly thirty years later, succinctly notes:

> Colonel Berdan was slightly wounded by a piece of shell.

The following day Division Commander General Porter, along with his staff, visited Colonel Berdan's Headquarters and complimented him for the actions of the 1st Regiment on the battlefield. No mention, whatsoever, was made of Berdan's "wound." Immediately following their engagement at Groveton, the SharpShooters retired to the vicinity of Fort Corcoran, near Washington. They had travelled full circle, coming back to the site of their Camp of Instruction, which they had left five months earlier.

The lull in the action persuaded General Porter to grant Berdan his wish to travel north on recruiting duty. An order was signed on September 6, detailing Berdan and Lieutenant George Marden to recruiting service. But, rather than leaving for the north, Berdan sought medical attention in Washington, instead.

Major Trepp, second-in-command of the 1st Regiment, was also suffering from a debilitating illness, and chose this time to apply for an immediate resignation. This, it should be remembered, was Trepp's third attempt to resign his commission and escape the command of the one he despised so much, Colonel Berdan. This letter of resignation, dated September 9, 1862, was directed to none other than the Secretary of War, written from Trepp's sickbed in a Washington, D.C. hotel. We have no reason to disbelieve this honorable soldier, especially when he complains of "fever and chronic diarrhea:"

> In consequence of fevers and diarrhea from which I suffered in the Peninsula Campaign (since the month of June), a general debility has overtaken me in such a degree that I am unable to do duty in the field for months to come.
>
> I, therefore, feel it to be my duty towards my brother officers of the Regiment to tender, most respectfully, my resignation.
>
> C. Trepp
> Major

Above: *The SharpShooters lost a fine officer when Lieutenant Lewis C. Parmelee was killed at the battle of Antietam while trying to carry off a Rebel flag. He was struck with five Confederate bullets before he fell from his saddle.*

Trepp's resignation was endorsed by Doctor Francis Staenli, surgeon of the 7th Regiment of New York Volunteers, who said:

> I certify that I have carefully examined Major Caspar Trepp, and find that he is weakened in such a degree by the hardships of the last campaign and the ensuing sicknesses (dysenteria chronica and febris continua) that he will not be able to do duty for at least three months.

Regimental records indicate that Trepp's resignation was not honored, but he was ordered to convalesce in Washington. Meanwhile, the 1st Regiment of U.S. SharpShooters remained without the leadership of Berdan or Trepp.

On September 15, Doctor Clymer of the Washington Medical Corps signed a medical certification stating that Colonel Berdan was under his care for "hemoptysis," and would to unable "to return to his regiment without risk to his life, and is wholly unfit for duty." It was said that Berdan's wife, Mary, made haste to be at her husband's side, when she learned of his injury and resultant illness.

Meanwhile, action at the front continued. On September 5, Robert E. Lee's Army of Northern Virginia crossed the Potomac and entered Maryland, opening the first Confederate invasion of the North. Four days later, Lee split his forces and sent Stonewall Jackson to capture Harper's Ferry, Virginia, in preparation of a Confederate movement into Pennsylvania.

On September 12, what was left of the 1st Regiment of SharpShooters, 14 officers and 411 men, departed Washington for the field under the command of Captain John Isler. Berdan and Trepp remained in separate convalescent facilities in Washington. A number of much needed new recruits arrived from Wisconsin and Vermont to help fill the depleted ranks, but the SharpShooters fielded only about half of their original strength. On September 14, General McClellan broke through the South Mountain passes, in the Battle of Crampton's Gap and the Battle of South Mountain, forcing Lee to concentrate at Sharpsburg, Maryland. Two days later Jackson's force rejoined Lee at Antietam Creek.

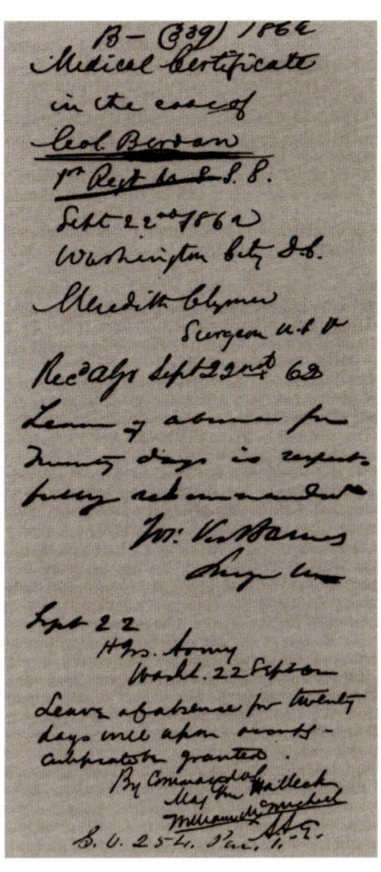
B – (339) 1862
Medical Certificate
in the case of
Col. Berdan
1st Regt. U.S. S.S.
Sept 22nd 1862
Washington City D.C.
Meredith Clymer
Surgeon U.S.V.
Rec'd Sept 22nd 62
Leave of absence for
twenty days is respectfully recommended
[illegible]
Sept 22
Hd.qrs. Army
Wash. 22 Sept
Leave of absence for twenty days will upon [illegible] application be granted.
By Command of Maj. Gen. Halleck
[illegible]
A.A.G.
S. O. 254, Par. 1.

Left: *Endorsements by senior officers on Berdan's medical certificate.*

Isler's men took part in the Battle of South Mountain on September 14, with no casualties. Post's 2nd Regiment of U.S. SharpShooters suffered two wounded as a result of their participation in the battle. This engagement was the prelude to one of the Civil War's greatest conflicts, the Battle of Antietam, Maryland, of September 16 and 17, 1862.

General Porter's V Corps, to which Isler's SharpShooters were assigned, was to occupy the center of the line of battle at Antietam. Surprisingly, the 1st Regiment of SharpShooters was not heavily engaged, and suffered only a single casualty. This great struggle, which proved to be the undoing of Generals McClellan and Burnside, found the 1st Regiment of SharpShooters held in reserve, a position in which they rarely found themselves during the war. The 2nd Regiment of U.S. SharpShooters did not fare as well. They were in the thick of the fighting at Antietam, suffering 66 killed and wounded. General Abner Doubleday, Commander of the 1st Division, I Corps, Army of the Potomac, reported that Post's 2nd U.S.S.S. were ordered to advance to the front, and engage the enemy troops that flanked the Union forces.

Second Regiment Adjutant Lewis Parmelee was among those who died here. It was said that he was shot dead while trying to capture a Confederate flag which was fastened to a fence post. Regimental Commander Henry Post was, himself, severely wounded during this battle, while trying to capture two enemy battle flags. Post never fully recovered from his wounds, and was medically discharged in November, 1862. The Sharp-shooters lost two fine officers.

All in all, the 2nd Regiment of U.S. SharpShooters lost 3 officers killed and 10 wounded, and 3 enlisted men killed, 48 wounded, and 2 missing during the two-day Battle of Antietam. This was the price that the SharpShooters had to pay when ordered to the front of the main body of troops in a major engagement.

On September 19 and 20, the 1st Regiment of Sharpshooters (still without Berdan or Trepp) were involved in heavy forays and skirmishes around Sharpsburg. The Regiment now consisted of less than half of its initial complement, with more than 500 SharpShooters wounded,

Below: *A money belt that Lewis Parmelee was wearing at the time of his death. It is remarkable that such personal items have survived nearly 150 years after the war.*

captured, sick, on detached duty, or having deserted. Fortunately for the Federals, Lee's Army retreated south, ending the Confederate invasion threat to the North for 1862.

During his convalescence in Washington, Colonel Berdan wrote to President Lincoln. He thanked him for recommending to McClellan that he be promoted to Brigadier General, not realizing that the Army of the Potomac Commander was soon to be relieved of his command. Lincoln's recommendation was soon to be moot. Berdan's letter does, however, give valuable insight into the status of the SharpShooters at that point:

Washington, D.C.
September 18, 1862

His Excellency
Abraham Lincoln
President of the United States

Sir:
General Marcy read me your note to General McClellan, in which you suggested the propriety of having one acknowledged head to the Corps of SharpShooters, and appointing me Brigadier General in command of them. Please accept my thanks. Could I please have the authority to increase it to a full brigade, or more? I should be very glad to accept the promotion, otherwise, I prefer to remain Colonel of one regiment.

Enough companies are now offered, with the approval of the Governors, provided they can be attached to my command to increase the corps to a full brigade. I am confident that with the proper authority I could, in a very short time, raise a regiment or a battalion from most, if not from everyone, of the loyal states. My present command is entirely inadequate to the demand for SharpShooters. I frequently had one regiment divided between five or six divisions, using one or two decimated companies, where a strong battalion could be used to great advantage. In my judgment, a regiment of these skillful rifle shots in each Corps D'Armee, for rifle pits, outpost duty, as Sharpshooters in time of action and as skirmishers to discover the position of the enemy, are almost indispensable.

An authority to raise a regiment or a battalion from each Loyal State would enable me to turn in the companies already furnished by the different states, and thus, remedy a difficulty we have always experienced in getting commissions. At present my regiments are made up of companies from different states. Therefore, no one governor has authority to commission the field and staff officers. This has always been a source of great trouble in my command.

It will be seen by the enclosed letter of the Adjutant General, that it is impossible for me to appoint a field officer in the present state of the organization.

I am now under medical treatment for injuries received in the battle of the 31st ult. and Surgeon Clymer informed me a few days since that it would be some time before I should be able to resume active duty in the field. He advised me to apply for a furlough, as a change of air is necessary to stop my hemorrhage. I had declined an earlier furlough, owing to the present state of my organization, but Surgeon Clymer has just obtained one for me without my knowledge or consent.

I dislike to avail myself of a leave of absence, as I do not have a field officer on duty in either of my regiments. I have only two captains remaining on duty, but should Your Excellency grant this application, it would enable me to fill all vacancies at once.

H. Berdan
Colonel Commanding U.S. SharpShooters

President Lincoln responded:

Colonel Berdan's SharpShooters are an irregular, in a sense, an illegal organization. Its field and staff officers have had no commissions. It is a good deal reduced by skirmishes, battles, and other hard service. As far as I know, there are no jealousies against it, and it is universally appreciated. I, therefore, propose that the Secretary of War, with the assistance of the Adjutant General and Colonel Berdan, put the corps into the most effective form, regardless of existing regulations. I will recommend to Congress to ratify it, giving commissions, pay, etc. from the time individuals respectively entered the service.

A. Lincoln

President Lincoln's endorsement to Berdan's plan meant that some improvements were forthcoming. While no final authority was ever given to increase the size of the SharpShooters, nor was Berdan promoted to general (at least not during the war), it appears that major improvements were made in filling officer vacancies. Meanwhile, Berdan's problems with higher authorities continued. The following letter implies that when he was injured, Berdan did not receive proper authorization to convalesce in Washington. Furthermore, the letter which was written in response shows that not even his regiment knew where he was, or why he was absent.

Headquarters – 5th Army Corps
September 21, 1862

Major General Morell
Commanding General:

On the report of your division, it is noted that Colonel Berdan is "absent without leave." The Commanding General desires to know the date of Colonel Berdan's absence, and the cause, if any there be.

Fred G. Locke
Lieutenant Colonel
Asst. Adjutant General

Berdan's U.S. SharpShooters Headquarters
September 22, 1862

Major General Porter
Commanding 5th Army Corps

General:
In compliance with your request, I beg leave to state that the reason of Colonel Berdan's absence from his command is not known to me. Colonel Berdan, on leaving the regiment at Washington City (Friday, September 12th), told me

that he had obtained a leave of absence for a few days, for the purpose of collecting rifles and accoutrements of his command. And that he would join us by Monday evening, the 15th instant.

J.B. Isler Captain
Comd'g. 1st Rgt. U.S.S.S.

Captain Isler saw and spoke with Berdan on September 12, and no mention was made, evidently, of a wound or of a need to seek medical attention. Furthermore, there is no mention of Berdan's medical problems in the Regimental Record Book, the unit's official record of movements, orders, departures, deaths and leaves. And yet, Berdan was, indeed, in Washington at this time, under the care of Army Surgeon Meridith Clymer, and attended to by his wife, Mary.

On September 22, Doctor Clymer forwarded an official medical certificate of Berdan's condition to the Surgeon General in Washington. It was favorably endorsed, suggesting that Berdan be issued a ninety-day medical leave of absence. It was further endorsed by Major General Halleck of Washington's Army Headquarters, reducing the total leave of absence to twenty days. On September 26, Major General Porter, Berdan's Commanding Officer of V Corps, sent the following endorsement to his superiors, acknowledging his medical treatment and excused absence.

Respectfully forwarded, with enclosures, to Headquarters of the Army of the Potomac, in connection with the recommendation for dropping from the rolls the name of Colonel Berdan. He had failed to report his presence anywhere, and having heard of him through the newspapers as apparently well, I made the recommendation thus forwarded. Knowing that officers should not, of their own free will, absent themselves, as such has been discharged by order of the Secretary of War.

I now wish to reverse that recommendation, as Colonel Berdan has obtained an extension of his leave from Headquarters, and being reported as sick.

F.J. Porter Major General
Commanding

Evidently, Clymer's medical certificate for Berdan did reach Porter's Headquarters. Berdan's whereabouts were finally known, but the circumstances surrounding his absence cast a shadow over his ability to command a regiment successfully. Captain Isler, still in charge of the 1st U.S. SharpShooters wrote to the convalescing Major Trepp of the Berdan incident:

Berdan's U.S. SharpShooters Headquarters
Camp near Blackford's, Maryland
Major Trepp
September 24, 1862

St. Charles Hotel
Washington City

Dear Sir:
Your note of September 18th came this morning to hand, and I have forwarded to proper quarter, its enclosure. As you are aware, Colonel Berdan left me in command of his regiment at Washington City. He stayed behind, as he told me, for the purpose of collecting Sharps rifles which belonged to his regiment, and pretended to have a leave of absence from the Commanding General. But now it turns out that it is not so, for General Porter wanted to know of his whereabouts and cause of absence from his command.

Of course, I did know nothing else but what Berdan told me, and reported accordingly. I certainly would have expected from Colonel Berdan to be straight forward towards me, for I must openly confess that my position is not to be envied. You know, yourself, that our regiment is hated by all that have to deal with it, and since we left Washington, we are one day with Butterfield, another day with Griffin, and sometimes with Martindale. Nobody seems to care much for us, and as we have no quartermaster with us, we often suffer for want of provisions.

In short, the old tale. I am gratified that General Porter is the only person that seems to take some little interest in our welfare. At least, in the last engagement he had common sense enough to let me have my own way in the use of his Command and at my own direction. We lost 2 men killed and 6 wounded. By yesterday's morning report, I have 314 men for duty, and 804 absent. Of Officers, there are 6, besides me.

Let me know what your intentions are for the future. Tell me candidly if you intend to remain, or if you have tendered your resignation, and intend to leave the regiment. Your decision will, in a great measure, guide my movements, for I must confess, but for you, I would have taken steps, long ago, to get away.

J.B. Isler
Captain

There is no surviving record of Major Caspar Trepp's reply, if any. Meanwhile, on September 27, Colonel Berdan, at long last, wrote a letter of explanation to his commander, Major General Morell:

Washington, D.C.
September 27th, 1862

Major General Geo. Morell
Commanding Division

General:
Enclosed, please find leave of absence for 20 days, obtained for me by Surgeon Clymer without my knowledge or consent. I am somewhat improved in health, but the Surgeon informs me that a change in air is necessary to my complete restoration. I have, as yet, so many things to do for this Corps with the limited time I am able to labor daily, that I shall be unable to leave for a few days.

There are now in the Convalescent Camp, at Alexandria, fifty recruits for my regiment, and more on the way. All of which will be sent forward as fast as they can be equipped. I regret, exceedingly, that I cannot be with you, and wishing you every possible success.

H. Berdan
Colonel Commanding
U.S.S.S.

p.s. I have had no attack of hemorrhage for the last two days, and think I am getting stronger.

Berdan continued his convalescence in Washington with his wife, Mary, at his side. Nearly a month later, on October 25, 1862, Army Surgeon Clymer wrote this prognosis:

> Colonel H. Berdan has been carefully examined by me and I find that he is, and has been since the 30th day of August last, suffering from disease of the left lung, the result of a severe contusion of the chest from a fragment of shell, received on that date. He is unfit for any military duty, and will not be, in my opinion, for the next ten months.

On October 2,1862, newly-promoted Lieutenant Colonel Caspar Trepp (recently returned to duty with the 1st U.S. SharpShooters), penned a very informative letter to the Adjutant General of V Corps. It gives valuable historical documentation on the origins of the various companies of SharpShooters, as well as the present status of the unit.

> Company A –organized in New York, and comprised entirely of Germans and Swiss. Number of enlisted men was 59. At present, 34. Captain and First Lieutenant positions vacant. Second Lieutenant Rudolf Aschmann promoted from Sergeant in October 1862.
>
> Company B – organized in New York. Number of enlisted men was 94. At present, 88. Captain John Wilson, promoted November 1861. First Lieutenants William Nash and William Elwenburg, promoted March 1862.
>
> Company C – organized in Michigan. Number of enlisted men was 99. At present, 75. Captain's position is vacant. First Lieutenant James Baker and Second Lieutenant Byron Brewer.
>
> Company D – organized in New York. Number of enlisted men was 33. At present, 20. Captain's position is vacant. First Lieutenant Charles McClain. Second Lieutenant Albert Ferret was promoted from First Sergeant of Company A in October 1862.
>
> Company E – organized in New Hampshire. Number of enlisted men was 69. At present, 47. Captain W.P. Austin. First Lieutenant Wm. Gibbs. Second Lieutenant's position is vacant.
>
> Company F –organized in Vermont. Number of enlisted men was 108. At present, 82. Captain Charles Seaton. First Lieutenant's position is vacant. Second Lieutenant Martin Bronson.
>
> Company G – organized in Wisconsin. Number of enlisted men was 93. At present, 63. Captain Frank Marble. First Lieutenant position is vacant. Second Lieutenant Charles Stevens.
>
> Company H – organized in New York. Number of enlisted men was 72. At present, 47. Captain W. Winthrop, promoted in September 1862. First Lieutenant Roswall Weston, promoted October 1862. Second Lieutenant Michael McGeough, promoted from Sergeant in October 1862.
>
> Company J – organized in Michigan. Number of enlisted men was 93. At present, 51. Captain A.M. Wilsch. First Lieutenant Coval. Second Lieutenant Sprauge. All officers are absent, sick.
>
> Company K – organized in Michigan. Number of enlisted men was 75. At present, 48. Captain's, First Lieutenant's and Second Lieutenant's positions are vacant.

Above: *An unidentified U.S. SharpShooter whose uniform has evolved in battle. Gone are the leather leggings, and neat kepi. Many men equipped themselves from the battlefield fallen.*

Field and Staff Officers;
Colonel Hiram Berdan – appointed by the War Department in July 1861.
Lieutenant Colonel Caspar Trepp –promoted from Major on September 22, 1862.
Major George Hastings – promoted from Captain on September 22, 1862.
Surgeon John W. Brennan – promoted from Assistant Surgeon in September 1862.
Acting Assistant Surgeon George Bernon – appointed by contract with the Medical Department in 1862.
Adjutant Lieutenant W.H. Horton – promoted from Sergeant Major in October 1862.
Quartermaster George Marden – promoted rom Second Lieutenant in October 1862.

On October 3, President Lincoln visited V Corps and reviewed, among others, the 1st Regiment of U.S SharpShooters. Historian Stevens later recalled that "while it afforded them much pleasure, it would have been more gratifying had they not been roasted for three hours in the hot sun." Evidently, the soldiers, SharpShooters included, were a sorry lot to behold. They were described as: "brown as a berry, with their weather-tanned faces, with tattered banners and faded clothes." "All," Stevens remembered, "which brought forth the fullest sympathy of the President."

The true picture of the SharpShooters, after only six months of action, portrays them in a sad light. Their once brilliant green coats, kepis and trousers were now faded, torn and thread-bare. Leggings, overcoats and hair-covered knapsacks had been long since discarded. Leather cartridge pouches, shoes, belts and canteens were cracked and flaking from constant exposure to the sun and to moisture. Bedrolls and tarred ponchos share the same fate. Uniforms or accoutrements that could not be mended were discarded, and replaced, if the SharpShooter was lucky, with new issue from the Regimental Quartermaster. But, as often as not, there were no new items available, and it was left up to the individual to clothe and equip himself from what could be taken from battlefield casualties.

Possibly the most scathing report ever written against Colonel Berdan was published in the *PENN YAN CHRONICLE* on November 6, 1862. The writer's name was not revealed, but knowledge of intimate events involving the Berdan SharpShooters would be known only to ranking officers of the unit:

THE PENN YAN CHRONICLE
The First Regiment of SharpShooters was composed of ten companies, four from New York, three from Michigan, one from Wisconsin, one from New Hampshire, and one from Vermont. Never was better material given into the hands of a Colonel, never was a regiment more abused. When the regiment went into camp at Washington in August 1861, Lieutenant F. Mears of the 9th Infantry was assigned to it as drill master. On the 27th of November, 1861, Mears, who in the mean time had been appointed Lieutenant Colonel of the regiment, drilled it for the last time, having resigned on account of troubles between himself on one hand, and Colonel Berdan and Major Rowland on the other hand.

Major Rowland subsequently resigned on December 12, 1861. At that time no regiment in the service could drill better than the 1st U.S.S.S. All the discipline the regiment ever had was entirely owing to the efforts of Lieutenant Colonel William Y.W. Ripley of Rutland, Vermont. Colonel Berdan never had, nor has he now (though he has been over a year in the service), military knowledge enough to conduct either a dress parade or an inspection.

At Harrison's Landing on the 24th day of July, 1862, the division of General Morell was reviewed by General Porter and General Morell, and on the next day the Corps of General Porter was reviewed by General McClellan. In conducting the regiment to the parade ground, Colonel Berdan gave the order "Unfix bayonets," while the regiment was marching at "right shoulder shift." When General McClellan passed in front of the troops, the Colonel paid no attention to him, but when the General was riding in the rear of the brigade, the Colonel gave the order "Present arms," from an "In-place, rest." Some of the men were even lying on the ground.

In the winter of 61 and 62, it became known in camp that Colonel Berdan intended to take the field in person as a Colonel. This caused a universal feeling of gloom and discontent. The men said, and they reasoned correctly, "Of what use is it that we are the best drilled regiment in the service, if we are to have a Colonel utterly incompetent even to review his own regiment."

I wish it distinctly understood that I charge Colonel H. Berdan with having discouraged, disheartened, and nearly destroyed one of the best regiments in the service, by his inefficiency and cowardice. It would take too long to minutely relate all the occurrences of the memorable Peninsula Campaign.

On the 14th of May, 1862, the regiment was ordered to fall in with 60 rounds of ammunition, and prepare to march immediately to meet the enemy. Colonel Berdan was absent from his regiment, living at the house of a Mr. Toler. It was raining furiously. Lieutenant Colonel Ripley sent the order to Colonel Berdan, but he did not leave the house, but said that he was sick, and that he, Ripley, must take charge of the regiment. The Colonel... did not rejoin the regiment till it reached Cold Harbor on the 23rd of May, at which time he suddenly recovered his health.

On the 27th of May, Lieutenant Colonel Ripley aroused the regiment at 3 A.M. in the midst of a furious rain storm. Sixty rounds of ammunition were given out, and at daylight the regiment marched to attack Richmond. Colonel Berdan remained behind, sick again, as did Adjutant Willett. The regiment marched 17 miles and fought the first half of the battle. All supposed that the battle ended, when Colonel Berdan came up from the rear, and assumed command. Soon after, firing was heard in the rear, and the regiment was ordered back, doublequick... When the regiment reached the woods where the rebels were posted, Colonel Berdan left, and rode back up the road, where he remained until the end of the battle.

The conduct of Colonel Berdan at the Battle of Hanover Court House excited wonder and suspicion, but the regiment was unwilling to believe that their Colonel was a coward. At the Battle of Mechanicsville, the firing had been heard for... several hours, and the order [to move] had been expected. The Colonel turned over the command to J. Smith Brown, who was acting as Adjutant, ordering him to take the regiment and hunt up General Griffin and fight with him. He said, in conclusion, "I am going back to camp to stay all night, and protect our poor sick from being butchered by the rebels. It would be horrible to have them slaughtered there." What sick, or what rebels he was talking about, none in the regiment could ever understand.

When the army retreated at daylight, the regiment passed by its old camp, where the Colonel was busily engaged with reporters, eating a breakfast of chicken, bread, coffee, etc., and the Colonel was dictating large-sized personal narrations. One would think that cowardice could go no further, but read on.

Lieutenant Colonel Ripley forced Colonel Berdan to the front, anyway. He posted the men, and retired, two hours before the next action commenced. The Colonel was not seen again that day on the battlefield. He was heard of away in the rear, trying to rally stragglers, where he became so excited as to shoot an artillery horse with his revolver. The next morning the Colonel was discovered under a tree with one of the Herald reporters, to whom he was relating his marvelous exploits of the day before. The Colonel afterwards materially modified his story. He tried to get it published, but the reporter quietly threw it away when out of sight.

At Harrison's Landing the Colonel persuaded a Frank Leslie artist to sketch a view of the battle, showing the Colonel in the act of halting 18,000 panic stricken officers and men. General Morell sent for him and forbade him to have it published, as it represented an untruth.

The Colonel first said that he had gone to the rear for ammunition. Afterwards he did not press that reason, for any intelligent sergeant could have obtained the ammunition, which, by the way, was not needed. He dwelt strongly upon what he did at the rear, without first explaining how he came to be there, when his regiment was in the front.

At the Battle of Malvern, Colonel Berdan again posted his regiment in the very front, and then retired, as usual, to the rear. He did not come near the battlefield again that day. His excuse was that he was trying to get some fresh beef for his men. The men were indeed hungry, but they had no time then to eat.

On Sunday morning Lieutenant Colonel Ripley rode up to the Adjutant and said:

"You see now what the game is. Berdan shoves us to the front to be killed for his glory. He dares not accompany his regiment into battle. He sends us to the very front, and the more we fight, the more of us are killed, and the greater is his glory, and he is always in the rear. It is a duty we owe ourselves, and to the regiment, to expose him."

Upon arriving at Harrison's Landing, four or five of Colonel Berdan's officers wrote a letter to General Morell, denouncing the Colonel, and especially his cowardice and incompetency. This letter was sent direct to General Morell, and was returned because it was not properly forwarded. Colonel Berdan immediately placed the officers under arrest, and by threats and promises, induced them to write a letter of retraction.

On the 29th of August, the Colonel claimed to have been wounded with a shell which struck him on the shoulder blade, although he has always refused to allow J. W. Brennan, Surgeon of the regiment, examine it. When the regiment arrived in Washington, the Colonel sent a dispatch to the Associated Press, saying that "Colonel Berdan was not so seriously injured as was at first supposed, but has recovered and is now on duty." Now I do not pretend to say that the Colonel was not wounded, but I do say that not one in the regiment ever saw his wound, nor could they detect any signs.

I have thus, briefly, alluded to some of the most important specifications to the above charge. Much more might be truthfully written of a similar nature, but the above is sufficient for anyone to decide upon.

The editor of the newspaper wrote the following editorial on the SharpShooter's condemnation of Berdan:

On our first page, we print a communication of considerable length, giving an account of the military exploits of Colonel Berdan, of the U.S. SharpShooters. If correct, as we have no doubt that it is, the Colonel stands exposed as a most despicable coward and humbug. It is astonishing that such an errant military quack could be tolerated so long in the army. In any other army but that commanded by the inflated "young Napoleon" [McClellan], he would have been cashiered out, long ago.

"Res Ipsa Loquitur" – the thing speaks for itself.

November 1862, found Colonel Berdan still "convalescing from his wounds" at the Willard's Hotel in Washington, D.C. On the 27, he wrote to President Lincoln, again requesting that he be put in charge of a new corps of the army, the SharpShooters. This, he believed, would stand with the other corps: infantry, cavalry, artillery, signal, engineers, etc., and only he, Berdan, should lead it:

274 F Street
Washington, D.C.
November 27, 1862

His Excellency – Abraham Lincoln
President of the United States

Sir:
During the summer and autumn of 1861, I raised a brigade of SharpShooters with the intention of using them as light troops. I, of course, expected to have the command with the rank of Brigadier General. They were thought, by General McClellan, to be too valuable to be kept together. Consequently, two regiments were sent to different divisions, and the balance were sent as independent companies, all without a commander of the whole. The independent companies did but little service, as they had neither field or staff officers to look after them.

The regiments rendered valuable service, and got along very well without a commander, until they became

***Above:** Unidentified Berdan SharpShooter.*

very much decimated. I had no trouble to recruit my regiment, as I had started the corps, and was the only one known to the public in connection with it.

Enough have applied to fill up all the companies in the corps, and more too, but they all want to go into a regiment that I command. They refuse to go in any other until I have a position by which I can instruct and look after their regiment or company, as well as the one I have now.

Consequently, Colonel Post has resigned, having only 110 men left. The independent companies are also going all to pieces, for want of someone that can recruit for them and look after them.

All with whom I have conversed with on this subject agree with me, as to the importance of having a head to the corps, as much so as artillery, cavalry, or the corps of engineers. In fact, more so from the fact that it is something new, and the duties are, therefore, less understood. I have reason to believe that Your Excellency is of the same opinion.

The time has expired in which the 43 new companies were to have been ready, and not a single company has been raised, except 5 or 6 which were about full at the time the authority was given. These were recruited, understanding that I would, in some way, be attached to my command. I am quite sure that no more companies can be raised until this difficulty has been obviated.

The difficulties growing out of the wants of a head to the corps increase as the ranks diminish. All of the best officers are anxious to get out of the corps before it sinks into disrepute. I must confess to Your Excellency, that I partake of this feeling, very much myself. Unless Your Excellency will take the responsibility of appointing a Chief to look after it, the same as all other corps have, that have to be used in detached service [sic]. I would prefer to have the command, and that too, before the corps falls to the ground.

I ask that you will either give me the command of the Corps of SharpShooters, after they are armed with such rank and assistance as you may think I am entitled to. Or that you give me the appointment of Brigadier General, to date from the first of December, 1861, the time my 2nd Regiment was mustered in. I have not been brigaded and, therefore, have not been in the regular line for promotion. This makes the above alternative necessary to enable me to get out of the corps without resigning, which I would very much dislike to do. Simple justice to myself would demand that I should give the public my reasons for such an act, and this I don't think I could do, without significant injury to the corps, and therefore to the service.

H. Berdan
Colonel Commanding 1st Regiment U.S.S.S.

The following day, Berdan wrote another letter to Brigadier General John Martindale, Military Governor of the District of Columbia, seeking his endorsement to the proposal.

274 F Street
Washington
November 28, 1862

General John H. Martindale
Military Governor
District of Columbia

General:
I have got to the end of my rope, so far as anything I can do for this Corps of SharpShooters, unless I am put in command of the whole, to instruct, recruit for, etc. For the want of a proper head, I am quite sure it will not do well. I

shall, therefore, try to get another command. I am not, as you know, in the regular line for promotion, so I shall have to make the application, I suppose, and as we all served side by side for months together. I would be glad if you would state on the back of this letter, what you know of me as an officer and a gentleman, and as to my ability, in your judgment, to command a brigade.

H. Berdan
Colonel Commanding
U.S.S.S.

General Martindale wrote this positive endorsement:

Colonel Berdan has served with me through the Campaign of the Peninsula, and for a time had his regiment of SharpShooters pressed in front of my brigade. I have never witnessed anything but zeal and energy and intelligence in the performance of his duties, and I know that his Corps, in repeated actions, had acquitted itself with much gallantry in action.

On November 7. 1862, Major General McClellan was relieved as Commander of the Army of the Potomac, and replaced by General Ambrose Burnside. Five days later, Major General Joseph Hooker was ordered to take command of V Corps, relieving General Porter.

The SharpShooters were not engaged in battle during the month of November. December found them preparing for winter encampment near Falmouth, Virginia, by constructing comfortable log huts. Historian Stevens would later write:

Much dissatisfaction was perceptible in the army: rations, often short, were of bad quality; clothing and shoes were worn out; and it was weeks before these inconveniences were remedied. The men had not been paid for six months, which put them in bad humor. To make things still worse, our knapsacks, which had been left on the Peninsula in August, were returned in a bad condition and emptied of their former contents. So that many lost valuables, in the shape of presents, journals, etc. Therefore, the temper of our regiment was not very enviable.

The Battle of Fredericksburg

Before the SharpShooters could settle into camp, they were pressed into service by their new Army Commander, Major General Burnside. The Right Grand Division was headed by General Edwin V. Sumner, the Center under General Joseph Hooker, and the Left under General William B. Franklin. The 1st Regiment of U.S.S.S. was attached to the 1st Division, commanded by General Griffin. It was under General Daniel Butterfield's V Corps. Lieutenant Colonel Caspar Trepp headed the regiment, as Colonel Berdan was still on medical leave.

The 2nd Regiment, U.S. SharpShooters was headed by Major Homer R. Stoughton, and was attached to the 1st Division of I Corps, of the Left Grand Division. Burnside ordered Franklin's Left Grand Division to move south of Fredericksburg, where they crossed the Rappahannock on the 11th of December. Hooker and Sumner crossed into Fredericksburg during nightfall and into the next day. Burnside planned that the main attack should come from the Federal Left under Franklin, with the battle commencing on December 13. Franklin's Division was, however, repulsed, despite the spirited assaults of Meade and Gibbon. Meanwhile, Sumner, backed by Hooker, encountered Confederate General Longstreet's Corps on Marye's Heights, a ridge behind the city.

The Union assault against the entrenched Confederates failed miserably. Of the 114,000 men engaged, the Federals suffered 1,284 men killed, 9,600 wounded, and 1,769 missing or captured. The Confederates lost 595 men killed, 4,061 wounded, and 653 missing or captured, out of 72,500 troops. The Federals could not dislodge the entrenched Confederates, and began a retreat on the evening of December 14, across the Rappahannock.

The 1st Regiment of SharpShooters was not significantly engaged at Fredericksburg, being held in reserve. Likewise, the 2nd Regiment of SharpShooters were only lightly engaged, served as skirmishers for a time, and suffered but one man wounded.

Winter Encampment at Falmouth

The SharpShooters returned to the encampment site near Falmouth, Virginia, remaining until December 30, when they were ordered on a reconnaissance mission. They were part of a detachment commanded by Colonel Barnes of the 18th Massachusetts, when they engaged Confederate cavalry troops and SharpShooters across the Rappahannock. The entire affair was without much incident, with the men soon back in camp, with several captured turkeys and chickens to show for their trouble.

Meanwhile on December 26, a most unpleasant incident occurred in which Lieutenant Colonel Trepp was humiliated by the recently returned Colonel Berdan, and, for the fourth time, tendered his resignation:

Camp near Falmouth, Virginia
December 26th, 1862

Col. H. Berdan
Commanding 1st Rgt. U.S.S.S.

Colonel:
This morning you called at my quarters, and ordered me to take a rifle and go out to drill in the manual of arms, under the instruction of 1st Lieutenant Nash. I obeyed the order. Afterwards, you overheard me in my tent, complaining of the order. You came in and showed me certain written orders, prescribing such drill for the line officers, and stated that they did not apply to field officers, but that you had merely requested, not ordered, the field officers to drill, and that you would require me to apologize for the language in which I complained.

I beg to correct you as to the fact that you did, in so many words, tell me to drill under the Lieutenant. It was no request, but an order, and as such I obeyed it, reserving my complaints till afterwards. Major Hastings also states that he

Above: *A remarkable picture of Confederate troops in an undamaged sector of Fredericksburg after they repelled the Federal assault. It was taken by Matthew Brady with a telescopic lens from the opposite bank of the Rappahannock.*

understood that it was an order to him, as well, and had no idea that it was a mere request, until afterwards. I decline, therefore, to apologize for having complained in indignant terms, at what I consider a humiliation put upon me by you.

In view of these facts, I hereby tender my unconditional resignation, with the request that it be accepted immediately. I have been in the military service from 1847 to 1857, in which period of ten years I have had chances to learn the manual of arms. Yet, I am willing to be instructed as a recruit or as Lieutenant Colonel of your regiment if commanded and instructed by yourself, but not by any line officer of this or any other regiment.

The orders brought to me after the drill were never shown to me before, and I had, therefore, no opportunity to demonstrate against being regarded as a recruit. If I am to be a recruit, then I was never fit to be an officer at all; still I was a field officer of your regiment since January 1st, 1862. I must confess to feel ashamed of myself, that after one year's service in the field, to be regarded by my Colonel as unable to instruct the manual of arms, and to be instructed in the presence of any or all the enlisted men of the regiment, by a line officer.

If you chose to instruct part or the entire regiment by yourself, I am always ready and willing to be instructed, whenever ordered so. I never made inquiry of the opinion of anyone about his views to my ability as an officer, but have tried to do my duty to the best of my ability and never expected to have to undergo the instruction of any part of military science by any officer below the grade I occupy.

I hope you will do me this favor and to accept my resignation.

Caspar Trepp
Lt. Colonel
1st Rgt. U.S.S.S.

Nevertheless, Berdan ignored Trepp's honorable request, knowing that Trepp was very much needed to command troops in the field. Berdan's insensitive callousness toward Trepp and other officers of his regiment demonstrated his own lack of military discipline and leadership ability. History records these events in the favor of Trepp, to the detriment of Berdan.

General Burnside, issued the following order:

> Headquarters – Army of the Potomac,
> Camp near Falmouth,Virginia
> January 14, 1863
>
> Special Orders No.14
> The regiments and companies of SharpShooters in this Army will form a distinct arm of the service, and will be under the command of Colonel Berdan, as Chief of SharpShooters, who will report directly to these headquarters. Detachments from this force will be sent, from time to time, to the different Grand Divisions on detached service, to be used as SharpShooters.

Berdan had received one of his two wishes: he was appointed Chief of SharpShooters, but still had not been promoted to Brigadier General. On January 19, 1863, General Burnside's Army of the Potomac began its second excursion across the Rappahannock, to attack the encamped Confederates. The 1st Regiment of SharpShooters began their march on the 20th, arriving about ten miles north of Fredericksburg, on the Federal side of the river, in the afternoon. A heavy rain fell that night, making most roads impassable. It continued raining into the following day. General Burnside's plan to attack the Confederates failed, as mobility became difficult, then impossible. The mud march was a disheartening blow to the Federal winter campaign hopes, and with the advent of another storm, the troops grudgingly made their way back to their encampment near Fredericksburg, arriving on the 23rd. The Army of the Potomac was dispirited, wet, hungry and tired, and so were the SharpShooters.

***Above:** Major General Ambrose Everett Burnside who was blamed for the senseless and costly attack on Fredericksburg.*

Burnside blamed his Grand Division Commanders for the failure of the movement, not the weather. On the 23rd, he issued orders, to be approved by the President, relieving Generals Hooker, Franklin and Smith from command. On January 25, in conference with President Lincoln in Washington, Burnside, himself, was relieved, along with Generals Franklin and Sumner. General Joseph Hooker was chosen to replace Burnside as Commander of the Army of the Potomac. A reorganization of the Army followed, abolishing the concept of Grand Divisions. Berdan's 1st Regiment of SharpShooters was reassigned from V Corps (under Major General Meade), to III Corps (under Brigadier General Sickles).

The SharpShooters settled into winter encampment near Falmouth, Virginia, in an area known as Stoneman's Switch. Camp life was difficult during these freezing cold winter days and nights, with few creature comforts. Colonel Ripley later spoke of spirited snowball fights, and other winter sports to keep the men amused, as best they could, while awaiting the spring offensive.

Lieutenant Colonel Trepp's Arrest and Trial

The animosity that existed between Berdan and his next in command, Caspar Trepp, knew no bounds. It manifested itself over and over again, primarily with Berdan as the antagonist. Whether it was jealousy over Trepp's natural leadership ability, or the love and respect that the SharpShooters openly showed to him, the record stands that Berdan disliked him immensely.

The long string of boorish insults sent Trepp's way by Berdan continued unabated, including such a trivial charge as stealing regimental stationery! On January 27, 1863, Berdan charged Trepp with just such a capital offense. Trepp, angered by the annoyance, wrote a three-page rebuttal, denying all, and quoted chapter and verse from army regulations. Trepp's frustration and subsequent refusal to be intimidated by Berdan only made the Colonel seek other ways to belittle his subordinate.

Berdan decided that he would inflict upon Trepp the ultimate indignity of a court-martial, charging him with cowardice in the face of the enemy. As ridiculous as it sounds, Berdan's charges went back more than seven months, to the SharpShooters' actions at Fort Davidson in early June 1862. The redoubt at that time was occupied by the SharpShooters, commanded by then Major Trepp. Enemy movements compelled the Federals to abandon the fort, after first destroying its rear face, making it useless to the enemy. Aschmann would later recall:

> We occupied an earthwork, called Fort Davidson, which had just recently been cast up and was equipped with a twelve-pound battery. The entire garrison was placed under the command of Major Trepp. Our duty consisted of standing in arms inside the fort for two hours before daybreak, every morning, in order to be prepared for

> enemy assaults. Also, small groups of 10 to 20 men sometimes had to join the outpost lines when minor skirmishes had broken out there. Our fort, as well as the camps of the rest of the troops, was situated so far to the front that even the enemy's small arms fire could reach them, and several men were wounded in camp.
>
> The enemy outpost line was barely 200 steps away from ours, so that the guards could callout to each other.
>
> Artillery duels and outpost skirmishes took place almost daily and often took on a serious character. At noon on June 27th, the enemy threatened to attack the entire line. Our two companies, therefore, had to leave the fort and go to the front. We returned to camp late at night. Our corps received orders to get ready for a retreat. At daybreak, our entire division pulled back about half a mile and took up a position that was advantageous, especially for the artillery. Only our two companies still occupied Fort Davidson, while half a company of engineers demolished its rear, to prevent it from giving cover to the enemy later on. When the engineers had finished their task and had withdrawn, we too returned to our division.

Colonel Berdan ordered the arrest of Lieutenant Colonel Trepp on January 25, 1863, and confined him to camp, awaiting court-martial. Berdan drafted charges against Trepp at that time.

General Orders No. 10 appointed a general court-martial to meet at the 3rd Division Headquarters on February 20, 1863, for the trial of Lieutenant Colonel Caspar Trepp. On February 1, Trepp realized that he must put up his own defense against Berdan's charges. He wrote to General Hancock, Commander of II Corps, requesting his assistance:

> I am exceedingly sorry to be compelled to annoy you with these lines, but the circumstances under which I am placed by the recklessness of Colonel Berdan necessitate me to address myself to you.
>
> Since October 6, 1862, Colonel Berdan has been under charges preferred against him for cowardice and other grave misconduct. He is now, I hope, on the point of being tried for his cowardice and misbehavior. In order to get us out of the way, he has arrested me, the Major of the regiment, and Captain Winthrope (both are brave officers and gentlemen in the very sense of the word, and civil life lawyers). Colonel Berdan is afraid of us all, as he knows we desire to have him prosecuted, and therefore, arrested us and served us with charges and specifications. One of the charges against me reaches back seven months to the 28th of June, or the day after our rifle pit affair.
>
> General, I do not pretend to be extraordinary in any situation, but I have done my duty as officer and soldier, when on detached service with General Smith's Division. I never was aware that I did receive any reprimand, neither by you, nor by General Smith. On the contrary, with soldier's pride, I recollect to have been complimented by you, as well as by General Smith.
>
> I wrote a similar letter to General Smith, with a few details, in regard to verbal orders given by him on that day. The object of this letter is to ask you to appear at my trial and to testify to my general character as an officer and soldier, while serving in that Division. The friendly way in which you remember me as often as we meet, encourages me to address these lines to you.
>
> Caspar Trepp
> Lieutenant Colonel
> 1st Regt. U.S. SharpShooters

And to General Smith, Trepp wrote:

> I am again compelled to trouble you about myself, and hope you will excuse me. It is of the greatest importance to me to have a statement from you about the verbal order given to me on the 28th of June, near the entrance of Fort Davidson.
>
> The charge preferred against me is a violation of the 52nd Article of War, and is as you well know, one of the gravest offenses a soldier can commit. The specification states that I shamefully abandoned Fort Davidson on the 28th of June.
>
> Your order was (I could swear to it), to abandon the fort as soon as the sappers had destroyed the rear face, and to march towards the camp of the 20th New York Regiment.
>
> As you are unfortunately absent, and my trial is to begin tomorrow, the 11th, will you please send me a few lines, stating what you remember of this order, and of what I did in pursuance of it. Also, what was my character as a soldier and officer while under your command. Also, whether you had occasion to give me honorable mention in your official reports. I can use your written statement in evidence, or can introduce it into my written defense.
>
> By doing so, you will deeply oblige me, especially as I am deprived of the testimony of General Hancock, he being absent.
>
> Caspar Trepp

On February 12, eighteen days after his arrest, Trepp petitioned his commander to be temporarily released from camp confinement, in order to gather statements from witnesses. Berdan refused, but forwarded Trepp's request on to the Judge Advocate of the case. The Judge Advocate informed Berdan that his department had nothing to do with the limits of Trepp's arrest, giving Berdan full rein to confine his movements in any way he wished. Berdan was to limit Trepp's ability to defend himself in every legal manner, but could not halt him from writing letters to others, seeking assistance. Major General William Smith, Commander of IX Corps, wrote a letter in Trepp's defense, stating:

> I can truly state that you did not shamefully abandon Fort Davidson on the 28th of June 1862, but that you left the Fort in accordance with my instructions. Also, I wish to express my surprise that anyone should prefer charges against you for acts performed while executing my own personal instructions.

The court-martial convened on February 20, and Trepp was represented by Colonel Vincent, Commander of the 83rd PV's. Trepp, as one might imagine, pleaded NOT GUILTY to all charges. Over the next few days, several officers and enlisted men were called as witnesses for the prosecution and for the defense.

On February 25th, the court was cleared for deliberation, then quickly found for the accused: NOT GUILTY ON ALL CHARGES AND SPECIFICATIONS. Trepp was acquitted. On March 2, the proceedings of the general court-martial were approved by higher headquarters, and Lieutenant Colonel Trepp was released from arrest and returned to active duty with his regiment.

Colonel Hiram Berdan's Court-Martial

On October 6, 1862, while Colonel Berdan was "recuperating from his wounds," formal charges were brought against him by Captain Benjamin Giroux, Commander of Company C, 1st Regiment of U.S. SharpShooters. Berdan had been absent from command for several months now, and Captain Giroux felt this an appropriate time to rid the unit of man he believed to be an inferior leader. The charges were forwarded to 1st Division Headquarters, then to V Corps Headquarters, and finally to Army of the Potomac Commander, Major General George McClellan.

CHARGES AND SPECIFICATIONS PREFERRED AGAINST COLONEL BERDAN, 1ST REGIMENT, UNITED STATES SharpShooters

CHARGE 1st: MISBEHAVIOR BEFORE THE ENEMY

Specification 1st: In this, that Colonel Hiram Berdan, 1st Regiment U.S. SharpShooters, at the Battle of Yorktown, on or about the 5th day of April 1862, while the battle was raging, the said Colonel Berdan abandoned his command and did take himself to the rear, entirely out of danger. And on or about the hour of six pm, did send a mounted orderly with verbal orders to his regiment to return or withdraw from the field to Camp, before the relief had arrived, which verbal order, when received by the officer in command refused to obey, until such time as the Commanding General had sent the relief to take possession of the field to be made vacant by the withdrawal of the 1st Regiment of U.S. SharpShooters. Said relief, having arrived at or about the hour of nine pm, being the 44th New York Volunteers, commanded by Major Chapin.

Specification 2nd: In this, that the said Colonel Berdan, on or about the 5th day of April 1862, at and during the Battle of Yorktown, between or about the hours of three and four pm, did take himself away and abandoned his regiment upon the battlefield, and neglected and abandoned his regiment without any orders or charge to the next officer in command.

Specification 3rd: In this, that said Colonel Berdan, on or about the 27th day of May 1862, did unaccompany his regiment on the march to the Battle of Hanover Court House, but abandoned his regiment to the Lieutenant Colonel Ripley, and that the said Colonel Berdan did make his appearance at Hanover Court House only after cessation of hostilities and victory won.

Specification 4th: In this, that said Colonel Berdan, without any sufficient cause or reason, failed to command his regiment at the Battle of Hanover Court House, but remained out of danger and took no part in said battle. This, on or about the 27th day of May 1862.

Specification 5th: In this, that said Colonel Berdan, on or about the 26th day of June 1862, at the Battle of Mechanicsville, Virginia, abandoned his command to his subordinates, and then and there, did take himself out of danger and far to the rear of the battleground, taking no part, therein.

Specification 6th:In this, that said Colonel Berdan did, on the 27th day of June 1862, at the Battle of Gaines Mill, Virginia, abandoned his command, and did take himself to the rear and across the Chickahominy River, and there remained with the teamsters of his regiment while the battle was raging, and took no part, therein.

Specification 7th: In this, that said Colonel Berdan did, on the 27th day of June 1862, during the Battle of Gaines Mill, mingled and concealed himself with the teamsters of said regiment, and there remained out of danger, and abandoned his command to his subordinates.

CHARGE 2nd: VIOLATION OF THE 52nd ARTICLE OF WAR

Specification 1st: In this, that said Colonel Berdan, on or about the 5th day of April, the 27th day of May, the 26th & 27th days of June 1862, respectively at the Battles of Yorktown, Hanover Court House, Mechanicsville and Gaines Mill, abandon his regiment while engaged in battle, did take himself far to the rear and out of danger, taking no part in said battles. But, in any case, abandoning his regiment to the command of his subordinates.

CHARGE 3rd: CONDUCT UNBECOMING AN OFFICER AND A GENTLEMAN

Specification 1st: In this, that said Colonel Berdan, on the 7th day of July 1862, in Camp at Harrison's Landing, Virginia, used violent language and gesticulations, without any cause or provocation toward Captains E. Weston and W.P. Austin, and toward Lieutenant Beebe, and placed the first two officers in arrest. Said Colonel Berdan, being then accompanied with two guards, and with pistol in hand.

Specification 2nd: In this, that said Colonel Berdan, on or about the 7th day of July 1862, did use personal and abusive language, without any just cause or provocation toward Captain B. Giroux. And that said Colonel Berdan did place in arrest and in close confinement, under a guard, the said Captain Giroux for eight days, and refused a court-martial, and a copy of the charges and specifications, after being demanded on the same day, by Captain Giroux.

Specification 3rd: In this, that said Colonel Berdan, on or about the 7th day of July 1862, order Captain Giroux to his place of confinement, while in company with Captains Weston and Austin, and Lieutenant Beebe, with pistol in hand, accompanied with two guards, and then and there used violent gesticulations and insulting language toward said officers.

Specification 4th: In this, that said Colonel Berdan did use personal violence upon the person of Corporal E.A. Wilson of Company C, 1st Regiment of U.S. SharpShooters, without any cause or provocation. This, on the march from the Chickahominy River to Williamsburg, Virginia, on or about the 17th day of August 1862.

Above: *A worried-looking Berdan faced a Court-Martial in late 1862.*

Specification 5th: In this, that said Colonel Berdan did, in a violent manner, make use of his sword upon the person of Private H.J. Stone of Company F, 1st Regiment of U.S. SharpShooters, without any cause or provocation. This, on the march to Warrenton, Virginia, on or about the 27th day of August 1862.

Conduct prejudicial to good order and military discipline:

Specification 6th: In this, that the said Colonel Berdan, as an officer in camp or field, has proven his inefficiency in all military tactics, even ignorance of the manual of arms, company and battalion drills, and of all evolutions of the line. That the said Colonel Berdan has proven himself neither officer, nor gentleman, by ignoring the rights and laws of preferment in appointing junior officers over their seniors, and arbitrarily adding their names to pay rolls, as for instance, in the case of one Lieutenant Gruin, and of the appointment of acting Quartermaster, a private soldier, then acting in the capacity of his private secretary. And of the indulgence of personal pique and choler in the illegal establishment of a full guard over the person and quarters of his officers for trivial offenses, and also by the menacing with weapons of line officers on occasions of simple and self-provoked altercations.

CHARGE 4th: COWARDICE

Specification 1st: In this, that the said Colonel Berdan did, on or about the 1st day of July 1862, at the Battle of Malvern Hill, abandon his regiment, and that during said battle, was not to be seen on the battleground or in command of his regiment. But, that the regiment was then and there commanded by Lieutenant Colonel Ripley. And further, that the said Colonel Berdan did abandon his regiment and take himself far to the rear and entirely out of danger, before or during the engagement.

Specification 2nd: In this, that said Colonel Berdan did, on the morning following the Battle of Malvern Hill, come to Captain B. Giroux, who was then on detached service to General McCall's Division (called the Pennsylvania Reserve), and requested of him to place a guard and to order all men of the 1st Regiment of U.S. SharpShooters to report to said Captain Giroux, and there to await further orders, said Colonel Berdan, not knowing where his command was situated, or having any knowledge of the same. This, at Harrison's Landing, Virginia, on or about the 2nd day of July 1862.

Captain B. Giroux
Commanding Company C
1st Regt. U.S. SharpShooters

Captain Giroux's charges and specifications against Colonel Berdan were approved by higher headquarters and eventually returned to Division level on February 1st, 1863. The four month wait found the accuser no longer a member of the U.S. SharpShooters, unfortunately. Therefore, a new unit officer stepped forward to bring charges, as they were known to him: Lieutenant Colonel Caspar Trepp. These were more correctly issued as counter charges, as Trepp was, at that very moment, under court-martial proceedings, himself.

CHARGES AND SPECIFICATIONS PREFERRED AGAINST COLONEL HIRAM BERDAN, 1st REGIMENT, U.S. SharpShooters

CHARGE: CONDUCT UNBECOMING AN OFFICER AND A GENTLEMAN

Specification 1st: In this, that the said Colonel Hiram Berdan, 1st Regiment U.S. SharpShooters, being in command of said regiment, having preferred charges and specifications against Lieutenant Colonel Caspar Trepp, 1st Regiment U.S. SharpShooters, for having shamefully abandoned a fort when on detached service in General Smith's Division, in command as Major of Companies A and I, did call one Henry Wolschlager, a private in said Company A, privately to Colonel Berdan's Headquarters and told him to caution the members of said company to be careful how they should testify and not to be too fast to swear that they left the fort last, as the men of Company I would testify that they left last, and had settled their minds on that fact, and Company A might get into trouble if they should testify to the contrary. Thereby attempting to tamper and intimidate witnesses expected to testify in defense of said Lieutenant Colonel Trepp. And having reference to the circumstances of the alleged abandonment of the fort by said Trepp.

Specification 2nd: In this, that the said Colonel Berdan, did call Second lieutenant Rudolf Aschmann, Commanding Company A, of said Regiment, privately to his Headquarters and said to him: "I understand that some of your men are going to be witnesses on the trial of Lieutenant-Colonel

Trepp's case tomorrow. Tell them to be cautious what they testify, and not to testify anything but what they know to be fact." That the said Colonel Berdan then asked when Company A left the fort, to which Lieutenant Aschmann replied: "last." And that said Colonel Berdan then said: "No! That is not so. Company I came out last. You cannot testify that you came out last. You must tell your men that if any of them should be caught in the cross-examination, they will be court-martialed. And I should be sorry that to happen to so good a Company as Company A. The President of the Court is a Brigadier General and officer of the regular army, and will be very particular." Thereby attempting to tamper with and intimidate witnesses expected to testify in said Lieutenant Colonel Trepp's defense.

Caspar Trepp
Lieutenant Colonel
1st Regt. U.S. SharpShooters

Trepp's charges against Berdan were filed with higher headquarters, and they were added to charges made by another U.S.S.S. officer, Captain Charles W. Seaton, Commander of Company F. Seaton redrafted the charges originally made by the now-departed Captain Giroux, regarding Colonel Berdan's alleged misconduct and cowardice. These, then, became the basis of the official court-martial proceedings against the Chief of SharpShooters:

CHARGES AND SPECIFICATIONS AGAINST COLONEL HIRAM BERDAN, 1st REGIMENT OF U.S. SharpShooters

CHARGE 1st: MISBEHAVIOR BEFORE THE ENEMY

Specification 1st: In this, that said Colonel Hiram Berdan, 1st Regiment U.S. SharpShooters, did, on or about the 21st day of June 1862, after starting with his regiment on the march for the battlefield at Mechanicsville, Virginia, return to the camp of his regiment near Gaines Mill and absent himself entirely from his regiment, leaving the regiment in charge of the acting adjutant, Lieutenant J. Smith Brown, no field officer being present. The regiment being finally taken into action by Lieutenant Colonel Ripley.

Specification 2nd: In this, that said Colonel Berdan did, on or about the 27th day of June 1862, near Gaines Mill, after the Army was drawn up for battle and his regiment in position awaiting the enemy, leave and remain absent from it while engaged, and from the engagement, only appearing on the field for a short time in the rear, and remaining during the action, or a greater part thereof, on the other side of the Chickahominy River, and did not rejoin his regiment till the next morning.

Specification 3rd: In this, that said Colonel Berdan did, near White Oak Swamp, Virginia, on or about the 29th day of June 1862, while his regiment was on duty and expecting an attack by the enemy, absent himself from his regiment and remain absent during the most of the day.

Specification 4th: In this, that the said Colonel Berdan did, on or about the 11th day of July 1862, at Malvern Hills, Virginia, after posting his regiment in the front, absent himself from, and go to the rear, saying that he was going to get some meat cooked for the men, and did remain absent from his regiment during the whole engagement, his regiment being actively engaged in the fight.

Specification 5th: In this, that the said Colonel Berdan did, on or about the 30th day of August 1862, on the battlefield of Bull Run, leave his regiment, while engaged, in the early part of the engagement, and did go to the rear and there remain, till the engagement was over.

CHARGE 2nd: CONDUCT UNBECOMING AN OFFICER AND A GENTLEMAN

Specification 1st: In this, that the said Colonel Berdan did, on or about the 29th day of August 1862, near Gainesville, Virginia, when it was expected his Regiment would go into action, leave the regiment without turning over the command to the officer next in rank, or giving any instructions to said officers, and remain absent a considerable time while the regiment was moved forward the field, and was being formed in line of battle.

Specification 2nd: In this, that the said Colonel Berdan has been in the habit of frequently absenting himself from his regiment for hours together, while on the march while on the Peninsula and in Virginia, during the months of May, June, July and August 1862, when it was possible that the enemy might be encountered, without turning over the command to the officer next in rank, and particularly on the 28th day of August 1862, near Bristoe Station, Virginia, when he left his regiment on the march, and did not return to it until after it had gone into camp, though an attack was thought probable from the enemy and the Division, including his regiment was encamped in position to receive such attack.

Specification 3rd: In this, that the said Colonel Berdan did, on or about the month of September or October 1862, write, or cause to be written, a letter to Lieutenant J. Smith Brown, who had lately been acting adjutant of the said regiment, requesting him to sign a statement prepared by said Colonel Berdan exculpating him from blame for the publication in a newspaper of his official report of the battle of the 30th day of August 1862, near Bull Run. Said statement, representing that he, said Brown, could only account for the publication of said report by supposing that the newspaper reporter had taken it from his, said Berdan's, tent when he, said Brown, was asleep. And when he, said Brown, had been reprimanded by said Berdan for his carelessness in leaving said report so exposed. Which statement, so prepared for said Brown to sign, as aforesaid, he the said Colonel Berdan, knew to be false.

Specification 4th: In this, that the said Colonel Berdan did, at camp near Falmouth, Virginia, on or about the 19th day of December 1862, at an inspection of his regiment, made by Lieutenant Colonel Bertram, Inspector General of the 5th Army Corps, on being asked by said Inspecting Officer why some of his companies were unprovided with bayonets, answer that "such companies drew rifles which had no bayonets and that there were no bayonets to issue with the rifles at the time. Said rifles being some that had been turned in by other men who had lost or thrown away the bayonets belonging to them." When the real reason was that said Colonel Berdan had given those companies the privilege of taking the rifles without bayonets, and the rifles were new when drawn, and provided with bayonets packed in the same boxes with the rifles. And that the said Colonel Berdan knew the reason given by him in answer to the inquiry by said Inspecting Officer was false.

Specification 5th: In this, that the said Colonel Berdan did, at camp near Falmouth, Virginia, on or about the 29th day of December 1862, write an official letter to Lieutenant Colonel Lewis Richmond, Assistant Adjutant General of the Army of the Potomac, asking to have the 2nd Regiment U.S. SharpShooters, which was then attached to General King's Division, transferred and placed under his, Colonel Berdan's command, stating as a reason for such transfer, that he had many hundred applications from recruits to join his command, and that the 1st Regiment of U.S. SharpShooters was full. And he desired to place the recruits so applying in the 2nd Regiment, which statement that the 1st Regiment was full was wholly false, then being on the rolls of said 1st Regiment not exceeding seven hundred and twelve enlisted men, of whom two hundred and ten were absent, as shown by the morning report of that day.

Charles W. Seaton Captain
Company F
1st Regt. U.S.S.S.

On March 2, 1863, Colonel Berdan was placed under arrest by order of Brigadier General Whipple, Commander of the 3rd Division, and made to answer to Captain Seaton's charges, At 9 o'clock on the following day, the official court-martial of Colonel Hiram Berdan commenced, Berdan immediately asked that all charges be dismissed, stating the following reasons:

> First, that I was not accountable or responsible to my inferiors for my absences from all or any part of my command,
>
> Second, that my commanding officers, who were familiar with the circumstances and the orders that I was under, were repeatedly informed of this, and similar complaints, but have never taken any notice of them,
>
> Third, that nearly every specification refers to time and place when Captain Seaton was absent from the regiment,
>
> Fourth, that Captain Seaton was in arrest by my order before the charges and specifications were referred to me,
>
> Fifth, that these charges and specifications do not contain an endorsement of my Commanding Officer, that would make him in any way responsible to me for the disgrace I would sustain by being court-martialed, should the charges not be sustained,
>
> Sixth, that these charges and specifications were not forwarded through the proper channel.

Berdan's plea was not accepted, and the trial proceeded the following day, with his pleading of *"NOT GUILTY"* to all charges and specifications. The following statements were made in the trial that followed:

> Captain Charles Seaton: "On the 26th of June 1862, Colonel Berdan disappeared as we approached the firing near Mechanicsville, On the 27th of June, Colonel Berdan was absent from the skirmishing, and was seen escorting the ill Lieutenant Colonel Ripley to the rear, for medical treatment, leaving no field grade officer in charge of the SharpShooters, Colonel Berdan was absent from the fighting all day on June 29th, and on July 1st, 1862,"
>
> Captain Charles D. Mclean: "The Colonel was not with our unit during the fighting on June 26th and 27th, and on July 1st, 1862,"
>
> Private Edward Trusk: "During the Battle of Gaines Mill Colonel Berdan was in the rear supply area, not at the front."
>
> Corporal Cassius Peck: "When Lieutenant Colonel Ripley told Colonel Berdan to see to the men, Berdan said to leave them to the Captains,"
>
> Lieutenant J, Smith Brown: "On June 26th, Colonel Berdan told me that he was going to the rear to protect the sick. On July 1st, I met Colonel Berdan in the rear, He said that he had gone for some fresh meat, and was having it cooked for the men. On August 30th, as soon as the fighting started, Colonel Berdan departed, saying that he was going to see General Porter,"
>
> Major George Hastings: "Colonel Berdan lied to the Inspector-General regarding the receipt of Sharps rifles without bayonets,"
>
> Captain James H. Baker: "Colonel Berdan told me to turn the bayonets in, as he had given us permission to use the rifles without bayonets,"
>
> Major General Butterfield: "Colonel Berdan was not with his command on August 30th, the second battle of Bull Run."

On March 10th, the court deliberated and found Colonel Berdan to be *NOT GUILTY* to all charges preferred by Captain Seaton. The following day, a similar verdict was passed down, regarding all charges preferred by Lieutenant Colonel Trepp. The Court further stated:

> The charges and specifications preferred by Lieutenant Colonel Trepp against Colonel Berdan were frivolous and vexatious, and the Court does recommend that Lieutenant Colonel Trepp be reprimanded by the Commanding General.

The Court stood adjourned on March 13th, and the proceedings were reviewed by higher authority, and issued two weeks later:

> The reviewing officer regards the evidence in the foregoing trial of Colonel Berdan in a different light from that in which it is viewed by the Court. The substance of the specifications is clearly proved. The Court has acquitted the accused, evidently upon the belief that his intention was not to tamper with or intimidate the witnesses. Admitting that no sinister design was intended, the acts in question were highly improper in their character. The proceedings of the Court are disapproved.
>
> By Command of Brigadier General Whipple
> Commander 3rd Division
> Henry R. Dalton
> Captain
> Assistant Adjutant-General

In the published verdict and review, it was stated:

Above: *A noticeably older looking Berdan emerges from his trial and a period of illness.He was cleared of the charges and able to resume his position as Chief of SharpShooters in March 1863.*

In reviewing the testimony of the proceeding case, the 1st, 2nd, 4th, and portions of other specifications of the 1st charge are clearly proved, yet the Court, for reasons stated at the close of the trial, gives a verdict of NOT GUILTY.

The reviewing officer regrets to differ from the opinion of the Court. The four companies in this case constituted the sole command of Colonel Berdan. A commanding officer is expected to be with his troops, especially upon the field of battle, and during an engagement. A proof of absence from his command at such a period is prima facie evidence of misbehavior, or, at least of neglect of duty, which requires explanation upon his part. But here the Court has interposed and informed the accused that it is unnecessary for him to produce evidence in his own behalf. This is greatly to be regretted. However, if the Court has committed an error in this matter, the accused should not suffer in consequence. Besides, while officers of integrity and honor, like those of whom the Court is composed, find nothing in the evidence adduced, calculated to cast a shade of reproach upon the accused, it is fair to presume that he also believed that he had done all that duty required of him under the circumstances. The reviewing officer is content to record his dissent from the principles upon which the Court based its decision.

The proceedings are hereby confirmed. Colonel Hiram Berdan is relieved from arrest, and will return to duty.

By Command of General Whipple
Henry R. Dalton, Captain
Assistant Adjutant General

General Whipple was not pleased with the circumstances that led to Colonel Berdan's arrest and trial, as evidenced by his letter, dated April 4, 1863:

> Charges have, for a long time, been hanging over Colonel Berdan, and by passing through successive Commanders and the Commander-in-Chief, have become well known to the Army.
>
> Moreover, Colonel Berdan shows a limitable ignorance of military affairs in supposing that by the course pursued, he could circumvent the acts of his superior and arrest a trial by a general court-martial, legally convened.

This was not the last word on this matter. Three weeks later, Lieutenant Colonel Caspar Trepp wrote to General Whipple, and asked if the court proceedings might be printed, for distribution. His intention was to quiet Colonel Berdan, who, it appears, was boasting to all that would listen, that his acquittal was *"a triumphant refutation of all that has ever been alleged against him."*

General Whipple ordered the proceedings published, and Colonel Berdan's boasts ceased forthwith. But this did not end the story. General Whipple, for reasons unknown, rescinded his disapproval of Berdan's court-martial on April 9th.

Chancellorsville and Gettysburg

On March 29, 1863, Colonel Berdan resumed his position as Chief of SharpShooters. Lieutenant Colonel Trepp, as next in command, was made Commanding Officer of the 1st Regiment of U.S.S.S., while Major Homer Stoughton continued to command the 2nd U.S.S.S. They and the rest of the Army of the Potomac were in winter quarters, in camp near Falmouth, Virginia. The camp was located on the east bank of the Rappahannock River, and north of the Confederate occupied city of Fredericksburg. Every soldier awaited clear weather and the coming spring offensive. Years later, Captain Rudolf Aschmann recalled this winter encampment:

Above: *A silver medal from the 2nd Regiment of Sharp-shooters possible awarded for shooting skill.*

> In the beginning of spring we constructed, close to camp, a beautiful rifle range where almost daily target practice was held. In the month of April, the troops even had a shooting match, in conjunction with other amusements such as sprinting contests, sack races, climbing, etc. Prizes worth $150, contributed by the officers in voluntary donations, consisted of a gold medal, worth $50, for the best marksman, and a silver one, worth $20, for the second best. There were also several smaller gifts of $10 each.
>
> As usual in winter quarters, time was spent on regular drills and other camp duties. Now, just like the other regiments, we too were required to provide a team of men for picket duty. Previously this had never been the case, except in an occasional emergency, when we had to assist the outposts during the day. But we could always return to camp at night. Since the outpost line was some seven miles from camp, the teams were relieved only every three days. A tour of duty usually took four days, what with the preceding parade and inspection, and marching back and forth.
>
> As we never took any tents along, in order not to expose the insides of our quarters to rain and snow, we often had to suffer terribly from the wretched winter weather. The huts at the outpost line consisted only of a miserable lattice-work of pine branches, and could give us little protection. Although the enemy's position was not in close proximity and he moved to winter quarters himself, still the number of people needed for field guard duty was so great, that each team had to take a turn every ninth day.

Of this very same period, Lieutenant Colonel Ripley stated in his memoirs:

> On the 5th of April, the 1st Regiment had a grand celebration to mark the anniversary of the advance on Yorktown, where the SharpShooters had been under rebel fire for the first time. Target shooting, foot races, jumping, and wrestling were indulged in for small prizes. General Whipple, the Division Commander, ac-companied by several ladies who were visiting friends in camp, were interested spectators.

Below: *Winter camp of the SharpShooters at Falmouth, Virginia in February 1863.*

Above: Lieutenant William P. Shreve (left) in the winter of 1862-63 shortly after he and Lieutenant Calef (seen at right) were added to Colonel Berdan's staff when he resumed his role as Chief of Sharpshooters. The soldier in the middle of the picture is unidentified.

On April 8th, the Army of the Potomac was visited by President Lincoln. After conferring with Major General Hooker, Lincoln reviewed portions of the command, including the SharpShooters.

Barely two days after resuming command, Colonel Berdan petitioned Headquarters of III Corps to allow him ten days leave to travel to New York on private business. He mentioned a legal case involving the sum of $12,000, wherein he had obtained a judgment in November 1862. He spoke of a new trial which was scheduled for the end of April, but did not mention its scope or purpose. Unfortunately, a search of the state judicial records failed to turn up such a case, so possibly Berdan was neither the defendant nor the plaintiff in the action. His request was approved by his superior, General Whipple, the 3rd Division Commander. Upon his return, Berdan resumed his position as Chief of SharpShooters, and Lieutenant Colonel Trepp assumed command of the 1st Regiment.

Around this same time Colonel Berdan requested additional target rifles for his command, stating that the regiment still had some in storage at the Washington Arsenal, Possibly these were some of the heavy-barrel target rifles brought by the newly enlisted SharpShooters in 1861. It is not known if higher headquarters ever agreed to this request, as there is no reply in the regimental papers.

One of Trepp's many duties with the regiment during this time was supply, and to that end he had no peer, Surviving records prove that he believed strongly in unit and individual accountability. The following inventory gives us an accurate picture of the weaponry and accoutrements carried by the 1st Regiment on March 31, 1863:

Sharps rifles (cal,52)	426
bayonets	247
bayonet scabbards	255
leather cap pouches	426
leather cartridge boxes	426
metal cartridge box plates	c.322
leather cartridge box belts	c.409
metal belt plates	c.344
leather gun slings	316
leather waist belts	c.426
metal waist belt plates	425
firearm screwdrivers	165
gun wipers	100
wiping rods	12

In late April, Berdan resumed his quest for promotion to brigadier general. He forwarded a petition for his promotion, signed by officers of the 1st and 2nd Regiments of SharpShooters, to higher headquarters. Berdan also wrote to the President, as evidenced by the following letter from Army of the Potomac Commander, General Joseph Hooker:

Headquarters, Army of the Potomac
April 21, 1863

For His Excellency,
The President of the United States

My President:
Colonel Berdan handed me, this evening, your note of the 16th inst. respecting his promotion. I have had no opportunity to judge his services personally. I am informed by his Commanding Officers that he talks better than he acts. In all events, no wrong or injustice will be done him by allowing

his claims to rest until after the next fight. My sense of duty then will allow me to recommend him for promotion.
Joseph Hooker
Major General Commanding

The Battle of Chancellorsville

As spring approached, detachments on both sides penetrated each other's lines, testing the other in anticipation of the battles that would follow. General Hooker, untested Commander of the Army of the Potomac, was expected to be decisive in his offensive operations, unlike the actions of his predecessors. He received direct encouragement from President Lincoln during the Commander-In-Chief's visit to the Army of the Potomac from April 5th to the 10th.

On April 12th, Hooker wrote Lincoln, informing him of his battle plan to move across the Rappahannock River, attack and turn the Confederate left. His cavalry would make a wide sweep, hit Lee's rear echelons, cut Confederate communications with Richmond, and harass any troops seeking to retreat. It was a bold plan, and would take Hooker's infantry more than two weeks to begin their movement.

Most of the Army of the Potomac, under General Hooker's immediate command, some 70,000 men, began to march northwest and crossed the Rappahannock, upstream from Fredericksburg. The remaining Federal troops would hold Lee's Confederate Army in position, while Hooker's main force would approach from the rear. The 1st and 2nd Regiments of SharpShooters prepared for the pending action by drawing eight days rations and sixty rounds of ammunition per man, and by turning in all of their winter clothing and camp baggage.

Major General Reynolds' I Corps, Major General Daniel E. Sickles' III Corps, and Major General John Sedgwick's VI Corps moved south and east of Fredericksburg still on the Union side of the Rappahannock River, to hold Lee. As part of Sickles' III Corps, the SharpShooters marched down river in the late afternoon of April 29th, to a position opposite and south of Fredericksburg. The SharpShooters held this defensive position with III Corps through the afternoon of the 30th. The weather was rainy, but surprisingly warm for late April.

Meanwhile, the larger part of Hooker's Army of the Potomac had completed its march northwest, then south and had crossed the Rappahannock, then the Rapidan Rivers, to positions near the small town of Chancellorsville, Virginia. Much of their force was in position by mid-afternoon on April 30th. General Hooker had succeeded in moving a large Federal force to Lee's left and rear, without opposition and apparently unnoticed. A bold Federal attack to the east would catch Lee's Army of Northern Virginia against the river, with the Union I, III, V, and VI Corps, ready to halt any escape southward toward Richmond. However, this massive operation, with its aggressive strategy, never took place.

With the Chancellor house as a focal point, Hooker assembled Major General Darius N. Couch's I Corps, Major General George G. Meade's V Corps, Major General Oliver O. Howard's XI Corps, and Major General Henry W. Slocum's XII Corps. Approximately 60,000 men were now in the vicinity of Chancellorsville, ready to continue the offensive maneuver, unless discovered by Lee.

Above: *Major General Daniel E.Sickles whose III Corps the SharpShooters were attached to at Chancellorsville.*

Most of Lee's Army of Northern Virginia was still near Fredericksburg, observing Major General John Sedgwick's VI Corps to the east. When Lee received intelligence about Hooker's movements on April 30th, he decided to move most of his army in an attempt to engage Hooker's main body at its present position near Chancellorsville, nearly twenty miles to the west. Lee left Major General Jubal A. Early's force of 8,596 Confederate soldiers in place to oppose Sedgwick's VI Corps of 23,667 Federal troops.

General Sickles' III Corps (still with Sedgwick's VI Corps) received orders from Hooker to march to Chancellorsville. Therefore, the Corps, including the 1st and 2nd Regiments of SharpShooters, left its position on the east bank near Fredericksburg at 2pm, and marched nearly twenty miles, northwest and parallel to the Rappahannock River, approaching the United States Ford. There, the soldiers bivouacked for the night, ready to cross in the morning.

A captured Confederate courier's dispatch proved conclusively to Hooker on April 30th, that Lee was now aware of the Union surprise advance to Chancellorsville. A captured Confederate engineering officer's diary was additional proof that the Army of Northern Virginia anticipated that a fight would probably occur at Chancellorsville. Hooker, in a fateful decision that has been questioned over and over again, decided to halt the offensive, and draw his force into the best defensive position possible. This, he believed, would invite Lee to attack him. He put this plan into effect over the objec-

***Above:** First Lieutenant Benjamin S. Calef, Regimental Quartermaster of the 2nd U.S. SharpShooters, photographed on the heights near Centerville, Virginia.*

tions of his esteemed Corps commanders, who felt that they should maintain the offensive and boldly strike Lee from the rear. Hooker did not listen, and ordered his Corps commanders to make no advance.

At 7:30 A.M. on May 1st, III Corps began crossing the Rappahannock River on Federal pontoon bridges at the U.S. Ford. Since the Corps consisted of over 18,700 men, it took several hours to complete the movement. The SharpShooters finally crossed at 9 A.M., then proceeded south, until they took up assigned positions in the area the men called "the wilderness," near Chancellorsville.

By noon, Meade's V Corps was on Hooker's left flank, and moving east along the River Road toward the strategic Bank's Ford. The 2nd Division, under Sykes, had advanced east along the Old Orange Turnpike, alone, and would run headlong into McLaws' Division of Confederate infantry. Slocum's XII Corps was more concentrated, along the Orange Plank Road. Couch's II Corps centered its forces in the vicinity of the Chancellor house, except for Hancock's Division which had been sent forward to support Sykes. Sickles' III Corps was just arriving from the north, and was also in the area of Hooker's headquarters at the Chancellor house. Howard's XII Corps occupied positions along an east-west line at the extreme right flank of the Federal forces, in the vicinity of the Wilderness Church, and was, in essence, held in reserve.

By mid-afternoon, Slocum's XII Corps was squarely against the Confederate forces of Anderson's Division. Sykes' 2nd Division of Meade's V Corps was in danger of being cut off, so this division, Hancock's Division and the XII Corps were ordered to fall back into more secure defensive positions closer to the Chancellor house. Humphreys' and Griffin's Divisions of Meade's V Corps were already several miles east, and advancing toward their objective, Bank's Ford. They were summarily recalled to Chancellorsville by Hooker in mid-afternoon.

Darkness found the Union troops in a convex line, stretching on the north from Scott's Dam, south to the Great Meadow Swamp, then west to the Wilderness Church. The SharpShooters were formed into two lines as skirmishers in front of the III Corps. They were positioned just east of the

Chancellor house. There they remained until midnight, when they were ordered to the rear, on the road to the United States Ford, and bivouacked for the night. Hooker had lost all of the tactical advantage that his initial offensive had given him. Lee, with barely 47,000 men at his disposal, was surprised and confused by Hooker's decision to go on the defensive, but pressed forward into the afternoon of May 1st.

A late night conference on the evening of the 1st found Lee, Stuart and Jackson planning the next offensive strike. Lee, master strategist that he was, boldly decided to split his forces once again, ordering Lieutenant General Thomas "Stonewall" Jackson to take 26,000 men and attack the exposed right flank of Hooker's Army (Howard's XI Corps), still in static positions of defense and in reserve. Lee planned to attack Hooker's front with the remaining 11,000 Confederate infantry and artillery troops at his disposal, in a feint to draw attention away from Jackson's primary flank attack. It was a daring plan, and full of the risks that come of fragmenting already outnumbered forces.

Saturday morning, May 2nd, found Brigadier General David B. Birney's 1st Division of III Corps at Hazel Grove, about 2 miles southwest of Chancellorsville. Federal observers posted in tall trees spotted the early movement of Jackson's column about 8 A.M., as they were crossing an exposed ridge about a mile to the south. They reported that the enemy was headed "away from the front." When it was within range, about 1,600 yards, Clark's artillery battery was ordered to fire, in an attempt to disrupt the column's advance. But incredibly, Jackson's movement continued, nearly unabated, for more than three hours.

At about 9:30 A.M. a message was sent by Hooker to Howard, reminding him that XI Corps was positioned to repulse only a frontal attack. He directed his Corps commander to examine the area of his exposed right flank, and to be prepared if an attack should come from that direction. Unfortunately for the Army of the Potomac, Hooker's message was worded more like a suggestion than an order, and was not heeded by Howard.

Later in the morning, Howard wrote to Hooker of his observation of *"a column of infantry, moving westward on a road parallel* [to his own] *...and* [to the] *south."* Further, he wrote that he was *"taking measures to resist an attack from the west,"* but no evidence of this preparation exists. Jackson's movement to contact, therefore, came as no surprise to XI Corps.

In mid-morning, Major General Sickles, III Corps Commander, was ordered to make a reconnaissance to his front and left. The 11th Massachusetts and the 26th Pennsylvania were detailed for this mission, each with a detachment of skirmishers from Berdan's SharpShooters. In his after-action report, Colonel William Blaisdell, Commander of the 11th Massachusetts Infantry, chastised the "cowardice" displayed by some of the SharpShooters detailed to accompany this reconnaissance:

> I censure in the highest terms the conduct of some of Berdan's SharpShooters, who were sent as skirmishers. It was impossible to keep them to the front, and I was obliged to send some of my own men to the front, as skirmishers, armed only with smoothbore muskets.

This unfavorable report was one of very few condemnations ever made regarding an element of Berdan SharpShooters. Indeed, their service throughout the war was exemplary in all respects. About noon, Colonel Berdan was ordered by Brigadier General Birney to conduct a reconnaissance-in-force through the dense woods southeast of their position. They were *"to advance cautiously toward the road travelled by the enemy column, and to harass the movement as much as possible."* As they proceeded, enemy skirmishers fell back and regrouped at the knoll at Catharine's Furnace (referred to by Berdan as "the foundry"). The firepower from the SharpShooters' breechloading Sharps rifles overpowered the Confederates, and many surrendered. Meanwhile, several brigades of infantry in Sickles' III Corps swung south and east, using their left flank almost like a pivot, following Berdan's advance.

Except for Howard's XI Corps, the entire Union force at Chancellorsville now faced southeast. It confronted what the troops thought was Lee's main army, one mile to the east, but they were mistaken. In his after-action report, Colonel Berdan mentions "the retreat of a wagon train, moving down the road," What he saw was not a retreat at all, but the tail-end of Jackson's movement to outflank the Union line. Berdan had seen the supply wagons, ambulances and ammunition carts of a large Confederate force moving south and west along Furnace Road.

Had Berdan been able to accurately report what was occurring to his front, the battle could have ended differently, Had Hooker received positive confirmation of a major Confederate movement, intent on attacking his exposed right flank, he would have had sufficient time to move General Howard's troops to meet them. He also would have had time to bolster the army's right flank with troops then in reserve, and to recall Sickles' III Corps back into an east-west defensive line, Berdan's failure to complete a successful reconnaissance was a serious oversight, with disastrous ramifications for the Army of the Potomac, and for the military career of General Hooker,

In typical fashion, Berdan reported capturing *"365 of the enemy, including 10 officers,"* Major General Sickles, however, later disputed Berdan's figures, and said that the SharpShooters only captured 100 of the enemy. Meanwhile, Stonewall Jackson's three-mile-long column had proceeded south on Furnace Road, then northwest, utilizing part of Brock Road, and finally turned east on the Old Orange Turnpike to face the right flank of Howard's XI Corps. At 2:45 P.M. a major commanding an outpost on Howard's extreme right flank sent an urgent message that should have been heeded:

> A large body of the enemy is massing in my front. For God's sake, make disposition to receive him.

The message was repeated 15 minutes later, but still without reaction from the Commander of XI Corps.

Throughout the day Lee maintained pressure on Hooker's main line with constant skirmish assaults to draw attention away from Jackson's upcoming attack on the Union right. At 4:10 P.M., Hooker sent an order to Sedgwick's VI Corps to cross the river, capture

Above: *First Lieutenant William P. Shreve*

Fredericksburg, and pursue the enemy. Hooker was mistakenly, convinced that the Army of Northern Virginia was beginning to flee.

It had taken Jackson nearly all day to move his infantry into attack positions. They were finally in line of battle by 5:15 P.M., with only a few hours of daylight left in which to fight. The brilliant flank assault that ensued caught XI Corps totally unprepared. The Union right crumbled, and nearly thirteen thousand men retreated in panic toward Hooker's main force near Chancellorsville, despite Howard's heroic attempts to rally them.

The Confederate battle plan was nearly flawless, but for the natural confusion encountered by men fighting in scrub brush and thickets by twilight. It was under these adverse conditions that the triumphant Confederates suffered their major casualty, an accidental shooting by their own men, of one of the South's greatest leaders, Stonewall Jackson. He was mortally wounded at 9 P.M. on the evening of May 2nd, while riding in a forward battle area.

Around midnight Berdan and the other III Corps troops that were around him were ordered to withdraw. Under the light of a nearly full moon, the men fell back to the position they had occupied earlier in the day. They would soon be aware of the disaster that had befallen Howard's XI Corps. At the same hour, General Birney's 1st Division attacked the Confederates on the Union right, stopping their advance.

On Sunday, May 3rd, mortally wounded Jackson was unable to continue to lead his command. Lee chose Confederate Cavalry General J.E.B. Stuart to take charge and continue to push the disorganized Federals from the west. Lee attacked from the east, and the Confederate semi-circle tightened on Hooker's Army.

At morning, Berdan's SharpShooters were recalled from General Birney's command, and attached, directly, to General Whipple. The 1st Regiment of SharpShooters was posted in the woods, on the right of the Plank Road, and were ordered to advance firing. Berdan stated that they drove the enemy skirmishers back, claiming to have taken "more than 318 prisoners." The advance halted when they encountered the main body of the Confederate infantry, forcing them to withdraw. Berdan's 2nd Regiment had been held in reserve.

Throughout the morning the fighting see-sawed back and forth. Hooker then ordered his troops at Hazel Grove to withdraw, allowing Confederate infantry and artillery to assume the newly abandoned positions.

On Sunday afternoon a detachment of 120 Sharp-shooters under the command of Captain Wilson was posted near the building utilized as a Federal hospital. They drove the enemy from the immediate woods and acted as pickets for V Corps. Soon after, Wilson's SharpShooters were ordered by General Sickles to move left, and establish a picket line in front of III Corps, which they did. Meanwhile, Berdan's main body of 1st and 2nd Regiments of SharpShooters dug hastily constructed earthworks alongside the main infantry forces of III Corps.

Stuart's and Lee's infantrymen finally linked up and hammered Hooker's Federals to the north. Lee's relentless Confederate attack forced Hooker to withdraw his army toward U.S. Ford. There they set up more secure defensive positions with the Rappahannock on their left, and the Rapidan on their right.

Operating on orders from Hooker to push Major General Early out of the way and hasten to Chancellorsville to attack Lee from the rear, Sedgwick succeeded after two unsuccessful attempts. His VI Corps forced Early from the heights above Fredericksburg. In response, about noon, Lee had to send a portion of his force south to oppose the advancing Sedgwick. Lee was unable to deliver the knockout blow against Hooker, whose forces were converged around Chancellorsville. The engagement against Sedgwick occurred at Salem Church, and lasted until dark. On Monday morning, May 4th, a detail of Berdan SharpShooters was summoned to advance closer to the enemy's line and silence opposing SharpShooters, who were wreaking havoc on the Union troops. Ten volunteers advanced, forcing the Confederate marksmen back to their main line, and silencing their well aimed guns.

Lee's Army was now in full command of the battlefield. Major General Jubal Early's men had recovered from their defeat the day earlier, to advance north and attack Sedgwick's rear at Salem Church. Nearly cut off from the rest of the Army of the Potomac, Sedgwick found it prudent to retreat to the relative safety of the other side of the Rappahannock, during the evening I hours of May 4th.

Also on Monday evening, a tragic mistake occurred, as elements of the 11th New Jersey Infantry accidentally opened fire on the 2nd Regiment. Four SharpShooters were wounded before the New Jersey troops realized their mistake and ceased fire. The posting of Berdan SharpShooters as skirmishers, ahead of the main body of troops, had its inherent risks. Just before darkness, the SharpShooters retired across the river, along with the remainder of Sickles' III Corps.

The following day, May 5th, the rest of Hooker's defeated Army retreated across the Rappahannock and the Battle of Chancellorsville was over. General Robert E. Lee's army had defeated Hooker's vastly superior force through innovative planning, deception and execution. Hooker lost the battle, and eventually his command, but Lee had lost Stonewall Jackson. This was to prove a deprivation from which the Army of Northern Virginia would never recover. No Confederate General could match Jackson's dash, charisma, leadership or effectiveness, except, perhaps, for Lee, himself.

Chancellorsville Losses

Berdan's 3rd Brigade at Chancellorsville consisted of both the 1st and 2nd Regiments of SharpShooters. In his after-action report, Berdan boasted of capturing "683 prisoners," and having expended "over 60 rounds of ammunition per man." While the number of prisoners seems high, it is surprising that the number of rounds expended was so low, especially considering the amount of front-line action seen by the SharpShooters.

Berdan reported that one officer, Lieutenant Byron Brewer of C Company, 1st Regiment was killed, along with the loss of ten enlisted men. Five officers were wounded, including Major George Hastings, Captain James Baker, Captain Frank Marble, and Lieutenant William Horton. 54 enlisted men were wounded, and another 12 were counted as missing or captured.

Of the 133,868 Federal troops engaged, 1,606 were killed, 9,762 were wounded, and 5,919 were reported missing or captured. There were an estimated 60,000 Confederate troops engaged, with 1,665 killed, 9,081 wounded, and 2,018 missing or captured. Despite nearly identical losses, this battle was, without a doubt, a success for the Confederacy, and yet another defeat for the Union. The confidence of the soldiers of the Army of Northern Virginia reached new heights, while the morale of the Army of the Potomac reached unprecedented depths.

Hooker's defeated Federal Army recrossed the Rappahannock River, escaping Lee's infantry. An untimely downpour soon turned the roads and trails into mud, further diminishing the spirits of the men in blue and green. Berdan's 3rd Brigade was part of this dejected group, who found their way back to their encampment at Falmouth, Virginia. So the Army of the Potomac rested, cared for its wounded, and readied for the continued offensive. They were not aware at that time that it would be Lee's offensive, not their own, that would soon come.

Berdan's Behavior: Another View

The following documents reveal for the first time what may be the true story of Colonel Berdan's actions at the Battle of Chancellorsville. The letters were discovered in Lieutenant Colonel Trepp's Volunteer Service File, but do not appear in the official Regimental Record Book of the SharpShooters. Nevertheless, Berdan's less than exemplary field leadership throughout 1862 tends to make Trepp's account more believable than that of his commander:

> Judge Advocate-General's Office
> Washington
> May 11,1863
>
> My Dear Trepp:
> Yours, by hand of Quartermaster Calef, is just received. I rejoice to hear that you are all safe. I will take charge of the Major's baggage, which Calef has brought up to Brown's Hotel.
>
> Do not prefer charges against the party to whom you allude. Instead of this, make up an account of his proceedings, in full, of the late battle – formally written out and signed by all the officers cognizant of the facts. Stating also that he was court-martialed for similar conduct on repeated occasions before. Copy the remarks of General Whipple in reviewing the proceedings.
>
> Address to Hon. E.M. Stanton and send it to the War Department direct, by mail. I assure you from what I learn here, that this is the best course, and one often pursued in similar cases. If you could send up with your Chancellorsville paper, a full copy of the record at his court-martial, it would be well.
>
> On these facts, the Secretary will order him to be struck from the rolls at once. This is the best, by far, the best course.
> H.H. Winthrope

Trepp was later to follow Winthrope's advice and write directly to the Secretary of War. But first, he communicated with the severely injured Major George G. Hastings, Commander of Company F, 1st U.S.S.S., (who had been sent home to New York to recuperate) about Berdan's leadership problems. Evidently, Trepp was gathering evidence against his commander, in preparation for a letter to the Secretary of War. Hastings commented:

> Early in the morning on May 3rd, the Regiment was posted in line of battle in the woods, a few hundred yards west of the road leading from Chancellorsville to the U.S. Ford. Two companies, B and I, were deployed as skirmishers about 150 yards in advance of the regiment. The timber was small, but so close that it was impossible to see far in the woods.
>
> On my way to the rear, after I was wounded, I met Berdan on the field, but out of sight of the enemy. From the time I was sent forward to the skirmish line I did not see H.B. until I passed him at the rear.
>
> I authorize you to sign my name to any proper paper signed by yourself and others addressed to the President, remonstrating against H.B.'s promotion, or against his having the control of more SharpShooters.

Around this same time, Trepp also wrote to the Adjutant General of III Corps, expressing his concern over Berdan's cowardly actions at Chancellorsville earlier in the month:

Headquarters 1st U.S.S.S.
May 22, 1863

Lieutenant Colonel O.H. Hart
Assistant Adjutant General III Corps

Colonel:
I have the honor to ask that the official report of Colonel Berdan's Commanding 3rd Brigade, 3rd Division, III Corps, concerning the actions of 2nd and 3rd May, 1863, may be furnished me, or that I be allowed to make a report of the part taken by the 1st Regiment of U.S. SharpShooters in those actions, for the following reasons:

1st. In the engagement of 2nd May, from the time when 50 rebels surrendered to a portion of my command, about 1 o'clock pm, until about an hour before dusk, Colonel Berdan was not on any part of the line, to the right of the foundry. His report, consequently, of what occurred on that portion of the line can only be made from information derived from line officers or enlisted men. As that portion was under my command, and as I was, necessarily, in the discharge of my duties up and down the line constantly, I alone can give correct information of what there occurred. I have not been asked by Colonel Berdan for any report of what occurred on the line, and I am fearful that the names of officers and men who were conspicuous from courage and gallantry have been omitted.

Above: *Edwin M.Stanton [1814-1869] was Lincoln's second Secreatry of War, replacing Simon Cameron in January 1862.He held this responsible position during the rest of the war and was said to have to have assumed near dictatorial powers after Lincoln's assassination in 1865.*

2nd. The report of the action of May 3rd, by Colonel Berdan cannot be complete, as at the commencement of the engagement, he left the 1st Regiment entirely under my charge, and marched off with the 2nd Regiment U.S.S.S. At no time during the action did he return to the front, occupied by my Regiment as skirmishers. His knowledge of what occurred on that portion of the line must, therefore, be exceedingly limited, and perhaps, incorrect, as I have had no opportunity of presenting the facts within my knowledge, which are necessary to a complete report. In justice, therefore, to the officers and enlisted men in my command, I would, respectfully, urge that this application be granted.

C. Trepp
Lieutenant Colonel
Comdg. 1st U.S.S.S.

The III Corps Adjutant General urged Trepp to complete such a report, but there is, unfortunately, no evidence that it was ever acted upon, or placed into the official records of the SharpShooters. It was not until June 1st that Trepp would finally write a condemnation of Berdan directly to Secretary of War Stanton:

Since the formation of this regiment, its commanding officer, Colonel Hiram Berdan, has in many instances, and in various ways, been guilty of conduct unbecoming an officer and a gentleman (as the documents which I have the honor to transmit will show), and has otherwise shown his unfitness for his position. After various and fruitless attempts on the part of a number of officers of this regiment to have his case properly and fully acted upon in the field, I have the honor to make this memorial.

The first instance to which I would call attention occurred at the Camp of Instruction, Washington, D.C. in 1861. The detailed facts of which are marked exhibit 1. Exhibit 2 contains General Orders Nos.30 & 31, 3rd Division, 3rd Army Corps, in which, although Col. Berdan was acquitted by a court-martial, the receiving officer, General Whipple, regarded many of the specifications as clearly proved.

Exhibit 3 is a detailed statement of the conduct of Colonel Berdan during the late engagements on the South side of the Rappahannock on the 2nd and 3rd of May, signed by officers of the Regiment, cognizant of the facts therein stated.

As the great length of time between the dates at which some of these charges against Col. Berdan are alleged to have occurred, and the time at which they were brought before a court seems to require explanation. I would state that during the Peninsula Campaign this regiment was either actively engaged or else serving in detachments of companies at remote points, thus making it impossible for the officers and men to consult or advise as to the proper course to pursue. From September 16, 1862, until December 17, 1862, Colonel Berdan was absent from his command.

In regard to the charges and specifications, I would state that they were not brought before a court because I so confidently believed that the charges and specifications would be entirely sufficient to cause the dismissal from the service of Colonel Berdan, that it would be unnecessary to prefer them in addition. I also feared that I might be consid-

***Above:** General David B.Birney ,Commander of III Corps who endorsed and passed on Berdan's request for promotion.*

pressing these forward in conjunction with the others, when I was only really endeavoring to do my duty and to promote the interests of the service.

Further, our Division Commander, the late Brig. Gen'l. Whipple knew of these facts and approved of my course in the matter.

C. Trepp
Lieutenant Colonel
Commanding 1st U.S.S.S.

Trepp's letter was dispatched directly to the Secretary of War, without going through the usual time-consuming channels. It would prove to be a key element in denying Berdan a promotion, an act that wounded the Chief of SharpShooters far more than Trepp could imagine.

Berdan's Continued Quest for Promotion

It may be recalled that on April 12th, Berdan had forwarded a petition to higher headquarters requesting an immediate promotion. It was allegedly signed by numerous officers and men of the 1st and 2nd Regiments of SharpShooters. Not receiving a favorable reply, the self-centered Chief of SharpShooters decided to change his tactics and send a letter from the officers of the U.S. SharpShooters direct to President Lincoln, requesting not that he be promoted, but that the SharpShooters be filled and expanded. A larger force, the President might conclude, would need a leader with a rank higher than Colonel:

3rd Brigade, U.S.S.S.
3rd Div., III Corps
Camp near Falmouth, VA.
May 21st, 1863

To His Excellency
Abraham Lincoln
President of the United States

We, the undersigned officers of the 1st and 2nd Regiments of U.S. SharpShooters, having been in service nearly two years, and believing that the Corps of SharpShooters has proved itself to be an efficient and valuable arm of the service, and that its good qualities are duly appreciated by the Commanding Generals of the Army, and of the various corps and divisions in which the whole or detachments of this command have served, and believing, further, that even if the decimated companies now in service were filled up, we should not be able to meet the demands for SharpShooters for special service, would respectfully ask that authority be granted to increase the companies composing this command, from the States in which the were raised, to at least a battalion of four companies from each State represented.

The aggregate force of men present for duty is about five hundred. We would respectfully suggest that the recruits for these companies, whether volunteers or drafted men, be tested in accordance with General Order No.149; Adjutant General's Office – 1862 by officers who know and appreciate what is required to keep this special arm of the service in the highest state of efficiency, which can be done only by filling the ranks with practical SharpShooters.

(signed by 18 officers and non-commissioned officers)

Colonel Berdan added his endorsement to the letter allegedly written by his subordinates:

Respectfully forwarded, approved. In my judgment, the interests of the service demand that the force of SharpShooters in this Army should be increased. The petitions seem to have overlooked the fact that New York and Michigan have already furnished a battalion. I think that these States would readily furnish another battalion each.

As the Command is so much reduced, a competent commissioned officer with a sergeant could, in my judgment, be detailed without manifest injury to the service to test the men in each state, without which I fear the efficiency of the organization could not be sustained.

I would recommend that each battalion have an assistant surgeon and be under the command of a major, and the battalion adjutants and quartermasters be taken from the second lieutenants of the line.

H. Berdan Colonel
Commanding

Major General Birney, Commander of III Corps approved Berdan's proposal on May 29th, forwarding it to higher headquarters. The letter's final endorsement was by Major General Hooker, himself. Berdan's influence over certain superiors is baffling, but cannot be overlooked. Somehow, he changed Hooker's mind about him, as evidenced by the General's endorsement:

Above: *Major General Joseph Hooker poses with his white horse.*

I concur in the foregoing remarks. The services of the battalions of SharpShooters, as represented in this army, entitle them to great respect, and have enlisted an interest in their specialty and a desire for an increase in its organization in the mind of every officer who has had an opportunity to witness their skill and efficiency when properly directed.

In my opinion, no man who is not a sportsman and a good rifle shot should be permitted to enter the battalion of SharpShooters, and its officers should be active, enterprising and experienced woodsmen. When filled up with this class of officers and men, no body of troops can be more useful in the campaign before us. To secure this object, it, therefore, seems not only expedient, but necessary that the officers enlisted with raising new battalions or with the selection of recruits to fill up the old ones, should have, in addition to this fondness for this service, actual experience in the field as SharpShooters. In no other way can they know the precise character of the men required for this service.

For this reason, provided the governors of the States in which it is proposed to establish recruiting rendezvous make no objection, I recommend recruiting for each battalion be superintended by its commanding officers.

Joseph Hooker
Major General Commanding
Army of the Potomac

Without knowing of Berdan's alleged cowardice at Chancellorsville, Hooker recommended that the Chief of SharpShooters be promoted:

Headquarters – Army of the Potomac
May 29, 1863

To His Excellency
The President of the United States

Mr. President:
A few weeks ago, I had the honor to receive from your fair hand a note in relation to the promotion of Colonel Berdan. It now gives me great pleasure to recommend him to your favorable consideration for promotion to the rank of Brigadier General, for distinguished service at the Battle of Chancellorsville.

Joseph Hooker
Major General Commanding

Berdan was now relentless in his pursuit of higher rank. If Berdan had been as aggressive on the battlefield as he was on paper, he would have deserved his promotion. Nevertheless, he penned the following letter to one of President Lincoln's personal secretaries:

Headquarters – 3rd Brigade
3rd Division, III Corps
Falmouth, Va.
June 4, 1863

Mr. John G. Nicolay

Dear Sir:
You will greatly oblige me if you will present the enclosed to His Excellency, the President, for his official action, with as little delay as possible. I have now been in service nearly two years without having any commission and I deem it due to my family that I should have a commission that in case I should fall upon the field, that they would be able to receive a pension.

A movement of the army is imminent, and that it may occur at any day is cause for my anxiety that there should be no unnecessary delay in this matter. Please be kind enough to inform me what action, if any, is taken on the subject, and oblige.

H. Berdan Colonel
Commanding

In all probability, Berdan's letter reached the President about the same time that General Hooker's letter of May 29th was received. Evidently, the President was influenced, and wrote the following endorsement on the back of Hooker's letter, but makes no mention of a promotion:

I think Colonel Berdan ought to have a Commission of some sort.

A. Lincoln
June 6, 1863

The matter was turned over to the Army Adjutant General's Office, where Berdan's full record could be investigated and action taken. It was there that Lieutenant Colonel Trepp's untiring denunciations of Berdan were most effective. When the Office looked into Trepp's allegations, they concluded that there was enough of a question about Berdan's leadership that promotion to Brigadier General was denied.

Lee Takes the Offensive

Hooker's Army of the Potomac remained in camp near Falmouth, Virginia throughout the month of May and well into June before marching orders came. The SharpShooters broke camp on June 11th, having been reassigned to Ward's 2nd Brigade of Birney's 1st Division of III Corps. The Federals, it seems, were now in pursuit of Lee, whose main elements of nearly 75,000 men had left the Fredericksburg area on June 3rd, headed in a westerly direction. Lee soon turned north, first to Culpepper, then to Front Royal, and then to Winchester. There were frequent minor skirmishes every day, but Hooker's main body was nearly a week's march behind Lee, with no way to quickly react to the Confederate master strategist's moves. It soon became clear that Lee was to invade the Federal north, bringing the war onto their soil. This would give the farmlands of Virginia time to heal and produce much needed food for soldier and civilian, alike.

Because of excessive losses within the Army of the Potomac from battlefield casualties and from the mustering out of some nine-month regiments, the division was broken up. Berdan's 1st and 2nd Regiments of U.S. SharpShooters were made a part of General J .H. Hobart Ward's Second Brigade, General David B. Birney's 1st Division, and General Daniel Sickles' III Corps. Evidently, Berdan received orders that he, as Chief of SharpShooters of both regiments, could report directly to Birney, bypassing Ward. In essence, the Berdan SharpShooters were a separate brigade.

On June 16th, Lee's forward elements crossed the Potomac and continued north through Maryland. By the 26th, Confederate General Early's men entered the small, but important crossroads town of Gettysburg, Pennsylvania. The following day, Lincoln replaced the ineffective Hooker with Major General George Gordon Meade. The Army of the Potomac was already across the Potomac, in the vicinity of Frederick, Maryland, when they learned of the Confederate advance to Chambersburg and York, Pennsylvania.

On June 29th, the Federal cavalry under Generals John Buford and Judson Kilpatrick met elements of the Confederate advance at Gettysburg. All the while, Berdan SharpShooters continued to march north with the main body of the Army of the Potomac. They reached Bridgeport, Maryland on the 30th, and heard heavy firing to the north: the Battle of Gettysburg had begun.

The Battle of Gettysburg

Sickles' III Corps arrived on the Union battle line at Gettysburg on the evening of July 1st. They were positioned on the left of the nearly three mile long Federal line, awaiting the enemy's advance. On the morning of July 2nd, General Sickles was ordered by Army of the Potomac Commander Meade to place his Corps on Cemetery Ridge, his right flank connecting with II Corps, and his left flank extending south toward the Round Tops. Berdan received instructions from his division commander, General Birney, to post the 2nd Regiment (Major Stoughton commanding) on the division's left, to act as flankers, and the 1st Regiment (Lieutenant Colonel Trepp commanding) some 300 yards to the front, to act as skirmishers. They were not at that time in direct contact with the enemy, as all firing was to the north. Elements of General Buford's cavalry were in evidence throughout this area, exchanging small arms fire with enemy pickets until they were recalled in the early morning. Essentially, the Emmitsburg Road was free from action for nearly the entire morning, save the occasional shots from enemy SharpShooters.

About 7:30 A.M. Colonel Berdan received orders to send forward a detachment of 100 SharpShooters to determine the enemy's movements. Berdan accompanied B and H Companies, but it was Lieutenant Colonel Trepp who posted each of the men in position on the crest of the hill west of the Emmitsburg Road. Berdan and Trepp then withdrew,

Above: *Private John C.Page Company F [Vermont], 1st U.S. SharpShooters.*

Above: *Two privates from Company B [New York], 1st U.S.S.S. from left to right: Private Philip E. Sands, enlisted July 10, 1861, who died after being wounded at the Wilderness and Private John W. Kenny who was severely wounded at the Battle of Harrison's Creek, Virginia and was given a medical discharge, September 16,1864.*

without fulfilling the purpose of their reconnaissance. Whether this was due to Berdan's cowardice, or ignorance of the directives cannot be determined.

These 100 SharpShooters, meanwhile, remained in their posted position nearly all day under the command of Captain John Wilson. They withdrew at 5 P.M., and only after all their ammunition was expended.

When he returned to the main body of SharpShooters, Berdan ordered Major Stoughton, commander of the 2nd U.S. SharpShooters, further south to cover the ravine at Plum Run Gorge, near Round Top, and to keep a watch for the enemy from the most southerly direction. Stoughton placed Company H on the hill, Company D in the ravine, and Companies A, C, E and G in a line' perpendicular to Peach Orchard Road. Companies B and F were held in reserve. The 2nd U.S.S.S. held these positions until nearly 2 P.M. Meanwhile, Colonel Berdan returned to the relative safety of the position of his 1st U.S. SharpShooters, east of the Emmitsburg Road.

General Sickles worried about the poor defensive position occupied by his III Corps. Part of his line ran along low ground, somewhat swampy in front, then rose to a crest along the Emmitsburg Road. He became convinced that he could not successfully defend this position if attacked by a sizable force. Since the enemy's strength was unknown at this time, he decided to take action. Before he left for a meeting with General Meade he acted on a suggestion of Chief of Artillery Henry Hunt to order General Birney to send out a reconnaissance-in-force forward of III Corps.

Some controversy exists over whose suggestion it was to initiate this reconnaissance. Sickles, Birney and Berdan each would later claim it as their idea.

General Birney dispatched his own aide-de-camp, Captain J.C. Briscoe, to personally carry the order to Berdan to take out another detachment of SharpShooters, to advance further in front of the Federal lines than before. Berdan and 100 SharpShooters were accompanied by 210 officers and men of the3rd Maine Infantry Volunteers, who followed in support.

Captain Briscoe joined the reconnaissance, possibly because he was ordered by Birney to observe Berdan in action. The reconnaissance advanced, but it was Trepp who again commanded the advancing SharpShooters. Berdan, because of Birney's orders, was in a truly unfamiliar position, at the forefront of impending action. The reconnaissance proceeded southwest down the Emmitsburg Road, in full view of enemy pickets, until they were at a point opposite the left flank of III Corps, then swung north. The SharpShooters were deployed in a line running nearly east and west. The element moved in a northerly direction, nearly parallel to the road, and entered the thick woods on Warfield Ridge in skirmish order.

By noon, shortly after entering what was known as Pitzer's Woods, forward elements of the SharpShooters encountered Confederate skirmishers and drove them back several hundred yards through the thick stand of oak and chestnut trees. There, Trepp's SharpShooters encountered the advancing flank of Brigadier General Cadmus Wilcox's 8th, 9th, 10th, and 11th Alabama Infantry, who were headed east toward Emmitsburg Road to take up positions. This July 2nd surprise encounter, and the firefight that ensued, were the first indications of a major engagement on the Federal left.

Trepp's SharpShooters (Company D, F & I) battled the Confederates from positions in the thick woods, catching the enemy in the open. Wilcox would later report:

> The 11th Alabama advanced in the open field, and received a heavy volley of musketry on its right flank and rear from the enemy, [which was] concealed behind ledges of rock and trees in the woods. The 10th Alabama moved forward promptly, and soon encountered a strong line of [enemy] skirmishers. A spirited musketry fight ensued...

Colonel Hilary Herbert, commanding the 8th Alabama Infantry would add:

> The sudden volley caught the 11th Regiment in the midst at the open field. and they fell back in some disorder. The 8th and 10th Alabama advanced in line...

Meanwhile, Colonel Lakeman's 3rd Maine, 200 Infantrymen strong, advanced to the sound of the firing and took up positions alongside the SharpShooters. Trepp's men had, quite naturally, already occupied the best firing positions, leaving many of the Maine troops exposed to enemy musketry fire. The fighting was at a range of less than a hundred yards, and lasted but ten minutes. Wilcox would later say that *"it continued for some 15 or 20 minutes."* Historian Stevens described the confrontation as follows:

> It was a trying occasion for our men, but Colonel Berdan riding in front of the line, quickly took in the situation, and knowing that time gained them was everything, dispatched Captain Briscoe to our Generals, Birney and Sickles, a mile away, to warn them of the danger – the threatened assault upon our left.

As more of Wilcox's men advanced, the firing became more pronounced, causing Berdan *"to fall back, firing"* and retreat under the cover of the woods. The reconnaissance, having accomplished its mission of locating the enemy, withdrew to more secure positions east of the Emmitsburg Road. Wilcox's men pursued for only a short distance.

The detachment of SharpShooters lost 1 officer killed, 2 wounded, and 16 enlisted men killed, wounded or missing. The 3rd Maine Infantrymen lost a total of 48 killed, wounded, or missing. It was a costly reconnaissance, but it was to alert Sickles of the Confederate movement along his front.

The actual engagement took place between noon and one o'clock, by all reputable accounts. Berdan, unaccustomed to the terror of front line action, hurried to report in person to General Birney, arriving sometime before two o'clock. After years of relatively safe rear echelon duty, Berdan had been thrust into the thick of fighting. He was not about to allow a subordinate to take away any attention that he felt he should deserve. Berdan wanted the glory (and the brigadier's star) for himself.

He reported to Birney *"three columns in motion, in rear of the woods, changing direction, as it were, by the right flank."* To Berdan, Wilcox's men must have appeared as legions, as if the entire Confederate army was advancing toward the III Corps, ready to flank the Union left.

Ironically, Longstreet was indeed moving thousands of troops to attack the Federal left. Berdan did not see them, although years later he would contend that he did. In fact, Berdan would boast that he, personally, discovered Longstreet's advance. He claimed that his encounter with Wilcox slowed Longstreet's movement long enough for

Above: *General Sickles learned of the movement of the Confederate troops against the union left from Berdan's reconnaissance.*

General Sickles to order forward his III Corps to the Peach Orchard, to more suitable ground to oppose the enemy. Historian Stevens compounded the erroneous belief, by writing:

> Three hundred men, firing 10,000 rounds in 20 minutes stopped the advance of 30,000 foes.
>
> No greater display of heroism, no more self-sacrificing spirit of patriotism can be cited in the annals of war, than was the courageous attack of Berdan's 300 on the marching columns of 30,000 foes. And surely, it may be fairly said to be a turning point in the Rebellion.

The *"30,000"* was Steven's reference to the mistaken belief that Berdan had discovered Longstreet's flank march, and had delayed it long enough for General Sickles to order III Corps forward to deny the strategic Peach Orchard Ridge to the enemy. Nothing could have been further from the truth, as it was Wilcox's Alabama Infantry that Berdan saw, not Longstreet's main body. Let us examine this further.

Berdan left no contemporary written record of his discovery of Longstreet at Gettysburg. In fact, it was not mentioned until he proclaimed it in a battlefield reunion speech in the late 1880s. Extracting key segments from these late-in-life speeches, one finds Berdan prone to considerable puffery.

> About 11 A.M. on July 2nd, I approached General Sickles [they probably never met that day] about sending out a reconnaissance, which was immediately approved. I recall that I was some 300 yards ahead of my men [pure fiction, not supported by his longstanding history of cowardice on the battlefield] and I was mounted so as to see over the undergrowth. I came upon Wilcox's Brigade, leading Longstreet's column [which it was not] marching south through the woods. Rather than withdraw and risk losing the Round Tops [rhetoric of an old man lusting after glory he never received in actual combat], I gave the command: "Follow me, advance firing," although outnumbered 20 to 1. [This quote was, we believe, never uttered or recorded prior to this speech!]

General Longstreet, unfortunately, added to Berdan's misrepresentation by agreeing with the allegations. At the 1888 Gettysburg Reunion Longstreet said:

> The firing in question saved Sickles and the day. It caused me a loss of 40 minutes, and could I have saved 5 of those minutes, the battle would have gone against Meade on the 2nd day.

A brief review of Longstreet's actual march on July 2nd, 1863, will clarify this situation. By late morning the Federal Army occupied positions on Cemetery Ridge from beyond Culp's Hill, down to Little Round Top. The Confederate forces massed on Seminary Ridge. Lee ordered Longstreet's Corps to attack the Federal left, while Ewell's corps was to attack Cemetery and Culp's Hills. There were strategically costly delays. Longstreet opposed Lee's plan, and seemed in no haste to carry it out. At 5 A.M. on the morning of the 2nd, Longstreet's Corps, with McLaws' and Hood's Divisions, was in the vicinity of the Herr Tavern. By noon, they had moved about one mile southwest, to a point on Herr Ridge. They marched southwest, about 1 3/4 miles, to the vicinity of Black Horse Tavern, when McLaws and Johnston crested the ridge. They immediately noticed the Federal signal station on Little Round Top, 3 miles to the southeast. It was then about 1 P.M.

Fearing that they might be observed by the Federal Signalmen on Little Round Top, Longstreet (in a move oft criticized) ordered his troops to retrace their steps, returning to their initial start point on the north end of Herr Ridge. The entire march measured seven and three quarters miles. Contemporary records of times and places allow us to measure that Longstreet's foot soldiers averaged about two-and-a-half miles per hour for the journey back to Herr Ridge. Then the corps travelled approximately four miles over uneven terrain, to reach their positions on Emmitsburg Road at about 3 P.M. on the 2nd of July.

General Sickles learned of Berdan's reconnaissance and of the movement of Confederate troops against the Union left. This may have been the decisive factor that compelled Sickles to move his men forward to more advantageous positions from which to repel an enemy attack. There is no evidence that Sickles was aware of Longstreet, only that his frightened Chief of SharpShooters saw *"legions of the enemy advancing."*

With these and other facts in mind, this author and historians Dale Gallon and Richard Sauers retraced Berdan's and Longstreet's movements on the Battlefield of Gettysburg. After much study and debate, we drew the following unanimous conclusions:

At no point in any area of Berdan's reconnaissance could the Longstreet Ridge near Blackhorse Tavern have been seen by any of Berdan's men. The entire reconnaissance took place between 11 A.M. and 1 P.M., while the actual firefight occurred around noon, or shortly thereafter, lasting only ten minutes.

Since Longstreet's Corps left their jump-off point on Herr Ridge at noon, they could not have arrived at the crest of the hill near Black Horse Tavern until at least 1 P.M., and probably later. Berdan's reconnaissance ended sometime around 12:30 P.M.

The terrain in the entire vicinity of Pitzer's Woods (where Berdan's action took place) is much lower that the ridge near Black Horse Tavern. Someone on the ridge can only see the tops of the trees at Pitzer's Woods, but cannot observe anything on the ground, beneath. Likewise, someone in Pitzer's Woods can see nothing to the northwest, at Black Horse Tavern.

Post Reconnaissance Action

After communicating Berdan's information to General Sickles, 1st Division Commander, Major General David Birney was ordered to relocate his front to meet the impending attack, and take the high ground of the Peach Orchard.11 The 1st Division advanced some 500 yards, and formed a new line of battle. His force extended from the base of Sugar Loaf Mountain (Little Round Top), to the Peach Orchard on the Emmitsburg Road. Unfortunately, this left a large gap in the Union line on Cemetery Ridge, and left Little Round Top virtually undefended.

Captain Baker, commanding the remnants of the 1st Regiment of U.S. SharpShooters, moved forward to the right

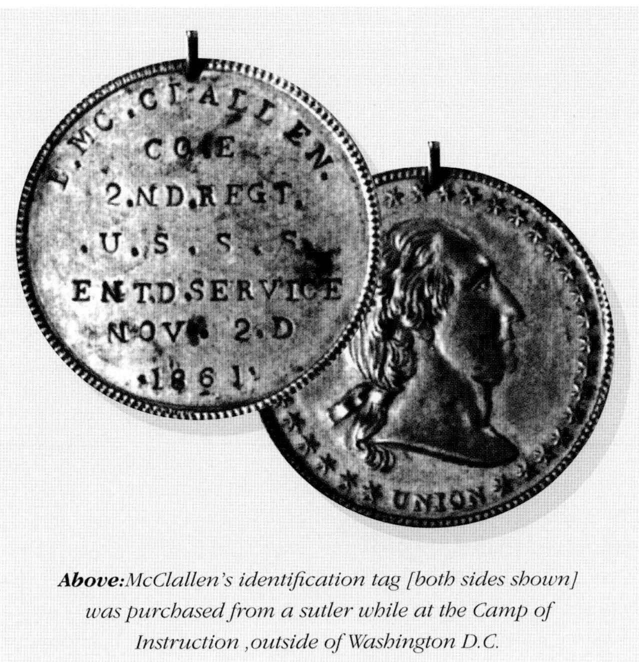

***Above:** McClallen's identification tag [both sides shown] was purchased from a sutler while at the Camp of Instruction ,outside of Washington D.C.*

of the Peach Orchard, to the right of the 1st Brigade. At the point of the heaviest fighting, Baker led a charge against the enemy, driving them across the field. The SharpShooters were ordered to the rear by Colonel Berdan only after their allotment of Sharps .52 caliber ammunition was reduced to fewer than 5 rounds per man in the late afternoon. Baker's men lost 3 killed and 5 wounded during this period.

Meanwhile, Major Stoughton's 2nd U.S.S.S. held the positions it occupied since early morning, not far from Devil's Den. About 2 P.M., General Ward directed Stoughton to move his SharpShooters across the ravine (Plum Run Gorge) and into the woods to his right. Then they advanced, moving south beyond Devil's Den, through the Wheatfield, to a branch of the Plum Run brook. Major Stoughton personally rode toward the enemy for about a half mile, and discovered Confederate soldiers advancing on his right. Longstreet's infantry had finally arrived on the Union left. It was now about 3 P.M., and Longstreet's infantry began its assault about an hour later.

The 2nd U.S.S.S. were soon engaged in the thick of the bloody fighting beneath Little Round Top. By 4:30 P.M. Robertson's Confederate brigade moved forward, facing Stoughton's entire front and flank. Holding advantageous defensive positions, the SharpShooters poured destructive fire into the ranks of Robertson's Texans. They delayed the Confederate advance long enough for General Warren to discover the vulnerability of the unprotected Little Round Top. The delay allowed the 140th New York Infantry to arrive in time to protect the Federal left flank.

The Federal VI Corps arrived on the field at about 2 P.M., after a forced march of 32 miles in less than 15 hours. General Meade ordered these exhausted troops to be held in reserve, replacing V Corps, whom he ordered to rush forward to secure the left flank. This strategic move probably saved the day for Sickles, and mitigated his decision to move his Corps forward without permission from Meade.

When General Sickles was severely wounded in the right leg by an artillery shell, the Corps command was passed to General Birney. The vacated Division command was passed to General Ward, and the Brigade command was given to Colonel Berdan.

On July 3rd, a detachment of 100 marksmen from the 1st U.S. SharpShooters was sent to cover the front of VI Corps. Captain Baker again commanded this group, and they remained there all day under constant fire. They advanced at nightfall, capturing eighteen prisoners. The remainder of Berdan's SharpShooters moved north with the rest of the Division to support batteries of V Corps. They were unopposed all day, as was Stoughton's 2nd U.S.S.S. Thus ended the action for Berdan's SharpShooters at Gettysburg.

In all, Berdan's 1st and 2nd U.S. SharpShooters suffered 92 casualties during the three days at Gettysburg: one officer killed, eight wounded and one missing; and ten enlisted men killed, fifty-two wounded, and twenty missing.

The SharpShooters After Gettysburg

Colonel Berdan's absence from the SharpShooters following the Battle of Gettysburg is shrouded with mystery, subterfuge, jealousy and contempt. Letters, reports, dispatches and telegrams during July, August and September found him in various places, performing various missions, with both military and personal overtones.

Following the Battle of Gettysburg, Berdan remained in command of Ward's 2nd Brigade until July 7th, but did not return to his SharpShooters. He petitioned the new III Corps Commander, Major General William H. French, for permission to travel north on recruiting duty. When he heard of this proposal, Trepp complained to the 2nd Brigade Adjutant that

***Above:** Private Byron Mc Clallen of Company E [Vermont], 2nd U.S. SharpShooters died at the Battle of Antietam ,September 17,1862.*

Colonel Berdan, two other U.S.S.S. officers and six enlisted men had already left for New Hampshire, New York and Vermont. Trepp, as Commander of the 1st U.S.S.S., was upset that Berdan gave himself this opportunity to get away from the war, without first re-establishing himself with the SharpShooters. Berdan had requested that he be listed as *"off duty."*

On August 7th, Corps Commander French wrote a letter to Berdan, inquiring as to his whereabouts, and ordering him to report immediately to the Recruiting Officer in New York State. Evidently the letter never reached Berdan, as he had already left Virginia, travelling east toward Washington, D.C. Three days later, Berdan's Division Commander General Birney, wrote to the Provost Marshal of Washington, D.C., telling him that the Colonel *"was on official recruiting duty, and that all possible assistance should be afforded him in this mission."* The same day, Birney wrote to President Lincoln, recommending Berdan for promotion to Brigadier General.

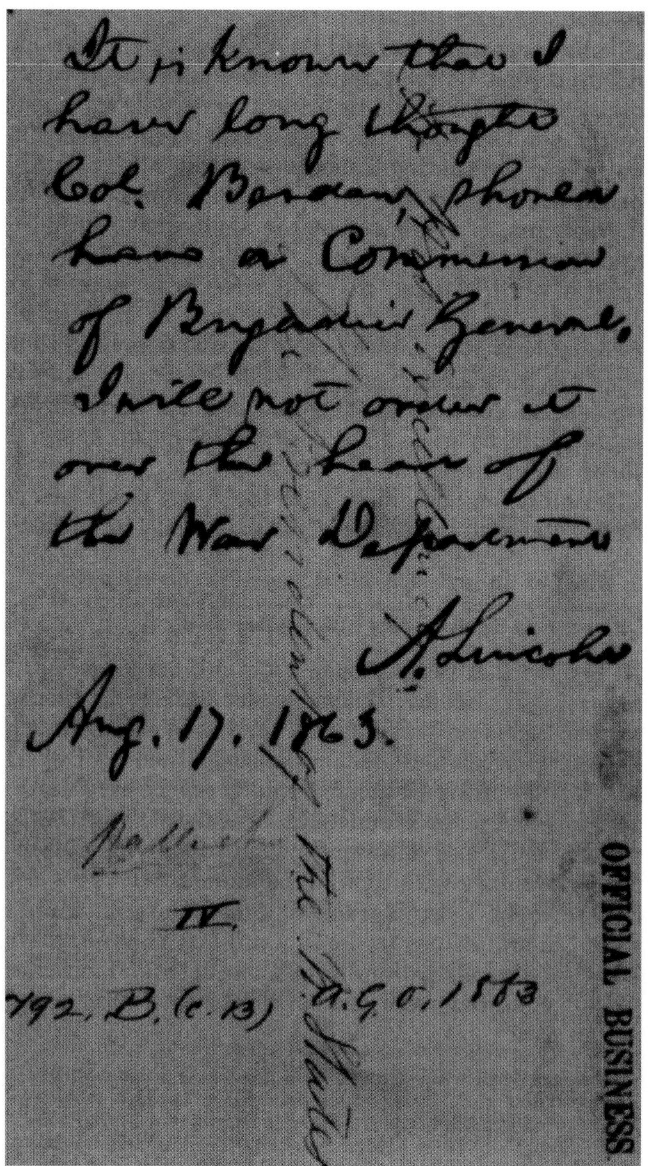

It is known that I have long thought Col. Berdan should have a Commission of Brigadier General, I will not order it over the head of the War Department

A. Lincoln

Aug. 17. 1863.

IV

792. B. (c. 13) A.G.O. 1863

OFFICIAL BUSINESS.

Above: *Here is Lincoln's note supporting Berdan's promotion to Brigadier General, a position that Berdan coveted.*

On August 11th, Berdan arrived in Washington, as ordered by General Birney, to confer with the Provost Marshal General about receiving replacement enlisted men for III Corps. Also, he conferred with officials of the Ordnance Department about procuring breechloading rifles for other regiments of the division. He remained in Washington for the better part of a week. Before he left, Berdan wrote a letter to President Lincoln responding to Trepp's accusations to Secretary of War Stanton on June 1st. The President wrote the following endorsement to accompany Berdan's letter, finally ending his wartime bid for a star:

> It is known that I have long thought Col. Berdan should have a commission of brigadier general. I will not order it over the head of the War Department.

On August 11th, Colonel Berdan traveled first to Vermont, and then to New Hampshire, on recruiting duty. It was not a coincidence that Berdan's family then resided in West Lebanon, New Hampshire.

A week later, Berdan wrote to Secretary of War Stanton responding to Trepp's accusations, and stated that he hoped to be exonerated. Some question then arose concerning Berdan's mission to the north, and the authority he had to recruit for the SharpShooters. His Corps Commander, General French, wrote:

> I shall direct Berdan and his party to return immediately.

Evidently, Berdan never received this letter, as he had not informed his regiment of his whereabouts. On August 31st, Berdan left New Hampshire, on his way to the Sharps Rifle Manufacturing Company in Hartford, Connecticut. There he discussed the procurement of additional firearms for his regiment. While enroute, numerous telegrams of inquiry were sent from Adjutant General Vincent to various recruiting commanders in New York State, requesting the whereabouts of Berdan. Each reply stated that his location was unknown. On September 2nd, Adjutant-General Vincent informed Major General Meade:

> Colonel Berdan has not reported for recruiting service in New York City. As soon as the department can find him he will be ordered to join his regiment.

On September 7th, Colonel Berdan finally arrived in New York City. Later he informed the State Recruiting Officer of his recruiting travels to other northern states, as evidence of the legitimacy of his absence. Two days later, Berdan was ordered to immediately rejoin his regiment in Virginia. However, Berdan decided to seek medical attention in Washington, D.C., prior to complying with this order. It is believed that Berdan had enough of the army life, and sought, now, to return to civilian life.

On September 11th, U.S.S.S. Surgeon J.W. Brennan examined Colonel Berdan and found him to be *"suffering from haemoptysis and diarrhea – the third attack this year."* Furthermore, that *"The Colonel needs quiet and rest, with no exposure to cold or sudden climate changes."* The following day, Army Surgeon George

Above: *A medal from Company H [Vermont] of the 2nd U.S. SharpShooters with its original ribbon.*

Jaquett recommended that Berdan be given *"an immediate thirty day medical leave of absence."*

Realizing that he was still being sought by high-ranking authorities, Colonel Berdan wrote to the Department of the East. He acknowledged Stanton's orders for him to return to active duty, but stated that his medical disability was prohibiting him from complying. Evidently, Berdan failed to inform his Division Commander of his whereabouts, as evidenced by the September 13th letter from Major General Birney to Assistant Adjutant General of III Corps. He submitted official charges against Berdan for taking personal time to be with his family in New Hampshire, while he was supposed to be recruiting for his regiment. *"The disobedience to positive orders is so glaring,"* Birney said, *"that I think an example should be made of the case. On his return he will be placed under arrest."*

Therefore, on September 28th the Army published an official notice in the *ARMY & NAVY GAZETTE:*

> The War Department, Adjutant General's Office made official notice of its intention to dismiss Colonel Berdan from the service if he did not report for duty within fifteen days.

It is clear that Berdan's superiors did not know of his claims for a medical discharge for service-connected wounds, or his presence at that time in Washington, On October 1st, Colonel Berdan was examined by Department of the Army Surgeon Jaquett, reaffirming earlier diagnosis by Doctor Brennan, He was issued a further 20 day medical leave of absence, legitimizing his absence from active duty with the SharpShooters.

Two weeks later, Berdan's immediate commander, Major General Birney, ordered a military commission to investigate the allegations of misconduct and dereliction of duty. Findings were issued on October 17th, which said, in part:

> Colonel Berdan was acting within the orders of his regiment and division while on recruiting duty during July and August. Furthermore, his infirmary made it impossible for him to continue these duties in September. This Court of Inquiry has decided that Berdan's defense was an acceptable and sound one, and all charges against him will be dismissed.

Berdan continued to seek medical aid in Washington, and on October 20th, the War Department issued Special Order No.470. This order, which was personally endorsed by President Lincoln, granted the Colonel a 50 day medical leave of absence for his service-connected disability. Later, on December 9th, Berdan was again examined by Department of the Army Surgeon Jaquett, who certified his continued disability, noting that he was still experiencing internal bleeding. He granted Berdan an additional 20 days medical leave of absence.

Colonel Hiram Berdan's tenure as Chief of SharpShooters was nearing an end. On December 20th, the commander of the 1st U.S.S.S., Captain Frank E. Marble, wrote to his division commander, Brigadier General Thomas, about Colonel Berdan. He quoted the provisions of Army General Order #100 (dated August 11, 1862), which stated that a soldier could be honorably discharged from the service if he was absent due to illness for more than 70 consecutive days. Colonel Berdan was honorably discharged from service in the Union Army on January 2nd, 1864, per Special Order No.1, Army Adjutant's Office. He received this severance because of *"physical disability."*

The question as to why Berdan sought to leave the SharpShooters may never be fully known. This author believes that the turning point for Berdan came in August 1863, when his request for promotion to Brigadier General was denied, with finality. It occurred when President Lincoln decided not to reverse Secretary of War Stanton's decision to withhold Berdan's star. Being unable to secure a promotion was tantamount to failure to this egocentric Chief of SharpShooters. There would be no further reason for Berdan to want to subject himself to the terrors of war for any purpose, other than a promotion. He was not a recognized military leader, a fact well established by superiors and subordinates, alike. And by virtue of his status as an independently wealthy man, he did not need the money, as the majority of active duty personnel did at this time. It was time for Berdan to leave the service and pursue his lifelong ambitions as an inventor.

The SharpShooters Without Berdan

Colonel Berdan's influence over the SharpShooters ended with the Battle of Gettysburg. The command of the SharpShooters fell to the true military hero of this unit, Lieutenant Colonel Caspar Trepp. It became his challenge to remold the regiment that had been decimated by war, sickness and fear, and to make them battle-ready once again. This would prove to be a thankless, a most difficult, and, indeed, a fatal undertaking for this young commander.

Following the Army of Northern Virginia's failure to win a decisive engagement at Gettysburg, Lee's army made good its escape south to Maryland, then retreated to the safety of Northern Virginia. General Meade's Army of the Potomac failed to pursue Lee, who went unharassed except for isolated cavalry skirmishes. Berdan's SharpShooters and the rest of III Corps finally left the Gettysburg area early in the pre-dawn hours of July 7th, having recovered their wounded and collected their dead. They marched south to the vicinity of Antietam, then through Harper's Ferry, on their way to Manassas Gap. There, on July 23rd, the SharpShooters took part in the battle known as *Wapping Heights*. The 1st U.S.S.S. lost one enlisted man killed, one officer and four enlisted men wounded, while the 2nd U.S.S.S. was held in reserve.

The SharpShooters camped in this strategic mountain pass location for over six weeks, giving the weary troops an opportunity to rest and recover. Colonel Berdan, Captain Wilson, Lieutenant Marden and six enlisted men returned to the north in an effort to recruit new men for the regiment. Colonel Berdan was never to return to the regiment that bore his name, and thus the command ultimately passed to Trepp.

On August 1st, Trepp sought to be relieved from duty for the fifth and last time:

Headquarters 1st Rgt. U.S.S.S.
August 1, 1863

Lieutenant W. Torbet
Assistant Adjutant General III Corps

Lieutenant Torbet:
I have the honor to tender my unconditional and immediate resignation as Lieutenant Colonel of this regiment, with the earnest request that it may be accepted. My reasons are that in a very short time I have to return to my home in Switzerland. The Army is now at a halt, and the regiment small, with full number of field officers. The efficiency of the regiment will not be affected at all by this change.

I would further state that I am not a citizen of the United States, nor did I give any declaration to become one. I have served in this regiment since August 2nd, 1861, to the best of my ability, and consciously to the Oath of Office.

C. Trepp
Lieutenant Colonel
Commanding 1st U.S.S.S.

Trepp's official letter of resignation was endorsed and forwarded all the way up to Army of the Potomac Commander, Major General George Meade. It was declined without comment, on August 5th.

To say that the 1st U.S. SharpShooters were a mere shadow of their original strength would be an understatement. As recruited, they began their Civil War duty with thirty-three commissioned officers and 981 enlisted men. On August 31st, 1863 the unit could muster only eleven officers and 261 enlisted men ready for duty. Fifteen officers and 233 enlisted men were absent, in confinement, sick, or on special duty away from the regiment.4

In September, Lieutenant Colonel Trepp suffered a final indignity when charges were brought against him by an unnamed General Officer who had inspected Trepp's command at Sulphur Springs, Virginia on August 24th. The charges brought against Trepp were:

1st: He did not properly instruct or command SharpShooter pickets, "allowing them to put aside their equipment and lounge about their posts without any restraint,"
2nd: He neglected to instruct certain officers on their specific picket responsibilities.

A general court-martial was convened on September 11th, at 1st Division, III Corps Headquarters, to deliberate on the charges against Trepp. He pleaded *"NOT GUILTY"* to all charges. The Court found him *"not guilty"* on the first charge, but *"guilty"* on the second, and ordered that he be reprimanded. Upon reviewing the decision, Major General Birney reversed Trepp's guilty verdict, ordered him released forthwith.

The SharpShooters continued their role as pickets and skirmishers for III Corps, but were not hotly engaged until the Battle of Auburn on October 13th. The 1st U.S. SharpShooters suffered only two enlisted men wounded in the charge and skirmish. On November 7th, both regiments of SharpShooters were engaged in battle at *Kelly's Ford*. The charge across the river and the firefight that ensued resulted in six enlisted men killed and seven wounded.

On November 8th, III Corps pushed on toward Brandy Station, with the 1st Regiment of SharpShooters leading the way. The action there was light, so the troops departed on November 26th, crossed the Rapidan River, and joined in the *Battle of Locust Grove* the following day. The marksmanship of the SharpShooters halted the Confederate advances of General Johnson's Division several times, but not without serious losses to their own men. The SharpShooters lost one officer and eight enlisted men killed, and twenty-seven enlisted wounded.

The Death of a Hero

The following cold and rainy morning III Corps marched toward Mine Run, Virginia. *The Battle of Mine Run*, on November 30th, proved to be one of the saddest and costliest that the SharpShooters would ever endure: their inspired leader, Lieutenant Colonel Trepp, was fatally wounded in action. As usual, the 1st and 2nd SharpShooters had been dispatched to the front, to lead the advance. The 1st Regiment lost six men, and the 2nd Regiment three.

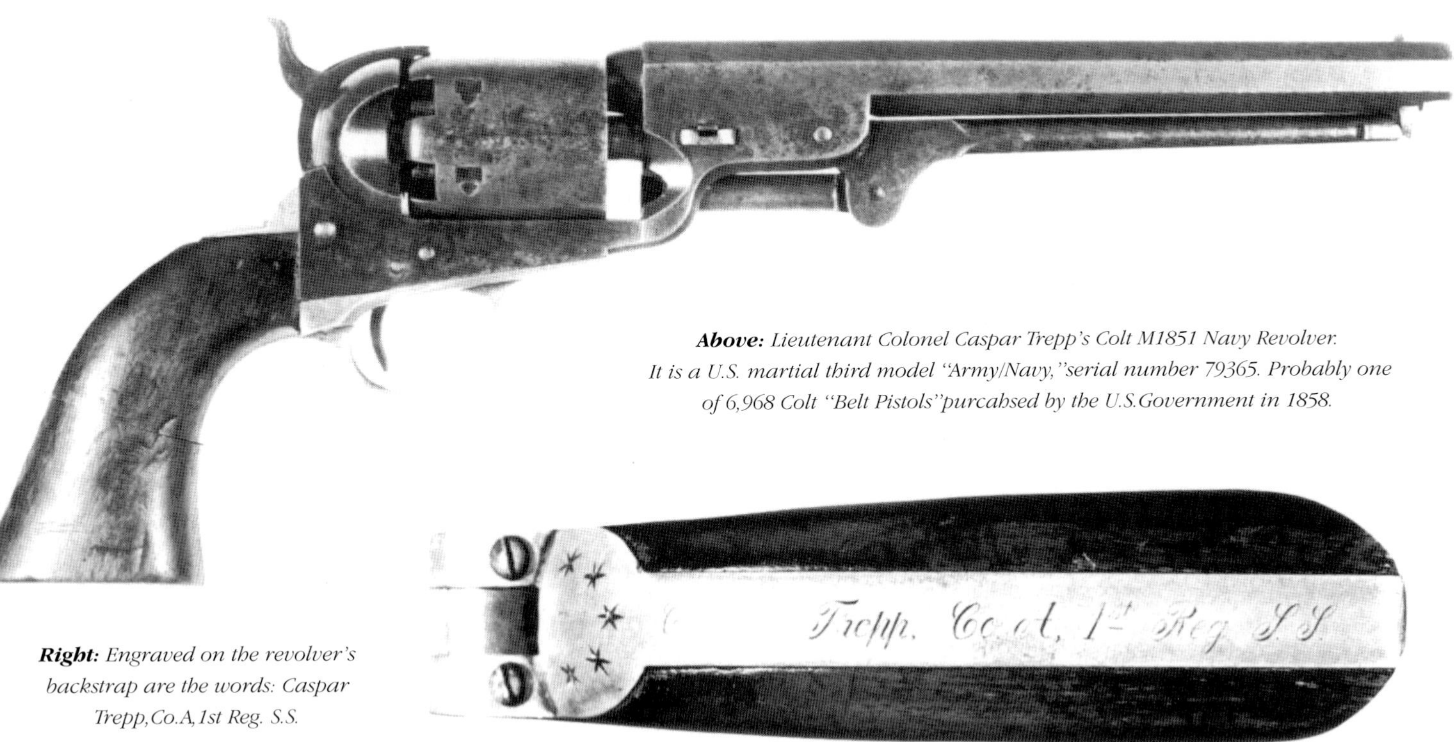

***Above:** Lieutenant Colonel Caspar Trepp's Colt M1851 Navy Revolver. It is a U.S. martial third model "Army/Navy," serial number 79365. Probably one of 6,968 Colt "Belt Pistols" purcahsed by the U.S. Government in 1858.*

***Right:** Engraved on the revolver's backstrap are the words: Caspar Trepp, Co. A, 1st Reg. S.S.*

Historian Stevens describes the action at Mine Run, Virginia in the following way:

> On the right of the line, the SharpShooters drove the enemy out of their rifle pits, doing considerable damage to the foe. At this point the regiment suffered the loss of its commander, Lieutenant Colonel Caspar Trepp, who while observing the situation in the front, was shot through the head, the bullet entering the red diamond on his hat.
>
> In his death the SharpShooter service lost a careful and skillful officer, one who had become well known throughout the corps for his promptness and efficiency in executing movements entrusted to him.
>
> He had been very active that morning from long before daylight, in the disposition of his command, and was very particular to caution his men not to needlessly expose themselves, but when the order was given to go forward to obey it. He appeared to me that morning to be unusually anxious, as if he feared dire results to his decimated regiment from the expected assault. He may have had a premonition of his own fate, as he was, at times, restless and nervous. He was buried three times: on the field, on Bott's farm at Brandy Station, and finally at New York City.

Major General Birney, Commander of the 1st Division, stated succinctly:

> I regret to say that the command has experienced a serious loss in the death of Lieutenant Colonel Trepp.

Colonel Thomas Egan, Commander of the 40th New York Infantry (to which the SharpShooters were attached) stated in his after-action report:

> Killed was Lieutenant Colonel Trepp, an officer of the highest merit, and one whose military knowledge and achievements have long been the admiration of all who knew him.

And the most poignant of all came from his friend, countryman and fellow officer, Rudolf Aschmann:

> On November 30th, before daybreak, our regiment was ordered to the front and deployed against the enemy as skirmishers. We were able to cross the Mine Run on crudely constructed bridges without meeting much resistance, but we soon encountered enemy outpost guards whom we chased out of several rifle pits, driving them back against their main line of fortification. When Colonel Trepp and I were watching the enemy from one of these pits to give orders for further advance, an enemy bullet struck him down right at my side. The deadly lead entered his left temple, emerged above his right ear and rushed past, missing my head by only a few inches, then buried itself in the sand about ten steps from me.
>
> Six men placed the body of our beloved Colonel on a stretcher fashioned of guns and a piece of tent cloth, and I accompanied it on our retreat, while the line followed slowly and in good order. After having received permission from my superiors to retire from my command for this day, I ordered Colonel Trepp to be carried to a field hospital where our regiment's surgeon cleaned and dressed his wound. Although he was totally unconscious, life had not yet left him. Only after midnight did his strong body finally succumb. The loss of this dear, fatherly friend affected me deeply. He was sincerely mourned by his superiors, as well as by the entire regiment.
>
> A crude coffin was fashioned from some boards and nails that we could obtain at a nearby farm, and in the afternoon Trepp's body was buried in the presence of the entire regiment. But soon after the ceremony I received word asking that the coffin be removed from the grave, since the

Division Commanding General [Birney] was providing a wagon to transport it back across the Rapidan, so that the fallen warrior would not have to rest in enemy soil.

As soon as I arrived in camp I applied for a three day leave, in order to take Trepp's body to Washington and have it buried there, unless his wife who lived in New York with her three children, requested that it be forwarded there. However, two days passed and we were forced to bury him in John Bott's family plot. We again exhumed it from its resting place, and I traveled to Washington that same evening, accompanied by the Colonel's Orderly.

We telegraphed the late Colonel's wife, who answered that it was her wish to have her beloved husband buried in New York. Therefore, we forwarded the body in a new coffin the next day. I much regretted that time did not permit me to attend Colonel Trepp's last funeral, in which he was honored by the Swiss community in New York.

The regiment and the Union cause lost their finest soldier.

Amen

Right and below: *George E.Albee enlisted in June 1862 as a member of Company G (Wisconsin) 1st U.S. SharpShooters. He was wounded at Groveton, August 30 1862 and received a medical discharge .He subsequently reenlisted in the Wisconsin Light Artillery and went on to serve on the Western Frontier after the war. Albee's Sharps NM1859 rifle,serial number 56745. It shows the original double set triggers, socket bayonet, and two SharpShooter silver corps badges inletted in the stock.*

The SharpShooters' Final Engagements

Since most of the ten companies that comprised the 1st Regiment of SharpShooters had been mustered into service in August and September of 1861, the majority of "three year enlistees" exercised their option and went home. Those who had been recruited in 1862 and 1863 remained with their SharpShooter companies, each of which had only a small fraction of their full allotment of one hundred men. First Sergeant Wyman S. White of Company F (New Hampshire), 2nd U.S. SharpShooters stated that Company A of the 2nd Regiment mustered out on August 14, 1864, with only twelve men remaining. Company C had only five men of the original 101 that had enlisted in 1861. Companies I and K had men that were recruited late, so they were assigned to other volunteer units.

On February 20, 1865, orders were received from the War Department to disband the remaining companies of the 2nd U.S.S.S. The following order from General DeTrobriand demonstrates the respect that was afforded the Berdan SharpShooters at this time:

Headquarters, 3rd Division, II Corps
February 16, 1865

General Orders – No.12.

The United States SharpShooters, including the first and second consolidated battalion, being about to be broken up as a distinct organization, in compliance with orders from the War Department, the Brigadier General commanding the Division will not take leave of them without acknowledging their good and efficient service during three years in the field.

REGIMENTAL STATISTICS

1st Regiment of U.S. SharpShooters

Original Strength....................................33 commissioned officers and 981 enlisted men

Total regimental enrollment during the war..................1,392 officers and men

Total Wounded...164 officers and men

Total Killed in Action..10 officers and 143 enlisted men

Total dead by disease while in service............................1 officer and 128 enlisted men

Where and when mustered in:

Co.			
Co.	A	New York City, New York	September 3, 1861
	B	Albany, New York	November 29, 1861
	C	Lansing, Michigan	August 21, 1861
	D	New Berlin, New York	November 29, 1861
	E	Concord, New Hampshire	November 14, 1861
	F	West Randolph, Vermont	September 13, 1861
	G	Madison, Wisconsin	September 23,1861
	H	New York City, New York	November 29, 1861
	I	Lansing, Michigan	March 4, 1862
	K	Lansing , Michigan	March 30, 1862

2nd Regiment U.S. SharpShooters

Original Strength........................24 commissioned officers and 785 enlisted men

Total Regimental enrollment during the war.................1,178 officers and men

Total Wounded...212 officers and men

Total killed in action...8 officers and 117 enlisted men

Total dead by disease while in service...........................2 officers and 123 enlisted men

Where and when mustered in:

Co.			
Co.	A	St Paul, Minnesota	October 5, 1861
	B	Lansing , Michigan	October 4,1861
	C	Pennsylvania	October 4, 1861
	D	Augusta, Maine	November 2, 1861
	E	West Randolph, Vermont	November 9, 1861
	F	Concord, New Hampshire	November 28,1861
	G	Concord, New Hampshire	December 10,1861
	H	West Randolph, Vermont	December 31,1861

> The U.S. SharpShooters leave behind them a glorious record in the Army of the Potomac since the first operation against Yorktown in 1862, up to Hatcher's Run, and few are the battles or engagements in which they did not make their mark. The Brigadier General commanding who had them under his command during most of the campaigns of 1863 and 1864, would be the last to forget their brave deeds during that period. He feels assured that the different organizations to which they may belong will show themselves worthy of their old reputation. With them, the past will answer for the future.
>
> By Command of Brigadier General
> R. DeTrobriand

In his book, REGIMENTAL LOSSES IN THE CIVIL WAR, Colonel Fox remarked the 1st and 2nd Regiments of Berdan SharpShooters were:

> ...the unique regiments of the war. Berdan's United States SharpShooters were the best known of any regiments in the army. It would have been difficult to have raised in any one state a regiment equal to Berdan's requirements. The class of men selected were also of a high grade in physical qualifications and intelligence. They were continually in demand as skirmishers, on account of their wonderful proficiency as such, and they undoubtedly killed more men than any other regiment in the army. In skirmishing they had no equal.

Right: *Lieutenant Perrin C. Judkins, Company G [Wisconsin], 1st U.S. SharpShooters, was killed in action at the Battle of Todd's Tavern, Virginia, May 8, 1864. He was killed while detached as an aide on brigade staff galloping gallantly to the front to encourage the troops to hold their positions.*

Postscript

Berdan had already been talking to gunmakers after he had left his command in July 1863, ostensibly to travel north to recruit for his decimated Corps of SharpShooters. It seems that he did not recruit a single man, but did visit a number of firearms manufacturers, including the Sharps Company and the Colt Factory in Hartford, Connecticut, the Remington Company at Ilion, N.Y. and the Edward Robinson factory in New York City.

By 1864 he was already designing and constructing a new firearm: a breechloading percussion musket. It never became a viable production item, but it was the first in the long line of weapons that this prolific and inventive engineer created.

Once he realised that the time for new percussion weapon designs was past, Berdan turned to the design of self-contained cartridges, and to weapons that would fire them. Initial ideas included a 'latch rifle', a rolling block system and various 'trap-door' conversions to existing muzzleloaders. His greatest commercial success was when the Russian Army took large numbers of his breechloading designs and associated cartridges.

Berdan went on to invent other devices, including an artillery rangefinder, shell fuzes, a naval torpedo and armored torpedo boat. He continued to court controversy and even managed to sue the U.S. Government, claiming that their Allin breechloading conversions of the Springfield muskets infringed some of his patents.

In the years after the war Berdan had continued to imply, both in speeches and in writing, that his own Gettysburg actions were the turning point of the battle. He lobbied both House and Senate for an appropriation for a commemorative statue at the site, to be called "The Turning point of the Rebellion." None was forthcoming. But he was gratified, that at long last, in 1868, President Andrew Johnson promoted him to brevet Brigadier General in acknowledgement of his wartime service.

The 25th Anniversary of the American Civil War commenced in April 1886. Thousands of members of the Grand Army of the Republic and thousands of Confederate Veterans, met at the sites of the battles in which they had fought twenty-five years earlier. The entire nation was caught up in patriotism and nationalism, as evidenced by the constant flood of articles on the Civil war in most every newspaper in America.

The ageing General Berdan attended the 25th anniversary commemorating the battle of Gettysburg on July 1st 1888. He was present at the Confederate General Longstreet's address, hearing that that the Berdan's SharpShooters "caused him a loss of 40 minutes, and could he have saved five of those minutes the battle would have gone against Meade on the second day!" Longstreet, unfortunately, perpetuated Berdan's mistaken contentions.

Articles and letters were published in the press, both for and against Berdan's interpretation of events. His planned memorial was never built, although many statues and memorials were built to honor other SharpShooter actions during the battle.

In 1890, the Survivors Association of Berdan's SharpShooters was formed in Boston, with over 200 charter members and General Berdan elected as first president. The association also appointed former Captain Charles Stevens as Regimental Historian and tasked him with writing their story. He prepared a 555-page Regimental History that was accurate and fair to both the 1st and 2nd Regiments of SharpShooters. Stevens was polite to Berdan, Rowland, and others who had some sordid moments during the war, few of which were alluded to in the book. His book is the source for many of the quotes in this one.

On May 6, 1891, General Berdan was elected a "Companion of the First Class, Original" of the Military order of the Loyal Legion of the United States (MOLLUS), District of Columbia. A fine honor, but still not enough for Berdan, and the fact that he appeared self-serving throughout his life may best be echoed by the following overture. On June 24, 1892, he wrote to the Department of the Army, Adjutant General's Office, requesting that his military records be reviewed. He asked if he might be considered for the Medal of Honor, for his actions on the battlefield at Gettysburg, July 2, 1863. Justice was served, as Berdan's request was denied.

Less than a year after he wrote, Berdan died of heart disease on March 31, 1893, while visiting the Metropolitan Club in Washington D.C. He was buried with full military honors at Arlington Cemetery, Washington D.C.

Historians may argue about Berdan's character and his military record, but not the effectiveness, skill, determination and heroism and of the unit he created. A unit that was born and disbanded within a few years, and one with an important place in the story of the Civil War.

Portraits of the SharpShooters

Captain Henry C. "Hank" Garrison, Commander of Company I [Michigan]. 1st U.S. SharpShooters was wounded at Gettysburg, July 2, 1863. He was honourably discharged, October 7, 1864, after completing his 3 year obligation.

Private Franklin H. Elwood, Company B [New York], 1st U.S. SharpShooters.

Private Charles Fox, Company F [New Hampshire], 2nd U.S.S.S. enlisted late in the war January 5, 1864 and mustered out on January 9, 1866.

Private William H. Chidsey, Company B [New York], 1st U.S.S.S.

Private John W. Chidsey, Company B [New York] 1st U.S.S.S. killed in action at Locust Grove, Virginia on November 27, 1863.

Private Isaac M. Baker, Company G [Wisconsin], 1st U.S.S.S., died of disease as a result of a severe reaction to a vaccination. He succumbed after being left with the Commissiary Dept. after action near West Point, Virginia, May 18,1862.

Sergeant Alexander J. Dupont, Company B [New York], 1st U.S.S.S. wounded at the Battle of Mine Run, Virginia, November 30,1863. Note the III Corps badge on the right breast of his four-button sack coat, and the barely perceptible chevrons on his sleeve.

1st Lieutenant Frank S. Wells, Company B [New York], 1st U.S.S.S., wounded at Kelly's Ford on November 7,1863.

Captain Albert Buxton, Company H [Vermont], 2nd U.S.S.S., was wounded in action at Gettysburg. He was killed eleven months later at the Battle of the Wilderness, May 6, 1864.

Lieutenant Gardner B. Clark, Company C [Michigan], 1st U.S.S.S. was wounded in action at Gettysburg, July 2,1863.Later promoted to Captain, commanding Company C.

Company B [New York], 1st U.S. SharpShooters. From left to right: Private James A. Byers [wounded at the Battle of Chancellorsville on May 2, 1863] and Private John H. White.

Private Alonzo Bernard, Company F [New Hampshire], 2nd U.S. SharpShooters.

Richard W. Tyler Company K [Michigan], 1st U.S. SharpShooters. Promoted to Company First-Sergeant, serving until May 25, 1864, when he was commissioned First Lieutenant. He was wounded at both the Battles of Groveton and Deep Run.

Sergeant Gilbert H. Prindle, Company H [Vermont], 2nd U.S. SharpShooters. Note the insignia on the top of his cap H and 2, depicting his company and regiment. He is wearing a holster on his left hip.

Sergeant Henry Lye, Company G [Wisconsin], 1st U.S.S.S., had been the company bugler. He was killed at Gettysburg on July 2, 1863.

Lieutenant Alvah A.Evans, 2nd U.S. SharpShooters.

Lieutenant Edwin A. Wilson, Company C [Michigan], 1st U.S. SharpShooters was wounded at Chancellorsville, May 3,1863. He recovered to lead his men at Gettysburg as Company Commander.

Frank E. Marble enlisted at Madison, Wisconsin in September 1861. He was elected First Lieutenant, later promoted to Captain and Company Commander. He commanded the 1st U.S.S.S. when both Berdan and Trepp were on medical leave.

Captain Edmund Weston Jr., commander of Company F [Vermont], 1st U.S.S.S. with the same cap insignia that Colonel Berdan was wearing: crossed rifles with "U.S." on top and "S.S" beneath.

Sergeant James S. Webster, Company G [Wisconsin], 1st U.S.S.S. In October 1862, made acting Sergeant Major of the Regiment. On March 27,1863, promoted to First-Sergeant. Slightly wounded in the head at Orange Road, Virginia, May 7,1864.

Private Loren S. Richardson enlisted into Company H; [Vermont], 2nd U.S. SharpShooters. Note the contrasting piping around the collar of the standard issue nine-button coat.

Private George R. Tower, Company H [Vermont], 2nd U.S. SharpShooters.

1st Lieutenant Henry E. Kinsman, Company F [Vermont], 1st U.S.S.S., wounded at the Battle of the Wilderness, Virginia, May 7, 1864. Honorably discharged, September 12, 1864.

Nathaniel Sessions enlisted in Company I [Michigan], U.S. SharpShooters November 24, 1861. Wounded near Petersburg, Virginia on June 18, 1864. Promoted to sergeant about the time the 1st Regiment of SharpShooters was disbanded, and transferred to Company E, 5th Infantry in late December 1864.

Private Douglas J. Pullman, Company B [New York], 1st U.S. SharpShooters.

Captain William "Horace" Horton was originally Sergeant Major of the 1st U.S. SharpShooters, later promoted to Lieutenant and then Regimental Adjutant. Historian Stevens wrote:"He was amongst the tallest and finest looking officers in the corps, and was very active and energetic in the heat of the battle."

Sergeant George W. Griffin, Company G [Wisconsin], 1st U.S. SharpShooters was wounded during the siege of Petersburg, and his foot was amputated soon after. He was killed during the Indian wars later in the century.

Company B [New York], 1st U.S. SharpShooters Private Frederick H. Johnson [left] was well respected for his markmanship. Private Matthew Morgan [right] was wounded at Chancellorsville, May 2, 1863 and again at Kelly's Ford, Virginia, November 7, 1863.

Horace Warner was Ordnance Sergeant, Company C [Pennsylvania], 2nd U.S.S.S. Appointed Regimental Quartermaster in February 1862.

William P. Shreve mustered into Company H [Vermont], 2nd U.S.S.S. in 1861. Appointed Quartermaster Sergeant and commissioned First Lieutenant in December 1862. When Colonel Berdan was made Chief of SharpShooters in 1863, Shreve was detailed to his staff.

Corporal Peter Wilker, Company A [New York], 1st U.S. SharpShooters.

Captain Dudley P. Chase, Company A [Minnesota], 2nd U.S.S.S. was severely wounded in the arm at the Battle of Chancellorsville, May 2, 1862. Surgeons amputated his arm but he died soon after of complications.

Private William H. Goodrich, Company F [New Hampshire] 2nd U.S.S.S. wisely huddled up with a scarf to keep out inclement weather in the field.

John "Captain Jack" Wilson commissioned First Lieutenant of Company B [New York], 1st U.S.S.S. promoted to Captain, commanding Company B. In early 1864, he ,being the highest ranking surviving officer, commanded the 1st Regiment of U.S.S.S.

The identity of this Berdan's SharpShooter Sergeant will remain a mystery as his details have been lost in the ensuing 140 plus years since the Civil War.

Acknowledgments

The author would like to acknowledge the following individuals for their assistance with this book:

Herbert Houze, former curator of the Cody Firearms Museum
Stuart Vogt, former curator at the Springfield Armory Museum
William Meuse, former curator at the Springfield Armory Museum
Russ Pritchard, Sr., former Directory of the Civil War Museum in Philadelphia
Wiley Sword, Historian and author
Jerry Russell, Founder of the Civil War Roundtables
Don Troiani, Artist Extraordinaire
Richard Sauers of Gettysburg, Pennsylvania
Dale Gallon, Artist in Residence, Gettysburg, Pennsylvania
Michael Music, retired Senior Archivist, National Archives of the U.S.
Bill Evans, former Archivist at the New York State Archives
Richard Carlisle, original photographs
Ronn Palm, original photographs
Art Buker, Berdan SharpShooter reinactor
Patrick F.Hogan,President, Rock Island Auction Company
Ed Cote, SharpShooter firearms
Art Frye, SharpShooter firearms
John Gunderson, SharpShooter uniforms
Paul Marcot, original research at the National Archives of the U.S.